TUNA

TUNA

CAPTAIN BILL SMITH

BURFORD BOOKS

Printed in the United States of America.

10   9   8   7   6   5   4   3   2

Library of Congress Cataloging-in-Publication Data
Smith, Bill, 1951–
    Tuna: an angler's guide to a great gamefish / by Capt. Bill Smith.
        p.   cm.
    ISBN 1-58080-082-3 (cloth)
    1. Tuna fishing.   2. Tuna.   I. Title.
    SH691.T8 S65   2000
    799.1'7783—dc21   00-040319

*To my sons Ben and Derrick, my true fishing buddies.
With the hope that we will pass on to you a healthier
and more prosperous ocean than we inherited.*

ACKNOWLEDGMENT

To my late grandfather, Nelson Demarest, my grandmother, Dorothy Demarest, and Uncle Nelson, Dorothy and Ned Demarest, Frank Payne, Frank Johnson Jr. and Frank Johnson III of Mold Craft Lures, Carl Darrenberg Jr., Norman Sanwald, J. Bennett Miller, Malcolm McClean, Bob Webster Jr., the late Capt. Greg Beacher, Melton Tackle, Hi Seas Tackle, Capt. Mike Potts, Walter Brigham and Walter Brigham, Bridgford Hunt, Lee Green at Stalker Outfitters, John Abplanalp, Tred Barta, Bob Hoose, Dick Tarlow, Ron Oehl, Gail Morchower, thank you.

I'm also grateful for the inspiration that came from the many anglers I've met on docks, in tournaments, and at dinners over the years who unfortunately must go unnamed. The angling community can be a very special place.

CONTENTS

Introduction   ix

PART 1   THE FISH
1.   What Is a Tuna?   3
2.   History of the Tuna   15
3.   Species Identification   39

PART 2   BEFORE LEAVING THE DOCK
4.   The Boat   71
5.   Boat Accessories   81
6.   Tackle and Equipment   91

PART 3   FISHING FOR TUNA
7.   Finding the Tuna   109
8.   Selecting and Using Lures   113
9.   Chunking and Chumming   123
10.   Live Baiting for Tuna   141
11.   Trolling for Tuna   145
12.   Downriggers   163
13.   More Tuna Techniques   169

PART 4   BOATING YOUR TUNA AND BEYOND
14.   Hooking and Boating Your Fish   183
15.   After the Tuna's Been Boated   199

PART 5   THE COMMERCIAL FISHERY
16.   Tsukiji Market, Tokyo   211
17.   Harpooning Tuna   219
18.   Tuna Conservation   223

Resources   231
Index   235

A good day's fishing: the author with a 1,065 pound tuna. Will such magnificent fish become a thing of the past?

INTRODUCTION

This is a book about a fish that I love; it's meant to be not a guide to catching tuna as much as a testament to a fish that has played a positive role for me throughout my life. Others can write about catching this fish much better than I can.

I caught my first tuna as a boy in the late 1950s off Montauk, New York, and it left such an impression on me that at each opportunity since I've read anything I could about them, chased them through the Atlantic and Caribbean, talked to others for endless hours, and looked at their pictures with the same awe as some schoolkid looking at photos of Mickey Mantle in Yankee Stadium. This book is my effort to repay these great fish for the substance that they have given my life in fishing trips, fish hooked, fish lost, and people met on docks and in bars around the world. It is in many ways a sad story because of what is happening to the tuna today; indeed, in shaping my life, tuna played a role in my career as a writer and environmentalist. It shouldn't be interpreted as a how-to book on catching tuna, or the final word on the politics or conservation of the tuna, which changes rapidly now. Nor am I trying to present myself as expert on tuna; there are many that know much more about them, their lifestyles, and catching them than I ever will. This book is simply my way to say thank you to these great fish. I hope they will add substance to my sons' lives, and to yours.

My love affair with the tuna began in the mid 1950s when I was about five years old. My family had a summer home on Shelter Island, a beautiful and then-rural island off eastern Long Island, where I now live year-round. The house is located on the water in a sheltered harbor, and we'd spend each summer there fishing, swimming, water-skiing, sailing, and playing in the woods and on the beaches.

My grandfather, who was an avid angler, always had a boat, and a few years before his untimely death he had a beautiful custom sport-fishing boat built. It incorporated the design features of some of the famous New England designs but was much bigger and had two very powerful engines. When he could escape the superficial business life of New York City, which was often because of his position, he used the boat for bay fishing, primarily for blues and weakfish. He and his captain Richard Halsey, a wonderful local man who became one of my grandfather's best friends, would spend hours together fishing, talking, cleaning fish, and having drinks afterward. Even when my grandfather became too sick to really fish, I remember seeing the two of them walking across the big front lawn and down the dock to the boat early in the morning. Of course, most times I was already waiting on the boat for them, and off we'd go for what were truly my formative fishing years.

After my grandfather died, my uncle Ned took over the boat, and with his circle of island friends we set off on some real fishing adventures, traveling off Montauk Point, Block Island, and Martha's Vineyard in pursuit of swordfish, or fishing in the United States Atlantic Tuna Tournament (USATT) from Block Island or Galilee, Rhode Island. When we swordfished we'd cruise at trolling speed, looking for their fins on the surface as they lay there sunning themselves, the entire time trolling feathers and cedar plugs to try to hook an occasional tuna—and to beat the monotony of trolling for a boy of 8 whose mind raced ahead to the great fish someday.

Back then we'd spot schools of tuna that to a small boy seemed endless; I'm told that they were at times acres in size. The water looked like white foam as they fed. Tuna were then considered a sort of junk fish, and no one really knew what to do with them, but because of their size and stamina they were prized as a sport fish. When we were lucky enough to catch one of these great fish, we'd clean it like a striped bass or bluefish, either filleting it or gutting it whole to bake later in the oven. Any giant bluefins we caught, usually during the USATT, were put in Frank Payne's pickup truck and hauled away to the Block Island dump for a fee, or towed out of Galilee Harbor after being weighed and dumped for crab food. Today, of course, it's a different story—a story unfortunately of the toll humans have taken on these magnificent fish.

Given the increasingly efficient technologies that have been developed, the fact that more and more countries are grabbing for a share of the ocean's fish, the refining of purse-seining, longlining, drift-netting, and pair-trawling techniques, as well as the waste generated by unknowledgeable "sport" anglers, once-vast schools of tunas have been greatly reduced. Bluefin tuna stocks today are estimated to be 10 percent of what they were just 20 years ago. Increased pressure is being put on the other species, too, as more of us increase our consumption of fish and advanced technologies make it easier and easier to catch entire schools of fish, instead of the occasional few.

It's become alarmingly obvious to me in my trips offshore that a change for the worse is taking place. Our waters are not teeming with life as they used to be, and this dramatic slide continues each season. Species of tunas and other fish are precariously close to collapsing. The average weight of a swordfish caught today on a longline is 65 pounds; 20 years ago it was closer to 300 pounds. This means that we are catching fish before they reach sexual maturity, and before they can reproduce. You don't have to be a scientist to see what will happen. When you think that out of the millions of eggs a mature female bluefin tuna lays each year, only two must survive to maintain the biomass, the tuna's decline is even more alarming.

If we are going to pass on a healthier ocean to our children and grandchildren, which is our responsibility, then we must eliminate the indiscriminate methods of fishing such as longlining, drift netting, purse seining, and pair trawling. We must also diversify our fisheries management committees so that those of us who know and understand the resource firsthand take the lead in implementing effective management programs. The government has tried and failed at this, and unless we get them out of the fisheries conservation business, all of us—along with our waters and the life they sustain—will suffer irreversible damage.

Equally important, more lines of communication and dialogue between the user groups (commercial and recreational) must be opened and cultivated. We can educate each other with our knowledge, and then hopefully educate the elected officials and government regulators who are charged with managing our fisheries but have failed so miserably. The finger pointing and name calling between recreational and commercial interests that many including the media and conservationists have perpetuated must end. When this happens all of us together as a force can ensure that future generations will have not only a good example to emulate but also fish to catch and an incredible lifestyle to experience. It's the lifestyle I've been fortunate to have, and through my life's work I hope our children and theirs will have it, too.

—BILL SMITH
Shelter Island, New York

PART I

THE FISH

1

WHAT IS A TUNA?

In his classic 1922 book *Tales of Swordfish and Tuna,* Zane Grey wrote that there were two types of tuna in the oceans—the yellowfin and bluefin. Today of course we know this to be false; we can now identify 21 different species worldwide belonging to the tribe Thunnini within the Scombridae family. This includes such lesser-known species as the slender, frigate, and bullet tuna, as well as the longtail.

Fifty-eight different species of tuna and related fish (see chart) belong in the order Perciformes. This order consists of many suborders, one of them being Scombrodidei. In turn the suborder is divided into various families. The family Scombridae, which consists of the fish commonly thought of as tuna is made up of two subfamilies. The one that I will be focusing on in this book is the subfamily Scombrinae. It includes the "true" tuna (Thunnini tribe), along with three other tribes of fish: the bonito, the various mackerel, and the lesser-known seerfish found only in areas such as the Indian Ocean and the waters surrounding Southeast Asia. All four of these tribes share similar physical characteristics, including:

- A body that's nearly round in cross section, rather than compressed
- An elongated shape somewhat similar to a spindle that's rounded and broadest in the middle, tapering toward each end

Odd as it may seem, the swordfish, all species of marlin, and the lesser-known spearfish are all related to the tuna as members of the Istiophoridae and Xiphiidae families. Their observed behavior is very similar, and they all share the tuna's migratory nature.

With their delicate colors and beautifully streamlined bodies, tuna are among the world's most beautiful and important fish. They have also evolved over the years to what appears to be the epitome of hydrodynamic refinement. With features such as recessed fins that retract into grooves and eyes that form a smooth surface with the rest of the head, they are true swimming machines capable of speeds of 60 or more miles per hour in quick bursts. Tuna must also swim continuously in order to pass oxygen-rich water through their gills and enable them to "breathe". Even at rest a tuna must travel a distance equal to its body length each second in order to take in enough oxygen to survive.

Primarily schooling fish, tuna are found in the tropical and temperate waters of the Atlantic, Pacific, and Indian Oceans as well as the Caribbean, Mediterranean, and Gulf of Mexico. They inhabit chiefly the open seas, rarely wandering into surrounding bays and harbors anymore. The exceptions are the smaller species, which are often found in harbors and bays and caught among schools of bluefish and striped bass by surprised anglers and giant bluefins, found at times in shallow-water, bays, harbors, and shoal areas. Still, for the most part these fish are at home in deeper, wide-open water.

They travel in the ocean's warm upper layers. As you'll see later, water temperature controls all aspects of a tuna's daily life. The ocean's upper layers, sometimes referred to as the mixed layers, are churned up as a result of waves produced by the wind's force. Wave movement then creates a fairly uniform temperature throughout. The mixed layers are separated from underlying cold water by a descending slope that can range in depth from 35 to 500 feet, depending on the geographic area of the ocean and season of the year.

LIFE CYCLE
A tuna begins its life as a small egg approximately 1 millimeter in diameter. It remains in the warm, mixed layer of water through the egg stage of

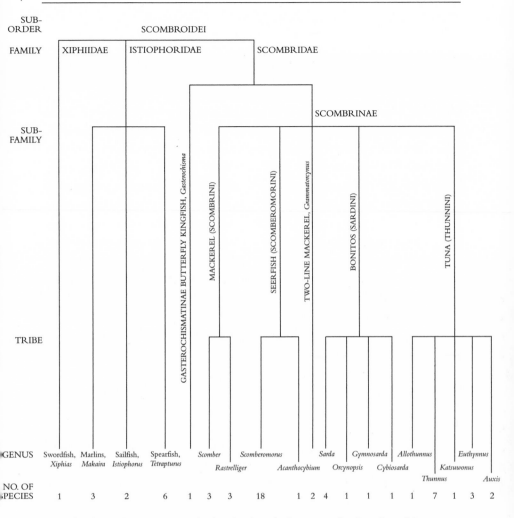

Tuna family tree. Tuna are most closely related to the bonito, mackerel, and seerfish.

its life. A tiny enclosed droplet of oil keeps the egg buoyant and ensures that it stays in the warmer water until the larva is hatched after about 3 days. At this point the larva is approximately 2½ millimeters or ⅒ of an inch in length. It will grow at an astounding rate. The Atlantic bluefin, for example, will increase its birth weight over one billion times before reaching maturity at nine years of age.

The fertility of a female tuna is amazing. She will produce approximately 50,000 eggs per year for each pound of her body weight. Thus a 300-pound fish could conceivably produce 15 million eggs annually! Unfortunately, few of these eggs will become fertilized or survive to the adult stage; larvae and young fish are easy prey for other fish and seabirds.

Only much later, as young adult fish, will they reach the top of the food pyramid with few enemies other than sharks and human beings.

PHYSICAL CHARACTERISTICS AND BEHAVIOR

The mature sizes of the various species of tuna are as wide ranging as the migratory routes of the fish themselves. The smallest of the species—the bullet and frigate tunas—rarely exceed 6 pounds. However, their cousin the Atlantic bluefin can easily reach a weight in excess of 1,000 pounds, while the more commonly caught yellowfin normally peaks at around 300 to 350 pounds.

Tuna are active predators of other fish, squid, and even crustaceans. They spend the greatest portion of their life in pursuit of food, an effort for which these fish are remarkably well adapted. Anyone who has ever witnessed a tuna chasing or crashing a trolled bait, swimming through a chum slick, or running off a reel after being hooked can attest to the fish's great speed and strength. As even the most inexperienced angler knows, there is no such thing as stopping a running tuna. The best you can hope for is to slow it down and eventually tire it out. Add to this the expertise you need to consistently catch tuna and you've got a great game fish.

In addition to its muscular, streamlined body, tuna have many other built-in characteristics that enable them to attain their great speeds. Extending just behind the tuna's head is the corselet (stomach–abdominal area)—a patch of specially modified scales capable of increasing the water's turbulence around the widest part of the body. These small scales greatly reduce the drag on the moving fish. In addition, the tuna's tail is powerful and crescent or lunate shaped. It works much like a ship propeller to provide maximum forward thrust.

Some species of tuna, such as the bluefin and yellowfin, possess slots into which their spinous dorsal fins can retract. This also reduces drag and adds speed. The spiny and soft-rayed dorsal fins of the tuna are separate; the soft-rayed dorsal fin is matched in size and shape by the anal fin located directly beneath it. Following each set of fins on a tuna is a series of finlets, usually yellow in color and varying in size depending on the species.

Throughout a tuna's life its body patterning and coloration will go through substantial changes. If you could compare a juvenile fish to an adult, the different body patterns would be obvious. Scientists believe that the temporary vertical bars found on tuna and bonito are actually fish's way to convey messages to each other in a school with regard to such things as the presence of nearby food or enemies. There is also much speculation in the scientific community that this body patterning holds the yet untranslated answers to such questions as a fish's age and sex.

In addition to being functional, the tuna's coloration and body patterning are extremely beautiful. The blues and greens found on the back grade into a silver color on the underside, which helps tuna camouflage themselves if necessary. Once the fish is removed from the water, these colors rapidly vanish until finally the tuna turns a drab charcoal color after death.

The internal makeup of the tuna has already provided researchers answers to many questions concerning things such as their nomadic lifestyle as well as their ability to swim incredible distances and to exhibit sudden bursts of speed and energy. Their respiratory and circulatory systems are particularly unusual among fish.

The tuna's circulatory system is very much like that of a human. Made up of the heart and numerous blood vessels, it is designed to retain or dissipate body heat as needed when determined by the tuna's activity level. Thus a fish that is inactive requires more body heat. As its activity level rises, though, so does its ability to dissipate body heat. While other species of fish maintain a body temperature very close to that of the surrounding water, tuna's body temperature will in most cases stay above that of the surrounding water by as much as 10 degrees. Researchers now believe that this phenomenon allows the tuna's muscles to make immediate use of the breakdown of sugar in the digestive system. This enables the tuna to exhibit sudden bursts of strength and speed much like those of a small child after eating a highly sugar-concentrated food or drink.

The tuna is able to maintain this unique above-average body temperature due to its high metabolic rate. This equally as unusual feature makes it necessary for the tuna to use more oxygen than any other species of fish, hence the constant swimming noted earlier, always with the mouth open. The continuous swimming also makes up for the tuna's lack of a swim bladder—a part of the body that aids in making all other fish buoyant. The tuna's pectoral fins act as hydrofoils, too, to counteract the tuna's weight and keep it from sinking.

Tuna are not "quiet" fish. While swimming the sounds that they make are not voluntary, but instead produced by their movement and feeding activities. They are also equipped with very good listening devices, sensitive chemical detectors, and—like hawks, wolves, and other high-speed predators—have binocular or stereoscopic vision that helps them in their pursuit of food.

The tuna's muscle system is what makes all this activity possible. When you clean a tuna you will notice both a white and a red muscle. The white muscle is the one used in the short, sudden bursts of activity, while the much larger red mass of muscle is what gives the tuna its incredible stamina.

This combination of speed and stamina has been confirmed by many tagging studies of tuna migratory habits. While it's impossible to determine a fish's exact route from the time it's tagged until it's caught again, scientists usually assume the shortest possible distance between the two points for the purpose of their data. From this information we now know that albacore and bluefin tuna undertake the longest consistent journeys— approximately 5,300 and 5,000 miles, respectively. A skipjack tuna tagged off the tip of Baja California was once recaptured some 6,000 miles away near the Marshall Islands. The more prevalent yellowfin tuna generally travel between 1,000 and 3,000 miles in one of their nomadic migrations.

But how do these remarkable fish do it—how do they cover vast featureless expanses of the ocean that are clearly differentiated only along the earth's vertical axis? Any available light they may have to navigate by disappears rapidly as the water's depth increases. Hydrostatic pressures may be highly important, even at moderate depths, as a guide to these fish, as may water temperature. These temperatures drop rapidly to uncomfortable levels once the fish passes through the thermocline, which guides the tuna in its travels. Aside from the vertical diversity, though, the higher levels of the oceans are trackless and featureless. So how do tuna orient and pilot themselves on their far-reaching migrations? Recently scientists have discovered small particles of a magnetic material named magnetite located near the nerve endings in tuna skulls. Speculation at this point is that these particles somehow permit the fish to navigate via both the earth's magnetic field and visual clues from the position of the sun. Current satellite-tag studies should help define the migrations of the larger tunas as well as understand how these remarkable fish choose their migratory routes.

THE TUNA'S COMMERCIAL VALUE

Tuna are among the most valuable commercial species of fish caught in the world today. In the United States only shrimp bring in more money than tuna, and not for long. The catches of tuna in just the Atlantic Ocean and Gulf of Mexico in 1998 were 40.5 metric tons worth just 169,667.00 compared to 1986's catches of 99.7 metric tons worth 372,831.00. In the larger picture, however, tuna may be more valuable as a recreational fish. Given recent declines in the swordfish population as a result of overfishing, as well as the regulations imposed on striped bass and other species in many states, tuna—known for their spectacular fighting abilities and excellent taste—are fast becoming the first choice of offshore angler.

Unfortunately this same overfishing which has decimated so many fish populations, now threatens to do the same to the tuna. These true nomads of the sea are caught by nearly 70 coastal and island nations commercially, yet over half the world's catch is taken by two countries, Japan and the United States. Methods of fishing range from the small coastal sailboats that troll crude handlines off the Maldive Islands to the giant purse seiners of Japan and the U.S. More than 95 percent of the fish in the tuna family caught commercially are caught one of four ways: hook and line, purse seining, pair trawling, or longlining. Fish caught by harpooning—which are considered commercial—are small in number compared to these four.

- Hook-and-line fishing accounts for more than 45 percent of the worldwide catch. This category includes live baiting, chunking, and trolling with artificial lures. It's now used by commercial and sport anglers alike, and both continue to experiment with new ways to catch these fish more effectively.

A purse-seiner in action. This fishing method accounts for nearly 30 percent of the tuna marketed worldwide.

- Purse seining is a highly efficient method that works best when the fish are formed in a school. A vessel that in most cases is being directed by a spotter plane from above will surround the school with a net that may be ½ mile or more in length. The boat then closes the ends of the net together by pulling a cable through rings attached to its bottom. A hydraulically powered pulley system then closes the net with the fish trapped inside. The fish are winched aboard, where they're unloaded, processed, and quickly frozen in the ship's hold. This method accounts for nearly 30 percent of the tuna marketed worldwide—an extraordinary figure when you realize that very few purse-seine boats are still fishing.

- Pair trawling is a relatively new and very efficient method of catching tuna, particularly the bigeye species. It is done primarily in offshore canyons, by two large dragger-type boats. These boats trawl a net up to 1 mile across and sweep the water of all tuna, birds, whales, porpoises, and any other fish that become entangled in this wall of death. I have talked to crew members of these boats who told me about cutting loose dead porpoises and whales that had drowned after becoming entangled in the mesh. From all indications it is a very dirty fishery; regulations pertaining to it need to be addressed.

- Longlining is rapidly gaining international popularity due to its high efficiency. Deep-water fishing is done with a main line that may extend up to 80 miles in length. Buoys are placed at intervals along its length to keep the giant line afloat. From this line hundreds of baited hooks extend on branch lines at depths from 50 to 500 feet. A single longline set may take up to a day. The one real problem with this method, which accounts for up to 30 percent of all tuna caught today, is that it catches many other types of fish. These other fish are usually thrown overboard dead because of a weak market price, or because regulations imposed on most foreign ships operating in the waters of the continental United States allow them to keep only the species they are licensed for. Thousands of swordfish, marlin, and sharks, many of them juvenile, are wasted each year. This alone should be reason to forbid longlining by all countries, including ours, yet our government and others allow it to continue.

This U.S. regulation is also extremely difficult to enforce due to the ships' and the tuna's mobility. During one trip, for example, some of the larger longline vessels may fish in the territorial waters of several different nations until filling their holds. In addition, so many different countries are commercial fishing for tuna that the paperwork and manpower needed for effective regulation is impossible.

Worldwide distribution of yellowfin, skipjack, bluefin, and albacore tunas.

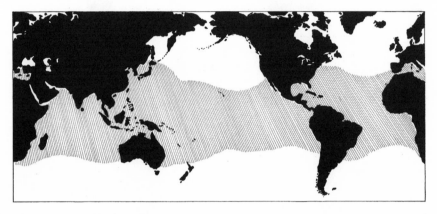

Yellowfin and skipjack distribution.

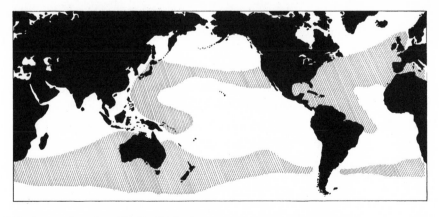

Northern and southern bluefin distribution.

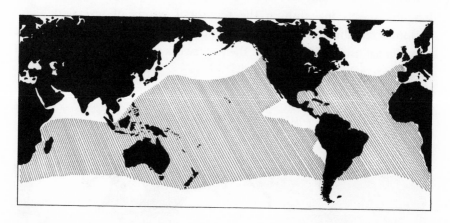

Albacore distribution.

As I mentioned earlier, the two fishing giants—Japan and the United States—account for over 50 percent of the world's catch and consume over 75 percent of it. Tuna is eaten canned in both countries, although in Japan the meat is also in great demand as sushi or sashimi—a traditional gourmet food eaten raw—which is rapidly gaining popularity in the U.S. as well. Thus the demand for tuna is increasing by leaps and bounds worldwide. Other countries that now consume over 20 percent of the world catch are France, Spain, Germany, and Italy. In the U.S. the demand has increased over 1,400 percent in the past five decades—more than any other type of food including fast-food burgers. The trend is expected to continue as ever-fitness-conscious Americans seek out the low-fat, vitamin-rich raw meat of the tuna. This should make it imperative that strict regulations protect the worldwide supply of these great game fish. Commercial anglers, recreational anglers, and consumers of tuna must recognize their obligations to the conservation of these great fish.

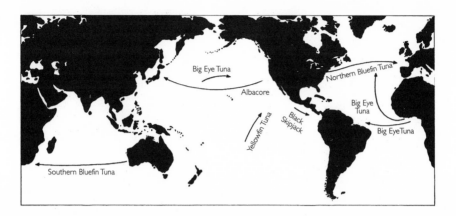

Migration routes of various tuna species.

2

HISTORY
OF THE
TUNA

The pursuit of tuna is referred to extensively throughout the world's written history. Enough valid evidence has been found to confirm that the ancient Mediterraneans, Polynesians, and Japanese all enjoyed tuna as table fare. Furthermore, there is enough sound information on hand to suggest that prehistoric humans caught and consumed tuna as a regular part of their diet. In the area of the United States now known as New Mexico and Arizona, skipjack tuna bones have been found buried in Stone Age mounds along with barbless hooks that had been fashioned from pieces of horn. These anglers sought out tuna using small dugout canoes in areas that we know today as Phoenix, Arizona, and Santa Fe, New Mexico. Equally as interesting are the images of tuna that have been found drawn on cave walls near France's Bay of Biscay. These date back to the Ice Age, confirming the tuna as one of the few fish consumed and recorded during this period.

COMMERCIAL FISHING
Ancient Rome and Greece
Before the collapse of ancient Rome, the Roman scientist Pliny the Elder wrote that Alexander the Great's fleet had once come upon a school of

tuna so vast that the ships were forced to advance into battle formation in order to make their way through! In addition, tuna were sold in surprisingly large quantities in the street markets of Caesar's Rome. They were netted commercially by methods very similar to today's purse seining and gill netting, but on a much smaller scale.

Aristotle wrote in his *History of Animals* that Greek anglers recorded movements and sightings of tuna schools and speculated about their migrations. In this timeless work Aristotle also discussed the "older and larger tuna," apparently referring to bluefins, which he said were "unfit for pickling" and hence cooked for servants or discarded. The same mentality was prevalent until the mid-1970s, when it was discovered that the Japanese had an insatiable appetite for bluefin flesh, and curiosity here in the United States resulted in an explosion of Japanese restaurants. Today these "fat old tuna" have sold in Japan for upward of $80,000 apiece.

There was also much conjecture on the part of the ancient Greeks about the cycles of these fish. When the schools of tuna were scarce, Greek anglers believed that they had "wandered deep into a place in the ocean where a giant oak tree could be found. There the tunas would feed on the tree's acorns until they finally exploded from becoming so obese" and hence depleted the schools. So much for early conservation theories.

The Spanish

The tuna and their movements also fascinated the Spanish. During the 18th century the Spanish cleric Fray Martin Sarmiento wrote a report about the tuna to the Duke of Medina-Sidonia, commander of the Spanish Armada. In it he stated, among other things, that "Tuna seem to have no native country, nor lasting domicile. All the sea is their native country. They are wandering fish."

Like the codfish in the United States, the Spanish involvement with tuna dates back to the earliest written accounts; the fish is intertwined in many ways in their culture. Throughout history coins of Spain have displayed images of the tuna, as does the town hall facade of the town of Cadiz.

Almadrabras

As far back as the 10th century tuna were trapped or netted near the Straits of Gibraltar by Spanish anglers who were granted permission to fish these waters by the king. These tuna were caught in huge stationary nets called almadrabras. It is one of the most ancient fishing techniques in written history, which through centuries has been practiced more or less unchanged. The nets are set in areas that take advantage of the migratory patterns of the tuna as they leave or enter the Mediterranean during the months of May, June, July, and August.

Several kilometers in length, almadrabras are placed perpendicular to the coast in order to create a series of labyrinths, shortcutting the route of the tuna and guiding them into the so-called death chamber or Red Matador. In addition to lateral nets, there are others in the bottom of the trap that, when lifted manually, allow the catch of the heavier bluefin species. Fish of over 2,000 pounds have reportedly been taken, but not in some time; the average weight of bluefin taken in the almadrabras is around 450 pounds. Once in the final chamber, the tuna cannot escape. This part of the trap is raised to the surface twice a day during the fishing season, which runs from April until October, and emptied. On the surface 10 different types of support vessels all manned with crews maintain the giant trap; their wide range of tasks includes hauling the death chamber to the surface and harvesting the fish from it. Historically these fish were salted down and stored in huge barrels until they were sold in markets controlled by the Duke of Medina-Sidonia. The Duke was able to amass an immense family fortune as a result of his control over all tuna sold in Spain.

The first migration, referred to as "from the right," is when the tuna are most plentiful and have the highest fat content and weight. At this time the tuna are coming in from the Atlantic Ocean to spawn. The second migration or run occurs in the opposite direction and begins in July when the tuna are returning to the Atlantic to feed and rebuild body strength, weight, and fat stores. The word trap is derived from the Moorish word almadraba. This word was introduced into Spanish culture in the eighth century, a result of the Moors' invasion of Spain. Outside the Straits of Gibraltar in the Atlantic there are eight almadrabras still in use by a semigovernmental cooperative. The famous almadraba of Barbate sits 2 miles offshore of the town of Cadiz. This trap has been fished for over a century now by Spanish anglers. It is anchored to the ocean floor in approximately 100 feet of water. Like today's fish traps, a pair of rope leaders almost 2 miles long are used to guide or "herd" the tuna into the traps four chambers as they swim south past the coast of Spain.

At one time this particular trap was the single largest and most productive trap in the Atlantic-Mediterranean region, averaging 18,000 bluefin tuna per year from 1929 through 1962, peaking in 1949 with a take of 43,500 individual bluefins! Today it takes about 2,000 fish a year, and that number is dramatically falling. Similarly, the Italians fished a set of traps in the Mediterranean called tonnare. At the turn of the 20th century there were just over 100 of these traps active in the Atlantic-Mediterranean region, catching an average of 10,000 fish each per season. By 1950 this had dwindled to only 30 traps, catching a total of 20,000 tuna annually; by 1981 the last of these traps caught only 500 fish!

Japan and the Tuna

An island nation, Japan has long relied on the sea for sustenance. Tuna have been fished commercially by the Japanese since the eighth century and some families in Japan can trace their involvement with the commercial tunary back 20 generations. Fish and shellfish have always played an important role in the Japanese diet, particularly in the years when Buddhist influence prohibited the eating of animal flesh.

The practices of live baiting, artificial lure trolling, and water spraying were common among Japanese anglers by the 17th century. The live baiting was done with baitfish native to the Japanese waters on hooks shaped from bone. Artificial lures were made from feathers and resembled those still used today. In water spraying—a system also developed by the Japanese and still in use today—anglers use bamboo dippers to scoop seawater, throwing it back overboard to attract and hold the schools of tuna. Today this is done primarily on Pacific Ocean commercial fishing vessels; water jets disperse the seawater out at high pressure, "foaming" up the surface and holding the fish around the boat.

Although now declining due to overfishing by commercial fleets, tuna remain an important aspect of Japanese life both economically and culturally. Not surprisingly, Japan is now the largest harvester of seafood in the world, taking 15 percent of the world's total catch. The Japanese people eat in excess of 13 billion tons of fish each year, or eight times more fish than Americans.

Still, because of the rapidly declining populations of bluefin stocks worldwide—as well as the strong demand for these fish in Japan, where they account for nearly half of the nation's protein intake—the Japanese have been forced to begin joint fishing ventures with other nations. In 1971 the Japanese devised the concept of airlifting tuna in chilled "coffins" from nations such as Taiwan, Australia, Norway, Canada, and the United States.

In that first year the United States shipped a total of 216 giant bluefins to Japan. Seven years later in 1978 that figure had grown to over

3,000 bluefins, and today it is in the 10's of thousands. This despite the ever-increasing wholesale prices, which have risen steadily from under $1 to today's $40 or more per pound.

Until 1971 when the Japanese first expressed an interest in our bluefin tuna, these fish were primarily a challenge to American sport anglers. Mercury contamination had kept tuna and swordfish from being sold in U.S. markets but the Japanese had ignored the risks and continued to import these fish.

The California High-Seas Fishery

This was the first large-scale commercial tunary in the United States. It began at the turn of the 20th century with boats in the 30-foot-plus range; by 1937 boat lengths had grown to upward of 100 feet, and there were 70 boats fishing from San Diego and surrounding ports that year. They caught an estimated 140 million pounds of tuna, up from about 5 million pounds in 1918, and laid the foundation for today's modern commercial tunary. This was done without nets, spotter planes, or modern technology, but with sheer instinct and experience as well as brute strength.

Crews in those days were predominantly Portuguese, though Japan, Italy, and Scandinavia were also represented. With few exceptions they fished for shares of the catch out of any money left over after financing the boat-construction loan and interest. This was done in a family type arrangement, with the prospective owners entering into a partnership with the cannery that would sell the fish to raise the necessary funds to build the boat. Costs in the 1930s were about $1,000 per foot. Usually a boat was paid off in about five years, but because of the wear and tear on a boat of this type as well as its wood construction, a long life for a tuna boat was about 10 years. Then it was either stripped and scrapped or rebuilt at a 1930s cost of over $30,000.

These boats would travel from southern California as far south as Costa Rica in pursuit of what was then referred to as yellowfin or skip-jack tuna.

SPORT FISHING

While the commercial tunary reaches back thousands of years and involves many different cultures, the tuna sport fishery is relatively new and primarily involves Americans and Canadians.

The first person to catch a giant tuna singlehandedly from a boat was Thomas Patillo, a Canadian schoolteacher. In 1870 he fished for tuna from a small dory in Nova Scotia's Liverpool Harbor. According to Van Campen Heilner, to whom Patillo related his experience, he used "thirty two fathoms of ordinary cod line, wound up on a swivel reel." Attached to the line was a hook fashioned from a piece of steel "three eighths of an inch thick, with a long heavy beard."

Using a whole herring as bait, Patillo hooked a giant tuna on his first attempt. The fish then towed his boat "across Liverpool Harbor, through a fleet of herring netters, swamping one and creating havoc with all the others."

"To his great disappointment," one of the irate netters cut Patillo's line, freeing the fish. His second attempt that day was rewarded with success as he brought to gaff a 600-pound "horse-mackerel."

In 1938 the daisy chain bait system was developed at Wedgeport, Nova Scotia. At first this extremely effective system was used primarily as a hookless "decoy" system that used mackerel and herring rigged together to resemble a small school of baitfish. The chain was then let out behind a boat to be taken by the rips or trolled until it attracted a hungry fish. The fish was then allowed to satisfy its appetite devouring the baits. At the same time a fully rigged bait was dropped back it, resulting more often than not in a hooked fish. Soon after this system was developed, one angler took nine giants in one day at Wedgeport.

The California Sport Fishery

During the 1880s California was experiencing a population and real estate boom like never before. With railway systems in place and most of the Native American population subdued, the transcontinental journey to the West Coast was no longer hazardous. Dr. Charles Frederick Holder, an affluent resident of Massachusetts and an accomplished writer, naturalist, and sportsman, was one of the Americans who decided to change his life and move west to pursue his interest in nature.

Prior to this, in 1878, Holder had been in New York City on business and during a break went to visit the Fulton Fish Market. There he saw a 1,000-pound-plus bluefin tuna hanging in one of the stalls and, upon inquiring, learned that it had been netted and then harpooned off the New England coast. He was completely taken aback by the size and power that he anticipated a fish like this must possess. So began a lifelong relationship between Holder and the tuna.

Twenty-one years later and now a California resident, Holder caught the first well-documented tuna off California's Santa Catalina Island, and big-game fishing as we know it began. Holder's first bluefin weighed 183 pounds and was taken on a 16-ounce rod with 21-thread line, rated at 24 pounds breaking strength. Like all tackle then, his reel had no drag system, and the only way for Holder to apply pressure to the fish was with a thumbstall, a leather sleeve that fit over the thumb. During the fight, the fish towed Holder's small skiff more than 10 miles in just over four hours.

Holder may not have been the first person to catch a tuna on rod and reel, however. It seems that two years earlier, in 1896, Col. C. P. Morehouse made the first tuna catch on rod and reel off Catalina Island. Additionally, one W. Greer Campbell is said to have taken a tuna on a crude rod-and-reel system in the same waters—off Avalon on Catalina Island—with some regularity. Both would go on to become fairly well-known figures in early sport fishing. Unfortunately, because there is no written documentation of their catches, Holder's fish is recorded as the first sport-fishing tuna caught in the United States. Although Holder's bluefin is small by today's standards, in 1898 with only "a simple winch attached to a standard boat rod," Holder became a hero in his own time. The following day, fresh with his success, he established the most famous angling organization in the world—the Avalon Tuna Club, or simply the Tuna Club. Morehouse and Campbell were founding members, as were Holder's friends Fitch Dewey, Dr. H. K. Macomber, Clifford Scudder, Edward Doran, and W. J. Landers. The Los Angeles press had a field day reporting Holder's milestone, which was made even more powerful in the public imagination by an unprecedented run of tuna off Catalina's shores. The press vividly portrayed Holder's catch as an event that "eclipsed all previous achievements in the line of angling for the big thoroughbreds of the deep," inspiring many other anglers of the time.

Holder was an interesting and innovative thinker who'd been drawn to the West Coast by his sense of adventure and its remoteness. His first fishing experiences as a boy on the East Coast had exposed him to a variety of freshwater species, as well as the most prized saltwater species of the time—the striped bass. Additionally, as a boy Holder had caught a tarpon on a trip to Florida's west coast, galvanizing his passion for all things related to the waters. When he first visited Catalina Island in 1886 on vacation, he immediately knew that this was a special place with a hold on him that he would never break. Within a day of his arrival Holder had sent back to Los Angeles for his fishing tackle to "bend in its quiet bays" as he wrote. He was astonished by the abundance of marine life there and the almost virgin quality of the bays, which—although teeming with life—had never been cataloged by "men of science." He wrote a friend that bald eagles, sea lions, vast fish schools, and whales could easily be observed from Catalina's shores.

He observed schools of bait frantically attempting to flee the huge schools of yellowtail and white seabass. Holder also watched as local fishermen using handlines pulled in yellowtails of 5 to 35 pounds as fast as they could retrieve them. This observation concerned Holder, who likened it to a slaughter, and compelled him to begin promoting the concept of conservation on Catalina Island, working to expand tourism while trying to maintain a balance with the island's environment.

The formation of the club in 1898 brought together the frontier spirit of the West and Holder's own strong and visionary sense of conservation in an effort to elevate the sport of angling to its highest possible standard. The original charter specified the "protection of the game fishes of Southern California" as the club's goal. In order to achieve this, Holder and his group established strict angling rules designed to give the fish what they considered an even chance for its life. Thus the club motto—"Fair Play to Game Fishes"—was chosen, and club rules drawn up eliminating the use of handlines if catches by club members were to be recognized. Violating this rule was also grounds for expulsion from the club. This was a very big step in the right direction, because handlining was then the primary choice of "sports." Soon after its formation the members of the club, under Holder's direction, began a very active lobbying effort on a state level against commercial-fishing interests in the waters surrounding Catalina.

Word of the Tuna Club and its mission quickly spread. Anglers around the world heard about these great fish off Catalina and wanted to distinguish themselves by following Holder's lead both as anglers and as conservationists. Within just two months two dozen of these men had traveled to Catalina in hopes of qualifying as active club members. (Qualifying required successfully catching a "leaping tuna"—actually a bluefin—of over 100 pounds on 24-thread line.) Then in 1899 Colonel Morehouse, never one to take second place in anything, returned to Catalina and broke Holder's record of 183 pounds by catching a 251-pound bluefin. This still stands as the heavy-linen-line record.

The club was located originally at the Hotel Metropole on Catalina Island, and in its early days became a center of activity for members and curious onlookers alike. Its huge porch overlooking the water became the site of pre- and postfishing activities. Because anglers could seemingly always be found on the porch recuperating from exhaustion, sunstroke, broken thumbs, and even a dislocated shoulder resulting from fighting tuna, the porch became known as the "tuna hospital." As you would also expect, it was also the place where anglers would gather to exchange stories, discuss tackle and techniques, and in general shoot the breeze about what was then termed the new Sport of Kings.

Today the club continues under the direction of historian Michael Farrior. A book on its 100-year history is planned, including its role in the development of the sport fishery at Catalina and the evolution of techniques that have influenced sport fishing throughout the world. The strong conservation ethic started by Holder is maintained as it was when Teddy Roosevelt, Winston Churchill, and Gen. George Patton fished there. Although the tuna are gone, marlin are still caught, the vast majority tagged and released. Monofilament line is not allowed for trophy fish—only linen or Dacron—and IGFA rules prevail here as they do elsewhere throughout the world.

New Jersey

The year 1913 saw the first gasoline-powered skiffs venturing offshore from New Jersey in pursuit of tuna. Using handlines, "knuckle-buster" reels, and hickory clubs, anglers trolled and jigged cedar and lead plugs for tuna. Because of the size and power of the species, as well as the primitive tackle, anglers purposely tried to avoid any fish over 100 pounds: Hooking up to one would surely mean a stripped reel and bruised knuckles.

Right around this time William G. Sheer and his son Otto became interested in catching some of these giant fish off the Jersey coast. The elder Sheer made quick friends with the area's commercial anglers by offering a bounty if they wired him in his New York office should they sight any of the schools of tuna so big that "they beat the surface of the water into a white foam for acres."

The commercial anglers were glad to inform the elder Sheer of arrival of tuna schools for two reasons. First, tuna interfered with their netting and handlining of the more valuable bluefish. At the time the tuna was looked upon as a menace by the commercial bluefishermen, who while chumming offshore for the schools of bluefish would often raise instead a large or giant tuna. When one of these "worthless monsters" was hooked, all hell would break loose as nets were ripped, lines broken, and at times

A contented angler from Seaside Heights, New Jersey, circa 1930.

skiffs overturned. Hooking up to one meant certain chaos for the commercial anglers, and they tried to avoid tuna at any cost. Also, the money that Sheer paid for the information was a welcome addition to any commercial angler's slim earnings.

Upon learning of the arrival of these schools, Sheer and his son would leave the city for the Jersey coast where they kept their yacht, the *Venture,* moored. Heading offshore, they would look for the commercial bluefishing fleets and schools of tuna. Once they were located Sheer would anchor alongside the small fleet and await the signal that tuna were there. This signal came when one of the anglers raised an oar from his small skiff.

Then Sheer and his son would climb into their specially outfitted skiff and join the fleet, chumming immediately with bunker, butterfish, silversides, sand eels, or anything purchased from the commercial fleet. When one hooked a tuna, their yacht would be pulled through the small commercial fleet as the battle raged. Even though the development of offshore tackle was in its infancy, the Sheers fished with the best available, including a specially made threaded wire line that the father-son team designed. Although the Sheers hooked and battled many fish this way, one for over nine hours, they were never successful in boating one.

Soon after the Sheers conceded defeat at the hands of these tuna, the famed Zane Grey heard of their efforts and tried the same tactics off the Jersey coast, again with no luck. Not long after these attempts, what became known as the golden days of sport fishing began. Names like Hemingway, Farrington, Lerner, Gifford, and Mitchell-Henry were at the forefront of sport-fishing news chasing tuna, marlin, swordfish, and other big-game species using the best tackle available as well as new and innovative fishing techniques that eventually gave birth to the world-class, high-tech tackle we enjoy today.

England

On August 27, 1930, some 50 miles off the coast of Scarborough, England, Mr. Mitchell-Henry caught the first bluefin tuna on a rod and reel in Europe. The fish weighed 560 pounds and was caught from a small skiff; this would soon become the accepted method of giant-tuna fishing in Nova Scotia and Newfoundland. That same day Mr. Mitchell-Henry also boated giant bluefins weighing 630, 735, 591, and 392 pounds. Quite a beginning for the European sport fishery!

Bimini and Cat Cay

In 1932 one of the most innovative sport anglers ever, Capt. Tommy Gifford, developed the outrigger in order to position baits off the sides of the boat and make them skip across the top of the water on flat-calm days to entice giant bluefins. Gifford had discovered these giants as they migrated north off the Great Bahamas Bank near Bimini and Cat Cay in 1932 and from then on spent as much time as he could pursuing them. In 1933 he boated the first giant bluefin ever off Cat Cay on a rod and reel, although his fish was attacked and mutilated by sharks during the battle— a very common occurrence back then due to the primitive nature of the tackle, lack of familiarity with boat running, and crude fighting-chair techniques.

In May of 1935 Ernest Hemingway boated a giant bluefin 11½ feet in length and weighing 509 pounds off Bimini. He was also the first person to boat one of these fish unmutilated by the scores of sharks that inhabit these waters. Soon after Hemingway's triumph, S. Kip Farrington followed suit and tuna fishing took its place in American sport fishing.

Cat Cay and Bimini were both to play an integral role in the development of the tuna fishery for recreational anglers. Cat Cay was originally deeded to Capt. William Henry Stuart by Queen Victoria in 1874 as payment for acting as supervisor of all lighthouses throughout the Bahamas. Captian Stuart lived there periodically until about 1915, when the cay was bought by an English bachelor, one Captain Haigh, who lived there for 16 years. Although he lived alone, Captian Haigh practiced the English tradition of dining in black tie each night in the manor house. He kept the island until his death; an unnamed engineer then took possession for a short time before selling it to Milos Strong in 1919. In 1931 Louis Wasey, an advertising executive from New York, bought Cay Cay from Strong and the tiny island, full of history, began to take its place in sport-fishing history.

Mr. Wasey used the island as a winter home and office. He refurbished the manor house, and then laid out a nine-hole golf course and two tennis courts. Wasey also turned a swamp in the middle of the island into a lake; he built a marina in a sheltered harbor with docks, electricity, live bait wells, and a freshwater reservoir. Wealthy types added 16 private homes, and a clubhouse and other infrastructure followed.

While all this was happening, the giant bluefins were continuing to migrate—as they had for millions of years—from the Gulf of Mexico through the Florida Straits and northward past Cat Cay and Bimini through the Bimini Trough. Each May around the dark of the moon and when the winds blew from the southwest the first procession of these magnificent fish, driven by the instinct to feed and spawn, streamed through "Tuna Alley" past Wedge Rocks, Pickett Rocks, Honeymoon Harbor, Cat Cay, Gun Cay, and Bimini on their Atlantic Ocean loop. These fish weighed between 300 and 500 pounds with some running higher. They arrived lean and hungry. Finished with their spawning, they were heading north to the bait-rich waters off Montauk, Cape Cod, and Canada to regain their strength and prepare to head south again to spawn in the endless cycle of their lives.

Wasey and a group of friends and business associates fished the steep edge of the Bimini chain, catching dolphin, wahoo, sailfish, and white marlin. This was truly virgin territory; most of the sport fishing of that time was being done off Palm Beach, Miami, and the Florida Keys, because of this area's convenience and productivity, but also because few people would risk venturing across the Gulf Stream in the sport-fishing boats of the time. Wasey used the state-of-the-art tackle-split Tonkin bamboo rods or disposable Calcutta rods and 72- or 54-thread line (216- or 162-pound test)—and still managed to boat endless fish. The group also accidentally hooked giant fish that they thought were marlins from time to time and the men were amazed at their ability to melt reels, break rods in half, and create total chaos in the cockpit.

Before long word of this got out. On February 28, 1933, S. Kip Farrington, fishing from Cat Cay as Wasey's guest, caught and boated a 155-pound blue marlin, the first one landed on rod and reel on the Bimini side of the Gulf Stream. Then in March of that year Wasey took out Mrs. Anne Moore, a friend from New York City, and she caught a 510-pound blue marlin. In May 1933 something happened that would change sport fishing forever: Marlin anglers found themselves surrounded by thousands of giant fish pouring through the edge. Many were hooked that year but none landed. Still, the legend had begun.

The next season Wasey, knowing the power of advertising, took a 502-pound blue marlin he'd caught across the Gulf Stream to Miami and dropped the 10-foot-plus fish on the dock to be photographed. Within two months some of southern Florida's best sport-fishing captains were braving the Gulf Stream to try the waters off Cat Cay and Bimini.

On June 1, 1934, Capt. Bill Gray, Fred Bennett, Bob Kleiser, and Gil Drake made their first crossing to Bimini on the *Reveler,* Gil's boat. Upon arriving they discovered the fishing pier full of people and buzzing with excitement. It seemed that half of Bimini had come to see the head half of a giant bluefin tuna brought to the dock by anglers Johnny and Archie Cass, whose boat was captained by Tommy Gifford. Their half weighed 350 pounds and had a 57-inch girth. It was fought on a huge metal reel with over 1,000 yards of 72-thread line, weighing 35 pounds and built by Miami machinist Fred Greiten, later of Fin-Nor. Because of the reel's extra-wide spool and huge line capacity, the angler was forced to wear leather wristlets up to the elbows so that the line would not burn or cut the forearms. It was the first reel to abandon the multidisc star drag in favor of a single, slow-turning disc mounted outside the solid-hand machined spool.

Other anglers from Florida gathered that day had 14/0 outfits on their boats, and even sash cord—over ½ mile of it, coiled up neatly in a washtub. But the most startling rig was the drum of ¼-inch bronze cable. It was to be retrieved by a winch mounted on the boat's motor in the event of a hookup with one of the monsters off Bimini and Cat Cay.

Returning to Florida the next day, Captian Gray told his crew that he was determined to return and prevail next time. "We headed back to the mainland, like the rest of them, with our tackle in a shambles, but with a strong resolution to return someday to even the score with bigger, better and stronger tackle," Gray wrote in his diary.

The next season in May 1935 Hemingway boated his tuna, followed by Farrington using his 22-ounce split Tonkin bamboo rod and custom-matched Vom Hofe reel. In his book *Fishing the Atlantic,* Farrington wrote that in 1936, 20 whole tuna were taken by anglers off Bimini and Cat Cay, with twice that many in 1937. "In '38 and '39 they really began to take them."

In order to accommodate the rush of anglers to Bimini, Mrs. Helen Duncombe and R. J. McDonald of that island started the Complete Angler in 1935. It was Bimini's first hotel and immediately became a focal point of sport fishing there. Nearby on Cat Cay, Wasey was so being deluged by friends who wanted to visit the island to fish that he decided to turn it into a recreational hideaway with an exclusive members-only address. The Cat Cay Club was formed in 1937 with its previously mentioned amenities. A world-class skeet range was included, and according to Farrington "some live pigeon shoots" as well.

The club stayed open for business from December until July 4, attracting a Who's Who of the angling community. Mr and Mrs. Michael Lerner of the Lerner Clothes Stores were among them. Later Lerner— who also had a home on Bimini—went on to find the Lerner Marine Laboratory there, affiliated with the Museum of Natural History and also the International Game Fish Association. Putting to rest once and for all the thought that women are not strong enough to boat large fish, Lerner's wife became the first woman to boat a giant bluefin, and in one month in 1938 in fact landed 11!

THE CAT CAY TOURNAMENT

The first annual Cat Cay Tuna Tournament, hosting 31 boats, was held in May 1939. Entrants boated over 62,222 pounds of bluefin, and on May 29, 1939, took 55 giants weighing 23,600 pounds. The winner of this historic gathering was Julio Sanchez, who personally caught 4,177 pounds of bluefin using a very sporting 39-thread line on a Fin-Nor reel.

Capt. Clay Kyle was one of the last sport-fishing captains to fish the Bimini Islands and the Cat Cay Tournament during these amazing years and through the 1950s. He likened the hookup of a giant bluefin to a "depth charge going off." White water flew everywhere as the bluefin hit the bait or lure.

"I'd fly with old man Chalk [of Chalk's Flying Service] in the old days when he'd bring bait and supplies to Bimini and Cat Cay on Thursdays. You could look as far as you could see, and there'd be fish—a brown river of fish" as tuna passed through Tuna Alley.

"In those days the number of tuna an angler could catch was limited only by the strength of the tackle and durability of the tackle," Kyle remembered. "There were millions of tuna [bluefins] then, and they would eat anything: belly strips with a feather, and mackerel and mullet, both belly-rigged." Anglers did best when the wind was blowing from the southwest. This was when the tuna would come in behind Dollar Harbor and Sandy Key, entering the shallower white-sand flats before heading out to deeper water. Anglers would try to bait them, keeping them up on the shallows as they were fought.

Before World War II such legendary captains as Tommy Gifford—fishing his boat the *Lady Grace,* usually with Mike Lerner—and Bill Fagin on *Florida Cracker* fished alongside Johnny Cass on the *Alberta* and Red Stuart on the *Sea Quest,* a 1938 Matthews powered by big Chrysler Crown engines and capable of 20-knot speeds. After the war there were many new faces at Bimini and Cat Cay, many of them fishing on Chris-Crafts. The *Restless,* owned by Stuart and Mary Carrew, was a 40-foot express boat powered by six-cylinder gas engines and also capable of 20-knots plus.

According to Captain Kyle, Snatch and Hal Abbott usually caught the first fish of the early tournaments. One year Snatch hooked a 400-pound-plus bluefin, boating it in just 8½ minutes. This was because he practiced the technique of actually herding the fish onto the flats, the favorite technique at Cat Cay. Given the strength of a bluefin, it's impossible to steer one unless you combine the efforts of boat and angler, which usually worked at Cat Cay. If the fish went its own way and got into the deeper water, the angler would usually break it off and head back to the shallows. Deep water gave the tuna a huge advantage, and there were so many of the fish that anglers didn't want to waste their time battling one for hours. Keeping it on the shallow bottom allowed the captain to maneuver the boat as he watched the fish move, and the mate to wire and gaff the fish much quicker.

Cat Cay became so famous for its tuna fishing that its wealthy clientele and residents were written up in a 1949 edition of the *Saturday Evening Post.* This magazine reported that an average week's stay at Cat Cay cost $1,800, while a woman's "proper" fishing outfit from Abercrombie and Fitch might run over $2,000. Tackle was also expensive then, with a reel costing over $500, a spool of silk line $50, and a good rod $150 or more. Everything considered, a trip there to catch a tuna might cost $8,000, quite a sum in 1949 dollars.

A boat captain's life at Cat Cay was quite different, though. Captains did not socialize with the members or guests, and by today's standards ran boats that were amazingly primitive. They had no generators, bait freezers, or large fuel capacities. Their fuel was stored in 55-gallon drums across from the marina; when it was needed, captains and crew members had to hump it over to the boat. They lived on the boats during tournaments, sleeping in the V-berths, and ate by themselves either at the dock or in the clubhouse away from the guests. They were a rough-and-tumble bunch of characters back then, but dedicated to each other if trouble broke out on one of their boats.

Today the vast schools of bluefins off Cat Cay and Bimini are gone. The occasional two or three and the occasional small pack have replaced them. Captain Kyle fished there for the last time in the late 1970s, discouraged that there were no fish. "There wasn't any sense in it anymore," he said.

Nova Scotia

In the fall of 1935 Michael Lerner—the New York sportsman who founded the International Game Fish Association—first fished the rips off Wedgeport, Nova Scotia. Lerner had heard of the great numbers of tuna that migrated to Wedgeport each August to feed on the vast herring stocks, staying until the end of September, when they would again turn south or cross the Atlantic.

Here in Nova Scotia sport anglers soon perfected a crude but effective method of catching these fish. They'd leave the docks each morning between 2 and 3 A.M. in Down East Novi-type boats built in Wedgeport to what was then called a Cape Island design. Each featured a crew of three—the captain, a wireman, and a chummer. All were local men who fished commercially and knew the waters intimately. The larger boats towed a small lapstrake skiff behind that in most cases later would land the fish. All of these Novi skiffs had a primitive but functional fighting chair that hooked fish could be battled from. The anglers traveled through the morning darkness to the treacherous Soldiers Rip at the entrance to Lobster Bay off Wedgeport, where they sought out the net or drift boats that fished throughout the night for herring. At dawn the commercial anglers would haul in their nets; herring would be everywhere, along with screeching gulls and boiling giant bluefin. At the time it was common to see acres of boiling 500-, 600-, and 700-pound bluefins jumping and playing on the surface as they fed on the herring and mackerel, which literally flew out of the water as they attempted to escape the hungry bluefin. As this scene unfolded the sport anglers who were waiting in their chartered boats would let out their baits behind the boat until a fish struck. These boats were positioned into the rip, motors running at full speed and yet standing still in the strong water. Per a gentleman's agreement, the number of boats was limited to 20, to keep things safe and give everyone a chance at a fish, but usually the number varied between 7 and 15. Each boat would fish two rods rigged with herring or mackerel baits and daisy chains of the same. These usually had no hooks and acted as teasers. When a tuna spotted them you could watch it pick one fish after another off the rigs, working itself into a feeding frenzy. One rod was positioned in the rod holder, usually on the starboard side, while the other was in the fighting-chair holder with the angler. Lines were let out about 50 or 60 feet behind the boat while a member of the crew chummed whole or half sections of herring. When a feeding fish was spotted, the chum man would keep the fish at the boat while a baited rod was passed to the angler in the chair. It would then be let out to the fish, and more often than not a hookup would occur. The angler could either strike the fish hard or let it run for a while to swallow the bait. In the midst of treacherous water, the skiff was pulled alongside, the angler took the rod, and into the skiff he climbed as line screamed from the reel. The skiff was turned loose, and the angler and a wireman were on their own, being towed around in the rips in what was quickly termed a Nova Scotia sleigh ride. Word of this exciting fishing quickly spread in the small, elite sport-fishing fraternity, and in no time Wedgeport was swamped with wealthy anglers who wanted to do battle with a giant bluefin.

The tackle of choice then was a 12/0 reel filled with 39-thread line and mounted on a balanced bamboo rod. A more sporting tuna angler might even try 24-thread line, but with the primitive tackle it was difficult. Others not wanting to take a chance might use 54-thread line, though it was frowned upon by this small, elitist group of anglers who considered themselves sports. The usual hook was a 10/10 or 11/0, slightly offset and mounted to a 10- or 11-thickness piano-wire leader of no more than 15 feet. This wire leader was attached by a swivel to a doubled fifteen-foot-length of the threaded line. The majority of fish were hooked in the corner of the mouth, which resulted in some long battles.

Another calmer method of taking giants at Wedgeport was to fish when the tide was slack. Again two rods were used with either piano-wire or cable leader. The boats drifted with daisy-chain-type teasers and a man chumming away. When a fish took the teasers piece by piece, a baited hook would be presented and the fight was on. The baited hook would be dropped back or free-spooled and held at a predetermined depth with the aid of a balloon, a piece of cork, or even a cola bottle with a corked end.

It was not uncommon back then to take multiple fish in a day; during an extended stay, many anglers might take 10 or more fish in a week's time, all over 500 pounds. In fact, on September 24, 1949, 75 giants weighing from 100 to 640 pounds were taken, the day before that 62 fish, and on September 22, 51! One George Beesch took eight fish in a day. But the best was September 25, 1949, when 92 giants weighing over 10 tons were caught, with a Dr. Ledow of Philadelphia taking 11. The boats could be hired for about $30 a day, and crews were given the fish, which were sold for 10 to 40 cents per pound to one of the Canadian or Boston canneries. This was a nice supplement to the lobster-based economy of the area, and the group of angers was welcomed back each year.

To give you an example of just how good the fishing was at Wedgeport, in September 1946, S. Kip Farrington caught 11 giant bluefins in 14 days of fishing with a total weight of 7,145 pounds, or an average weight of almost 648 pounds. Wedgeport remained the place to fish for giants until 1975 when, for reasons that no one yet understands, the fish stopped coming. In 1975 one fish was taken at Wedgeport; the following year, none.

Something very strange had begun to occur with the giant bluefins in the 1950s. The same tuna that once seemed endless at Wedgeport began to show up in the waters around Newfoundland, where they stayed for almost an entire decade. Then they started to really disappear from Wedgeport and Liverpool, Nova Scotia, showing up in big numbers at Newfoundland and Prince Edward Island. But even this fishery was not without problems. In 1966, for instance, 388 giant bluefins were taken from Newfoundland waters, and from then on that number declined until 1981, when only 3 giants were taken. Today Prince Edward Island proclaims itself the Tuna Capital of the World, with 50 boats operating out of the tiny harbor during the August and September season. Here, too, the tuna have seen better days. In 1974 North Lake had its best year with 578 giants boated, while in 1981 that number was only 55.

Recent reports indicate that a small number of bluefins are beginning to show up again each year in these waters and off Nova Scotia. Still, the reasons why elude us; speculation ranges from overfishing to water temperature changes to depletion of once-bait-rich waters. My sense is that it is all of the above, with poor water quality also a factor.

THE SHARP CUP

On September 11–13, 1937 the first International Tuna Cup Match—the Sharp Cup—was held at Wedgeport with teams from the United States and Great Britain competing. Started by S. Kip Farrington, the Sharp Cup was designed to be the Davis or Walker Cup of fishing. Farrington was not

S. Kip Farrington, East Hampton, New York, during the glory days of sport tuna fishing.

Chessie Farrington, Montauk, New York, 1951—by all accounts an even better angler than her famous husband. With her are Captains Tom Harms (lower right) and Red Stewart (standing).

known for a strong sense of humility, but nevertheless deferred to Alton B. Sharp of Boston, asking him to put up the trophy cup. Sharp was glad to do it. The competition was named for him and in the years ahead would become the most prestigious fishing competition in North America, if not the world. The first year only two countries competed, but the participants still brought an international flavor to the event. Anglers fishing on the Great Britain team came from places such as Kenya, Bermuda, Great Britain, and the Bahamas. Although amazing fishing preceded the tournament that first year, weather conditions were less than desirable. A hurricane had come through the area just days before, ruining the apple crop, downing phone and telegraph lines, sinking the schooner *Shelburne,* and raising hell with the schools of baitfish that were pushed out of their usual areas. Nevertheless five giants were landed in two days of fishing; the third day was called due to weather. A competition that would continue until 1975 was born.

Wedgeport also saw the development of another innovative technique for catching giant bluefins. The flying wedge was essentially a circle-shaped formation of boats positioned in the middle of a rip as they chummed mackerel and herring. The idea was to keep the boats together as much as possible, to keep the maximum of chummed fish in an area in the hope of raising bluefins and bringing them to one area of the rip. The first year of the Sharp Cup it worked very well, resulting in four fish hooked with three landed for the British team. The largest was 569 pounds. The British went on to win the cup that first year.

In 1938, because of pressure put on the Nova Scotia government by interests of the city of Liverpool, the match was moved there, much to the dismay of the participants. Liverpool's geography eliminated the use of the flying wedge—a technique that in addition to bringing in fish also gave everyone involved an equal shot at hooking up. In three days of fishing at Liverpool, Nova Scotia, no fish over 100 pounds were taken by the British, Cuban, and American teams. The Cubans took the trophy.

The next year the match returned to Wedgeport, with teams from the United States, Great Britain, Cuba, France, and Belgium set to compete. Instead and despite some excellent fishing prior to the starting date, the 1939 match was canceled due to problems in fielding full teams. It remained in limbo until after the war in 1947.

Now began the best years of the Sharp Cup; some years 19 teams from countries competed. A clubhouse was built at Wedgeport at the head of the fishing dock, and sportspeople and their families arrived from all over the globe. An annual clambake that coincided with the competition was hosted by Mr. and Mrs. Julian Crandall at their Argyle Lodge; its guest list read like a Who's Who of the early angling community: Hal Lyman, Van Campen Heilner, Oz Ownings, Ed Migdalski, Elwood Harry, the Farringtons, Lerner, and more.

In 1952 Farrington came up with the idea of taking the Sharp Cup one step farther. He wanted to start a tuna-fishing competition for college students. Again acting contrary to his reputation, Farrington got Tony Hulman of Terra Haute, Indiana, to sponsor the cup. Farrington did purchase it at Tiffany's that year though, and asked Ed Migdalski of Yale University, a great sportsman and angler, to spearhead the academic efforts related to the competition.

Colleges from the United States and Canada used to fish this tournament each August or early September, and in addition to three full days of fishing at Soldiers Rip were treated to a full roster of fishing-related courses. Teams stayed at the Grand Hotel at Wedgeport, and after checking in would walk down to the dock for team photos. Following dinner at the Grand, the lecture programs began and ran until 10:30 P.M., resuming at 5:15 A.M. They included such courses as Introduction to Big Game

A postcard from the 1950s proclaims Galilee, Rhode Island "Tuna Capital of the World."

Tackle, How to Fight a Giant Tuna, Using the Norwegian Jig, and the always-in-demand Identification of Fishes. Slide shows and lectures by guests were thrown in for added interest. When the fishing began, college teams from the likes of Harvard, Dartmouth, Trinity, and Yale stayed on the water for eight hours each of the contest's three days.

As you can see, it was a pretty mighty attempt at a highbrow fishing competition, designed to make good sportsmen out of trust-fund kids. But like the Sharp Cup that gave birth to it, the Intercollegiate Tuna Cup Match was doomed by the rapid decline of the bluefin stocks.

3

Species Identification

ALBACORE *(Thunnus alalunga)*

The Albacore is also called the longfin tuna, due to its long pectoral fins. When translated from the French, albacore means "yellowfin tuna." In Europe the albacore is called the white tuna. In the United States and elsewhere, it's packaged as the only "white-meat" tuna, also referred to as Chicken of the Sea. By far the most valuable member of the tuna family for canning purposes, the albacore has excellent flavor both from the can and on the grill. It's a strong-fighting game fish sought out by anglers worldwide for its fighting abilities.

Physical Characteristics

These fish, featuring longer pectoral fins than all other tuna, belong to the mackerel tribe. At times it may be difficult to distinguish the albacore from the small bigeye except for the albacore's long pectoral fins. A sharp white border on the tail fin is another distinctive feature. The albacore is also a plain fish with no streaks, spots, or squiggles. Though it has an iridescent blue line along its side when brought to the boat, this quickly disappears as fish are boated and dressed.

Between 7 to 9 dorsal finlets and 7 to 8 anal finlets; 25 to 32 gill-rakers on the first branchial arch; elongated fusiform (rounded, broadest in middle and tapering toward each end) body; caudal peduncle (section between tail and dorsal fins) slender, with keel on each side. Very long pectoral fins that reach back beyond anal fin, and to second dorsal finlets on adult fish. Caudal fin has white posterior margin in both immature and adult fish. Liver striated on ventral (lower) surface.

Coloration

The dorsal side (top) is a metallic dark blue, grading to greenish-blue near the tail. In live fish, there is a metallic bronze cast over the entire body. The ventral area (underneath) is a silvery white. The first dorsal fin is true yellow; the second dorsal and anal fins are light yellow. Finlets are all light yellow, edged with black. Anal finlets are a silver or dusky color.

Distinctive Features

The young albacore (less than 13 inches), has shorter pectoral fins than similar-sized yellowfin and bigeye tuna. Adults can be identified by their lack of white vertical stripes on the ventral side. Adult albacore can also be easily identified by their long pectoral fins, extending past the second dorsal finlet.

Size

The maximum length for a fully mature fish is about 48 inches. The common length is 16 to 43 inches. The hook-and-line record is 88 pounds, 2 ounces, caught off the Canary Islands in 1986. Commercial anglers report albacore catches of up to 100 pounds.

Geographic Distribution and Behavior

Worldwide distribution, with four separate stocks: the North Atlantic, South Atlantic, North Pacific, and South Pacific. The Atlantic and Pacific stocks, once thought to be different species, are now known to be a single species. Tagging on the West Coast has shown that these fish travel easily between America and Japan, covering from 100 miles in a day and many thousands of miles in a season.

Albacore are found in wider range of water temperatures (60 to 70 degrees) than most tuna. This is a very important factor in finding these fish. Adult albacore (over 35 inches) appear in tropical and subtropical waters, but the larger of these fish are generally found in cooler temperatures, with the smaller seeking out warmer waters.

Albacore are distributed throughout the Atlantic. In the western Atlantic they can be found from Cape Cod to Argentina, and in the eastern Atlantic from France's Bay of Biscay to the waters of South Africa and around into the Indian Ocean.

In the Pacific Ocean they can be found from Cedros Island off Baja Mexico northward to the waters off Canada. Pacific stocks are much larger than Atlantic stocks. Young fish are often found in enormous surface schools. Here both commercial and sport anglers seek them out.

Spawning begins in spring and generally ends in late August but can go on as long as October, depending on water temperatures. A single female fish can lay up to three million eggs each year, but predators will take their toll on most of these quickly. Once born, the juvenile albacore will gain the strength and speed characteristic of tuna quickly, reaching 6 to 8 pounds their first year.

Fishing Methods

Methods used to catch albacore worldwide include longlining, purse seining, and live and natural baiting using herring, anchovies, butterfish, mossbunker, and sardines. The latter is an extremely effective method. Trolling is also very effective with hexheads, Green Machines, jetheads, feather jigging, and jigged West Coast lures. The same tackle is used on both coasts by sport anglers. There is increasing pressure on the albacore stocks off the West Coast because of the large commercial fishery.

Growth Rate

AGE	LENGTH (IN INCHES)	WEIGHT (IN POUNDS)
1	21	7
2	25	12
3	30	20
4	34	30
5	37	37
6	39	48
7	41	54

ATLANTIC BONITO *(Sarda sarda)*
Physical Characteristics
Has wavy lateral line; body covered with minute scales, thicker and larger on corselet. Between 16 and 26 large, conical teeth on either side of upper jaw, 12 to 24 on either side of lower jaw. Also between 8 and 21 small conical teeth in single row on palate, with possibly additional small patch of teeth in patch on head of vomer. No teeth on tongue, and no swim bladder. Between 16 and 23 gill rakers on first gill arch. Large mouth with upper jaw reaching beyond rear margin of eyes.

Coloration
The back is steel blue or blue-green, with a silver-colored belly and lower flanks. Between 5 and 11 straight, oblique bars or stripes run from just below the lateral line backward to the dorsal fins. There are no spots, lines, or markings on the belly.

Distribution and Behavior
Found in tropical and temperate waters of the Atlantic Ocean from Nova Scotia to Argentina, and again from Norway to South Africa. Less commonly found in the Caribbean, Mediterranean, and Black Seas.

The Atlantic bonito spawns between March and July in Mediterranean, and January through April in the Atlantic. It feeds on squid, shrimp, and other invertebrates and can swallow relatively large foods for its size. It's also known to be cannibalistic.

Size
The all-tackle record is 16.75 pounds, caught off the Canary Islands.

Fishing Methods
Taken recreationally on light tackle and fly rods, and commercially via nets, purse seines, beach seines, and hook and line.

AUSTRALIAN BONITO *(Sarda australis)*
Physical Characteristics
Has 16 to 26 teeth in upper jaw, 11 to 20 in lower; 19 to 21 gillrakers on first arch. First dorsal fin has 17 to 19 spines. Dorsal stripes more horizontal than in any other species of small tuna, extending onto stomach area in some fish.

Distribution

Australian bonito are commonly found in the coastal waters of Australia from Queensland to Western Australia. They continually migrate along Australia's east coast from southern Queensland to eastern Victoria, Tasmania, and South Australia. Not to be confused with the leaping bonito, which is a tropical species and found primarily in northern Australian waters. Australian bonito prefer the coastal waters around inshore and offshore reefs, islands, ocean rocks, wharves, and rocky inshore areas. They school according to size, and mature from January through April.

Size

The Australian record is 16.5 pounds, but the species commonly runs between 11 and 9 pounds.

Fishing Methods

This surface-feeding fish has an incredible fighting ability for its size. It makes very good sport fish on light tackle or a fly rod. Live baits such as slimy mackerel and yakkas work well, as do whole, strip, and cut baits of the same plus garfish, yellowtail, pilchard, herring, squid, and other small baitfish. Try artificial baits such as any flashy or chrome lures, spoons, small hexheads, or flathead jigs. For fly fishing, Clousers and Deceivers are your best bet.

Rocky headlands and inshore reef areas where "washy" areas occur from wave action are good angling spots. Fishing at dawn is good and trolling from 5 to 7 knots works well. The best times of year are summer and fall.

BLACKFIN TUNA *(Thunnus atlanticus)*
Physical Characteristics

Pectoral fin moderately long, reaching below beginning of second dorsal fin. Eyes large in proportion to body size. Between 19 and 25 gillrakers on first arch, with average between 21 and 23, fewer than any other tuna.

Coloration

The back is metallic to blue-black in color, the belly is white, the fins are dark to dark silver, and the finlets are dusky in color with only a slight trace of yellow. Dorsal finlets sometimes turn yellowish at base after death.

There's no white rear edge on the caudal fin. A broad brownish stripe is found along the upper part of the side. The sides are uniformly silver-gray or feature pale streaks and spots in vertical rows.

Geographic Distribution and Behavior

Found only in the western Atlantic Ocean from Cape Cod to Brazil. Extending to just a couple of hundred miles offshore, these fish never cross the Atlantic, nor do they ever enter coastal waters. The blackfin's diet includes such items as other similar- and smaller-sized fish, squid, crustaceans, and planktonic animals found from the surface to great depths. It often competes for food with skipjack tuna, and is occasionally preyed on by them. Other predators include blue marlin, other larger tuna, and dolphin.

Not much is known about this species. The average life span is thought to be about five years.

Spawning occurs off southern Florida and in the Gulf of Mexico from April through November.

Growth Rate

A small species of tuna, the blackfin is commonly less than 10 pounds, with an occasional fish reaching 30 pounds. The world record, caught off Bermuda in 1978, was 39 inches long and weighed 42 pounds.

Fishing Methods

Blackfin tuna are taken in large numbers by commercial anglers in Cuba using live bait and poles, and are caught in large numbers by sport anglers from Florida to the West Indies. These fish prefer to strike at large bait; try a squid over a ballyhoo. Its flesh is delicious white meat and much sought after. It makes an excellent bait for blue marlin.

BIGEYE TUNA *(Thunnus obesus)*

Until fairly recently the bigeye was not recognized as a separate species; it was thought to be a subspecies of the yellowfin. The two do exhibit very similar physical characteristics, but the bigeye's second dorsal and anal fins don't grow as long as the yellowfin's. A primary distinction is the liver: In the bigeye it is striated on the bottom, and the right and left lobes are about the same size.

Physical Characteristics

As its name implies, this species has an unusually large set of eyes, though to the untrained this isn't enough to distinguish it from the yellowfin. The bigeye's pectoral fins are more than 80 percent of its head length and may reach to the second dorsal fin. The second dorsal fin and anal fins are moderate in size and never reach as far as those of the yellowfin tuna. The bottom of its liver is striated (see photo). Its tail fin is large and crescent shaped, with strong lateral keels between two smaller keels on either side of the caudal peduncle and slightly farther back. The scales are small except for the anterior corselet (stomach-abdominal area), and the lateral line is indistinct. The bigeye's body shape is semifusiform— roundish but slightly compressed. Like all tuna, its caudal peduncle is very slender, and its anal vent is oval or teardrop shaped, unlike the albacore's, which is round.

Between 23 and 31 gillrakers on first arch. First dorsal fin has 13 to 14 spines, second 14 to 16 rays followed by 8 to 10 dorsal finlets. Anal fin has 11 to 15 rays followed by 7 to 10 finlets.

Coloration

The back of the bigeye is a dark metallic blue color, which then gradually changes through a band of yellow or lighter iridescent blue, finally becoming a light bluish white on the lower flanks and belly. The first dorsal fin is a deep yellow, and the second dorsal and anal fins are blackish-brown or yellow in color, banded with black. The finlets are bright yellow with narrow black edges, and the tail and pectoral fins can be reddish-black or brown. A bigeye's tail does not have a white trailing edge like an albacore. In general a bigeye has no special markings on its body, although some fish may have vertical rows of white spots on the venter.

Geographic Distribution and Behavior

Found worldwide in the warm-temperate waters (60 to 80 degrees) of the Atlantic, Pacific, and Indian Oceans. Not found in the Mediterranean.

Bigeyes are schooling, pelagic fish that migrate seasonally over a very broad geographic range. Schools usually remain deep during the day, coming to the surface occasionally to feed, especially in warmer waters. Ideal temperature ranges to find them are between 63 and 72 degrees. The bigeye's diet consists of squid, crustaceans, and other fish such as mullet, sardines, mackerel, and smaller deepwater fish species. Each female will shed several million eggs per year during spawning, which occurs during the warm summer months in the Northeast and northern Pacific. In waters near the equator it may occur throughout the year.

Fishing Methods

This large species is prized for its fighting ability and dockside price. Its flesh is delicious and marketed canned, frozen, and salt-dried. Try deep trolling with artificial lures, jetheads, and hexheads, or rigged squid, mullet, and other baits indigenous to the region. Live bait fishing also works well, as does using downriggers.

Commercially, bigeyes are sought after by the Japanese and Koreans, who took over 100,000 metric tons of them from the Pacific in 1980. The reported world catch that year was 201,000 metric tons. In the Pacific they're primarily taken on longlines; a purse-seine fishery has been experimented with in the northeastern western Atlantic.

BLUEFIN TUNA (Thunnus thynnus)

A member of the mackerel tribe and one of the world's largest game fish, the bluefin is also known as the horse mackerel, tunny, leaping tuna, and great tunny. There's a single worldwide species of bluefins, although this was only recently agreed upon. An important food and game fish, it's noted for its size, speed, strength, schooling habits, worldwide distribution, and dramatic migrations. The most abundant Telostean fish commonly reach 500 pounds or more. This is undoubtedly the most powerful fish that swims.

Physical Characteristics

The body shape is robust, tapering to a pointed snout. Bluefin have shorter pectoral fins than other American tuna, and more gillrakers (31 to 43) than any other Thunnus species. The vertical surface of the liver is covered with the same striations seen on the albacore and bigeye.

Bluefin have two dorsal fins, the first retractable, the second stationary. Nine to 10 yellow finlets with black edges are found behind second dorsal fin, with 8 to 10 finlets behind the anal fin. The tail is lunate in shape.

Coloration

The body color is generally steel blue above with green reflections, blending to silver-gray on the vertical surface. In immature bluefins white spots and streaks are found forming vertical lines on the lower sides. The anal fin and finlets are yellowish; all other fins are dark. Living fish have a bright yellow band beginning at the snout halfway along each side of the body. This fades rapidly when the fish dies or is taken from the water.

Distinctive Features

A bluefin's body temperature may reach 10 degrees above that of the surrounding seawater. This internally generated heat cannot be dissipated through the fish's thick body muscles. A midlateral strip of dark red meat is created by an abundance of blood vessels along with a high accumulation of myoglobin. This dark meat is high in stored carbohydrates and may be a stored-energy reserve, helping the fish attain and maintain high speeds.

Size

Bluefins grow up to 1,500 pounds, with much speculation and rumor about 1-ton fish being caught in the fish traps of Europe.

Geographic Distribution and Behavior

Bluefin are found worldwide, mainly in temperate and subtropical waters throughout the Atlantic from the Bahamas to Labrador.

They join schools when just ½ inch in length and stay in schools throughout their 40-year life span, always according to size. Bluefins swim in a single-file, side-by-side, soldier-type formation or in an arc, hunter-type formation.

It is thought that they navigate by using the sun as their compass, and also by following electronic fields, scents, and currents. Fish tagged off the Bahamas have been caught again off Norway. The exact migration patterns are not known. However, recent advances in electronic tags show that the Atlantic stocks do travel from New England and Canadian waters to Scandinavia, to northern Europe, and then down the European and northern African coasts before returning to the Gulf of Mexico as was commonly speculated for decades.

Ironically, the high technology employed in longline fishing has been particularly helpful in keeping track of bluefin movements. For example, bluefin are almost nonexistent in the northwest Atlantic during the months July through October. All the catches that have been made were at or near the edge of the continental shelf. Then in the fall the bluefin move from their summer feeding grounds to their wintering areas, which are much more extensive. Longline fishing has revealed that dense concentrations of medium-sized and smaller fish congregate in areas from Hudson Canyon off New York to Lydonia Canyon off Georges Bank in October and November.

From May through mid-June the bluefins begin their dramatic northward migration along the edge of the shelf off Cat Cay in the northwestern Bahamas. It seems that this migration follows the path through the Old Bahamas and Santaren channels. At the same time these fish are migrating past Cat Cay, other large bluefins have also been taken in the northern part of the Gulf of Mexico. It was assumed until recently that this northward migration followed the Atlantic coast up to Labrador, but tagged fish caught off the coast of Norway now prove this to be false. In addition, recent longline catches have suggested that a large area east of the Bahamas extending from San Salvador to Walkers Cay and 100 miles eastward contains large concentrations of bluefins during this time period.

During May the bluefins are found in the same areas as during the winter months, only in larger concentrations. These areas include places such as the 1,000-fathom curve and an area just north of the Gulf Stream. In June the smaller and medium-sized fish move on to or close to the continental shelf, while the larger fish are taken on or near the northern edge of the Gulf Stream. This activity ends in early July to complete their yearly cycle.

North Atlantic bluefins differ from their cousins in the Indian Ocean. For this reason subspecific names have been assigned to the two. The Atlantic species is called *T. thunnus,* while *T. t. saliens* has been assigned to the others. Both species are taken from South African waters.

WESTERN NORTH ATLANTIC STOCKS

The bluefin's range extends over a vast area of the North Atlantic but depends on the time of the year, size of fish, and other factors. From July through October bluefins will take advantage of warm-water conditions and "summer" in northeastern and Canadian waters. November and December is their migratory period; and January through April, when water temperatures are at their lowest, is their wintering period. May through June is another migratory period.

From Cape Hatteras to Labrador, including the continental shelf, bluefins are usually taken commercially and by sport anglers from May until November. The large fish show up first during May and June, to be followed by the smaller fish in July. Medium-sized fish show up around New Jersey or Long Island in July, gradually making their way, via Cape Cod, to Nova Scotia by September. This midsized group is then the last to leave on the journey southward, following the large and small fish. By November these fish are usually well offshore, taking advantage of the warm waters of the Gulf Stream.

Geographic distribution of the various sizes differs as well. Small fish are usually found south and west of Cape Cod in coastal waters, while the larger fish are found north and east of eastern Long Island. Areas in which bluefin tend to congregate are the Mud Hole off New York Harbor, the southwestern ledge off Block Island, Butterfish Hole off Montauk, Stellwagen Bank off the northern edge of Cape Cod, Ipswich and Casco Bays in the U.S. waters, Trinity Ledge, the Tusket Islands (Wedgeport), and St. Margrets Bay in Nova Scotia, as well as Conception Bay, Newfoundland. The smaller fish cover a much wider range—from the Chesapeake Bay to Cape Cod—congregating in such places as the South Channel area east of Chatham in late summer or early fall, and Hydrographer and Vetch Canyons in the fall. Data supplied by spotter planes and swordfishing anglers indicate that these fish are headed southward from the Gulf of Maine.

From June through October bluefin tuna are found on the continental shelf between Cape Hatteras and Newfoundland. Generally the smaller fish are found near the southwestern part of the range, while the larger fish occupy the northeastern range. By November most of these fish have left the coastal waters, and large numbers of both small and large fish are found along the edge of the shelf off southern New England. This is the month that they begin the migration to their wintering grounds. Then from January through April great numbers of fish can be found over a large area that includes the Gulf of Mexico, the northern Caribbean, and waters from the southeastern corner of the Grand Banks to Puerto Rico.

EASTERN ATLANTIC STOCKS

During the summer small and medium-sized fish are abundant in France's Bay of Biscay, which is on a latitude parallel to our New Jersey-Cape Cod area. Larger bluefins are found along the coasts of Norway and in the North Sea, corresponding to our Gulf of Maine–Nova Scotia area.

During the spring and summer these fish make regular runs to the different approaches of the Mediterranean Sea, comparable to their runs through the Florida Straits. Four large bluefins tagged off the coast of Norway were caught again that same year off Spain.

Populations
Research has proven that two different populations of bluefins inhabit the two sides of the Atlantic. Many fish tagged in the eastern Atlantic have turned up in European waters, however, suggesting that these two separate populations can and do mix in small numbers at times.

Fishing Methods
Bluefins are taken with pound nets and purse seines in New England, and mainly by purse seines in the Pacific. Japan takes about half of the total world catch. Commercial fishing for bluefins in the northwestern Atlantic is increasing. Longline fishing is practiced in the Gulf of Mexico and northern Caribbean as well as waters from Cape Hatteras to Newfoundland. Both longlining and purse seining are devastating to bluefin populations.

Spawning
Spawning grounds are not well defined. Large fish have been caught in spawning condition from the Windward Passage in the Antilles, the Florida Straits, and the northern Bahamas from April to early June. Smaller fish in spawning condition have been found as far north as New England in June. The young grow rapidly, reaching about 8½ inches by July.

Indications are that bluefins spawn over wide areas of the western Atlantic. Giants are found in the southern areas during April and May, with medium-sized fish being found north of the Gulf Stream during late May or early June. Ripe female giants have been caught in the Windward Passage east of the Bahamas in April, while other ripe fish have been caught in late May through early June in the Gulf of Mexico. Juveniles less than 3 inches long have been caught in the same areas during the same time of year. In the northern areas, ripe, medium–sized fish have been caught along the edge of the continental shelf and toward the Gulf Stream off southern New England in June.

Large numbers of juvenile bluefins 12 to 15 inches in length have been observed moving northward through the Florida Straits in July. Throughout the rest of the summer and into the early winter months slowly growing fish can be caught here as well, although in progressively smaller numbers. Other bluefins have been caught in the Gulf of Mexico from September through December, all thought to have been spawned by the giant bluefins in the southern areas. In addition, small bluefins have been caught trolling off Hatteras sporadically from September through March, and large runs of these small fish have been known to occur from July through October from the Chesapeake Bay to Cape Cod, with September being the most common month. It is believed that these juvenile fish are the result of spawning fish in the northern and southern areas.

Growth Rates

Bluefin tuna grow at a very quick rate. The below chart represents the average age-length-weight relationship for the western North Atlantic tuna. These fish are aged by their otoliths—small bonelike structures in the interior ear—rather than by the scale system, because as a bluefin grows the annuli on its scales become indistinguishable. Bluefins can also be aged by circular depression found on a cross section of their vertebrae.

AGE (YEARS)	LENGTH (INCHES)	WEIGHT (LBS)
0–3 months	13	1.5
1	23	8.5
2	31	22
3	39	40
4	47	69
5	55	100
6	61	140
7	67	185
8	73	240
9	79	300
10	85	360
11	91	430
12	96	510
13	101	600
14	105	690

BULLET TUNA *(Auxis rochei)*

This small tuna species is very hard to distinguish from the frigate tuna.

Physical Characteristics

Short pectoral fins. Pattern of 15 or more fairly broad, nearly vertical dark bars in scaleless area behind pectoral fins on upper side. Scales form corselet around stomach-abdominal area on anterior (front) portion; no scales on posterior (following) portion.

Geographic Distribution

Worldwide in tropical and subtropical waters, including the Mediterranean and Black Seas.

Fishing Methods

There's no specific fishery for bullet tuna, though they are taken incidentally with other species around the world, usually by pole-and-line fishing but also in nets, small longlines, trawls, traps, and purse seines.

DOGTOOTH TUNA *(Gymnosarda unicolor)*

Physical Characteristics

Deep purple above and silvery below, with yellow finlets. There are no spots or other markings on the body. The dogtooth is not as deep bodied as other family members, and is easily distinguished by its peglike teeth and lack of body scales. It has 14 to 31 large, conical teeth in the upper jaw, and 10 to 24 in the lower jaw. There are 11 to 14 gillrakers on first gill arch.

Geographic Distribution and Behavior

Found throughout the tropical Indo-Pacific, including northern Australian waters and the Pacific islands. The species also ranges to the east coast of Africa off Madagascar, and the Red Sea. It's not found in Hawaiian waters. Australia's Great Barrier Reef area is thought to be a spawning region.

The dogtooth tuna or tagi is a highly migratory fish found along the edges of deepwater reefs and submarine ledges where the bottom abruptly drops off into deeper water. It either schools or is found alone; unlike their cousins, dogtooth are solitary fish. They're found in water temperatures ranging from 68 to 82 degrees.

Tunas of the World
Paintings by Ron Pittard

ALBACORE TUNA *Thunnus alalunga*

ATLANTIC BONITO *Sarda sarda*

AUSTRALIAN BONITO *Sarda australis*

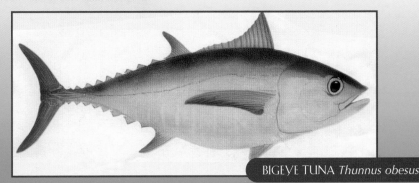

BIGEYE TUNA *Thunnus obesus*

BLACKFIN TUNA *Thunnus atlanticus*

BULLET TUNA *Auxis rochei*

DOGTOOTH TUNA *Gymnosarda unicolor*

BLACK SKIPJACK TUNA *Euthynnus lineatus*

EASTERN PACIFIC BONITO *Sarda chiliensis*

KAWAKAWA *Euthynnus affinis*

LEAPING BONITO *Cybiosardo elegans*

FRIGATE TUNA *Auxis thazard*

LONGTAIL TUNA *Thunnus tonggol*

NORTHERN BLUEFIN TUNA *Thunnus thynnus*

SKIPJACK TUNA *Katsuwonus pelami*

SLENDER TUNA *Allothunnus fallai*

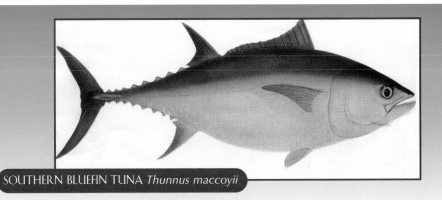

SOUTHERN BLUEFIN TUNA *Thunnus maccoyii*

SPOTTED TUNNY *Euthynnus alletteratus*

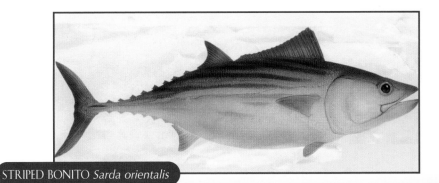

STRIPED BONITO *Sarda orientalis*

YELLOWFIN TUNA *Thunnus albacares*

SCHOOLING YELLOWFIN. *Copyright © William Boyce Photography*

YELLOWFIN APPROACHING THE BOAT *Copyright © Andy Hahn*

SAM TALARICO WITH A BLUEFIN TUNA CAUGHT ON A FLY OFF
MONTAUK, NEW YORK

Size
Reported to reach 300 pounds, although the 20- to 30-pound range is common. The world record is 288 pounds.

Fishing Methods
An excellent food and game fish, the dogtooth is a scaless white-meat tuna that puts up a good fight when hooked. It is commonly taken by trolling and drifting drop-offs with live, cut, or whole baits. Off American Samoa and once in a while around Guam dogtooths are commonly taken by handliners at night.

FRIGATE TUNA *(Auxis thazard)*
Physical Characteristics
Also called the frigate mackerel, this fish is part of the mackerel tribe. Distinguishable by two dorsal fins separated by a wide space, with 8 free finlets behind the second dorsal fin and 7 behind the anal fin.

The body has scales that form a corselet (stomach-abdominal area) on the anterior (front) portion with no scales on the posterior (following) portion. The pectoral fins are short. Between them is a fleshy flap almost as long as the pelvic fins.

The frigate is very difficult to distinguish from the bullet tuna. In both species an extension of the corselet follows the lateral line. The frigate's extension is no more than 5 scale rows wide under the second dorsal fin, while in the bullet it's 6 to 28 rows wide. Frigate tuna rarely reach more than 2 feet in length.

Geographic Distribution and Behavior
Found in the Indian and Pacific Oceans and from Florida to the Carolina coasts in the Atlantic Ocean.

Frigate tuna form dense schools of hundreds of fish. Their diet consists primarily of squid, crustaceans, and other small fish. They in turn are a favorite food of marlin and larger tuna.

LEAPING BONITO *(Cybiosardo elegans)*
Physical Characteristics
Short, relatively deep body. Rather large mouth; 13 to 22 large conical teeth on upper jaw, 10 to 17 on lower; 12 to 15 gillrakers on first arch.

Dorsal fins placed close together. Body mostly naked behind well-developed corselet, except for band of scales along bases of dorsal and anal fins. The Australian record is 2.5 pounds.

Coloration
The belly is pale or white, with several stripes similar to a skipjack tuna. The back is deep blue and covered with elongated black spots; the first dorsal fin is jet black, the anal and second dorsal fins are yellow.

Geographic Distribution and Behavior
Leaping bonito are commonly found in the northern coastal waters of Australia and Papua, New Guinea, and occasionally farther south along the east and west coasts of Australia. They prefer the coastal waters around inshore and offshore reefs, islands, ocean rocks, wharves, and rocky inshore areas. They school by the hundreds.

Fishing Methods
This surface-feeding fish is, like the Australian bonito, a great fighter for its size, especially taken on light tackle or a fly rod. It's a white-meat fish suitable for human consumption and often smoked.

There's no specific fishery for the leaping bonito, though they're used a lot by recreational anglers as bait for snappers and marlin. Fishing at dawn is good, and trolling from 5 to 7 knots works well. Live baits such as slimy mackerel and yakkas work well, as do whole, strip, and cut baits of the same plus garfish, yellowtail, pilchard, herring, squid, and other small baitfish. Try artificial baits such as any flashy or chrome lures, spoons, small hexheads, and flathead jigs. For fly fishing, Clousers and Deceivers are your best bet. The best times of year are summer and fall. Rocky headlands and inshore reef areas where washy areas are produced by wave action make for good angling.

LITTLE TUNNIES
Little tunnies are a group of fish intermediate between mackerel and tuna including the eastern Pacific bonito, plain bonito, black skipjack, Australian bonito, kawakawa, striped bonito, and spotted or little tuna. I will focus on the false albacore or plain bonito *(Euthynnus alletteratus);* the wavyback or kawakawa *(Eu. affinis),* the black skipjack *(Eu. lineatus);*

and the skipjack tuna *(Eu. pelamis).* They are difficult to distinguish from each other. All are members of the mackerel tribe. Their flesh is not favored for eating.

Physical Characteristics

Little tunies are medium-sized fishes that possess an armor-plated set of scales on the front of the body, while the rear is scaleless. Dorsal markings consist of broken horizontal stripes or bars. The two dorsal fins are narrowly separated, with the first being deeply concave. The teeth are conical. There are between 37 and 45 gillrakers on the first arch and 31 to 32 gill teeth.

The false albacore has no teeth on the vomer (a small bone in the roof of the mouth) and wavy lines on top. Its body shape is very similar to that of the albacore, but the false albacore has only a short pectoral fin. The largest ever caught on rod and reel weighed 27 pounds, off Key West, Florida.

The black skipjack may be distinguished by the 3 to 5 horizontal black lines on its back. Dark spots are found below the pectoral fin. Some fish may have faint stripes on the stomach. There are 8 dorsal finlets and 7 anal finlets. A double-pointed skin flap can be found between the pelvic fins. The upper portion of the body is dark blue; the stomach is silvery. The rod-and-reel record weighed 20 pounds and was caught off Clarion Island, Mexico; most of the black skipjacks caught weigh half that. The meat is highly valued in South American markets, but no specific fishery for these fish exists.

The kawakawa has teeth on the vomer and wavy lines on the back, starting at the end of the first dorsal fin and continuing to the tail. There are no stripes on the stomach. A small notch separates the dorsal fins. There are 8 to 10 dorsal finlets, 6 to 7 anal finlets, and double-pointed skin flap between the pelvic fins. This fish is dark blue on the upper part of the body, with a silvery white stomach. There are a variable number of black spots on the sides below the pectoral fins, with dark markings on the back. Wavy wormlike markings are also found on the back above the lateral line. The fish reaches about 3 feet in length.

Growth Rates

Little tunies in their first year of life reach average weight of 2 pounds and an average length of 15 inches. The extent of their growth is about 40 inches, after a maximum of 10 years. In the middle Atlantic the average fish caught is 2 years old and weighs 6 pounds, while the average fish caught in the warmer waters of Florida is smaller.

Geographic Distribution And Behavior

Found throughout the world's oceans in tropical and subtropical waters, including the Mediterranean, Black Sea, Gulf of Mexico, and Caribbean.

False albacore are found only in the Atlantic Ocean and Mediterranean Sea, ranging from Cape Cod to South America and including the Gulf of Mexico. In the eastern Atlantic they're found off Europe and Africa, south to Augold.

The black skipjack occurs only in the Pacific Ocean from California to Peru and west to the Galapagos. It's epipelagic and usually coastal.

The kawakawa is fairly rare off America's West Coast, but commonly found from Hawaii through the western Pacific and Indian Oceans. It's epipelagic and usually coastal, entering estuaries.

All little tunnies spawn year-round, with each female laying over one million eggs at a time. They're opportunistic feeders with a diet consisting of a wide range of crustaceans, squid, and other fish. They will compete for food with other species of fish and also with the dolphin that travel with them at times. When feeding, little tunnies either herd their prey into tight schools and picking out the stragglers, or crash into the pack devouring everything in their path.

Fishing Methods

Look for white water created by feeding action on the surface to locate schools. Little tunnies can be caught trolling, casting, or commercially with different netting techniques. Sport anglers catch these fish in a variety of ways, among them casting flashy lures and trolling ballyhoo or other small live and natural baits. They can be caught from the surf, off piers, while bluefishing, or offshore.

The red meat of these fish has good flavor when served raw. It will turn tannish-white in color when cooked by traditional methods such as broiling, and is much better when cooked Chinese style. Their primary use, though, is as sailfish strip baits or chunked for dolphin.

LONGTAIL TUNA *(Thunnus tonggoi)*

This species is sometimes referred to as the northern bluefin tuna in Australia. Juveniles are commonly mistaken for bluefins, yellowfins, or bigeyes. Therefore, records and catch statistics are thought to be somewhat inaccurate.

Physical Characteristics

A small fish very similar in appearance to the southern bluefin, the long-tail has a very deep, rounded body. The distance between the second dorsal fin and the caudal keel is longer than in any other tuna. The upper body is black with cobalt blue-purple hues throughout. The lower body is silvery white. Finlets are dark yellow, edged with gray tints. The caudal keel is black, with a short second dorsal and anal fin. Pectoral fins are longer than the bluefin's, but not as long as the head. Weights reach 100 pounds.

Geographic Distribution and Behavior

Found in the Indo-Pacific from Japan through the Philippines to Papua, New Guinea, New Britain, and the southwestern three-quarters of Australia, including New South Wales, Twofold Bay, and Freemantle in Western Australia. Also west through the East Indies to both coasts of India, the southern Arab Peninsula, the Red Sea, and the coast of Somalia.

They're commonly found in shallow inshore waters less than 60 fathoms deep near reefs or drop-offs and close to schools of baitfish such as anchovies and pilchards. Rarely found in the open ocean. Habitat: An epipelagic, neritic species, the longtail avoids turbulent waters and those with low salinity such as estuaries. Schools vary in size. The fish feed on many species of crustaceans, squid, and smaller fish.

Fishing Methods

This is a very fast fish, powerful and a great fighter on light or fly-fishing tackle. It's commercially fished off Japan, the Philippines, New Guinea, Indonesia, and Asia, primarily through drift netting, longlining, and trolling.

ORIENTAL BONITO *(Sarda orientalis)*

A small member of the bonito tribe.

Physical Characteristics
Easily identified by green backs and large number of oblique green stripes running horizontally along top half of body. Upper jaw has 12 to 20 teeth, lower 10 to 17; 8 to 13 gillrakers on first arch. Weights reach 6.6 pounds.

Geographic Distribution
Widespread in the tropical and subtropical waters of the Indo-Pacific and north to about 41 degrees north latitude. These fish are common in the northwestern and southwestern waters of Australia, particularly in late summer and fall and often accompanied by the leaping bonito. To the east they're found along America's Pacific Coast to Cabo San Lucas and the Galapagos Islands. They school with other small tuna and feed on crustaceans, squid, and other small fish.

Fishing Methods
This is a great recreational fish on light tackle or a fly rod. There's no defined commercial fishery, but the species is often taken with other small tuna in nets, in purse seines, by trolling, and via pole and line.

PACIFIC BONITO *(Sarda chiliensis)*
The Pacific bonito is a small tuna found both inshore and offshore; it's similar in size and coloration to the Atlantic bonito. It will often mix with or be found near other schools of tuna or mackerel. A large number of the Pacific bonito are canned on the Pacific Coast, but they're considered the least valuable of the tunalike fishes and cannot legally be labeled "tuna."

Physical Characteristics
Prominent horizontal or oblique stripes on back. Upper jaw has 18 to 30 teeth, lower 14 to 25; 23 to 27 gillrakers on first arch. Dorsal fins not widely separated; 7 to 9 dorsal finlets; 6 to 7 anal finlets. Between 17 and 19 spines on first dorsal fin; 20 to 27 gillrakers on first branchial arch. Large conical teeth. Body fully scaled, with scales in the corselet (stomach-abdominal area) larger. Upper jaw extends to rear of eye or beyond. Double-pointed skin flap between pelvic fins.

Coloration
Greenish-blue above with a silver underside and dark parallel lines running obliquely along the back.

Geographic Distribution and Behavior

Restricted to the eastern Pacific. The species is found from Chile to the Gulf of Alaska, but it's most common in the warmer portions of this range. It's found off southern California, especially from Santa Monica Bay southward. Northern and southern subspecies occur, separated by a tropical population. The southern subspecies ranges from south of the Gulf of Guayaquil in Peru to Talcahuano, Chile. The northern subspecies occurs from the Alaskan coast to Cabo San Lucas.

Pacific bonito spawn in batches off southern California and Baja from January through May. Each mature fish lays up to half a million eggs. Fish reach sexual maturity at 2 years, though some have been recorded as spawning at 1 year in cold-water areas influenced by thermal discharges. Older fish tend to live farther offshore. Other tuna, billfish, and sharks all prey upon them.

Growth Rate

The Pacific bonito grows to a maximum length of 4 feet. The average fish caught weighs 3 to 4 pounds, although they do get as large as 10 to 15 pounds. The all-tackle record is 23 lbs., 8 ozs., caught off the Seychelles Islands in 1975.

AGE (YEARS)	LENGTH (INCHES)	WEIGHT (POUNDS)
1	19	2
2	25	6
3	29	10
4	30	11
5	31	12
6	32	13

Fishing Methods

Pacific bonito are caught by trolling, jigging, or casting by sport anglers and commercially by purse seiners.

SKIPJACK (Katsuwonus pelamis)

A cosmopolitan species that gets its name from its practice of "skipping" over the surface as it chases smaller fish while feeding. Other names include oceanic tuna and striped tuna. Skipjacks are not members of the bonito tribe although they are often mistakenly referred to as Arctic or oceanic bonito.

Physical Characteristics

The skipjack's body is scaleless and its shape is fusiform, elongate, and rounded, with a short, sharply pointed snout. From 4 to 6 prominent, dark longitudinal stripes are found on the lower half of the body and stomach. Scales are found only on the front corselet (stomach-abdominal area) of the body. There are 53 to 63 gillrakers on the first arch. The first dorsal fin has 14 to 16 spines. The inner space between the first and second dorsal fins is never greater than the diameter of the fish's eye. The dorsal fin is connected at its base and contains 7 to 9 dorsal finlets and 7 to 8 anal. There's a short pectoral fin with no black spots below. A double-pointed skin flap is found between the pelvic fins. There are between 30 to 40 conical teeth in each jaw. These teeth are smaller and more numerous than the bonito's and very unlike the triangular, compressed teeth of the mackerel.

The skipjack is bluish to violet on the back, changing to silver below. The stripes on the belly and plain dark back distinguish the skipjack from similar species. Other smaller tuna species may have the stripes on the belly, but they also have markings on their back.

Geographic Distribution and Behavior

Found around the world in warm (64- to 82-degree) tropical and subtropical waters, often among other schools of tuna. Skipjacks swim in schools that may number up to 50,000 fish and are often seen on the surface feeding and jumping out of the water. Offshore fish are usually found on edges of continental shelves and occasionally inshore. In the Atlantic, skipjacks are often found near or in the Gulf Stream, breaking the surface as they chase bait. They're not found in the Black Sea.

Skipjacks spawn throughout the year in waters near the equator, but as the fish's distance from the equator increases, spawning tends to occur more in the summer months. Their diet consists of other fish, squid, and crustaceans. Cannibalism is common in schools. Their principal predators are other tuna and billfish.

Fishing Methods

The skipjack is one of the most important commercial fishes, particularly in the Pacific where they are of considerable economic value. The skipjack makes up about 40% of the world's tuna catch. Taken on the surface near Hawaii, Japan, and the Central American coast with purse seines, gillnets, traps, beach seines and even harpoons. Meat is red in color, excellent flavor either raw or when cooked. Marketed fresh, frozen, or canned, and in Japan they are dried.

Size

A warm-water fish, skipjack average two feet in length and five pounds body weight. They have been caught weighing up to 50 pounds and 42 inches in length commercially. The all-tackle record is 41 lbs. 12 ozs., caught off the island of Mauritius located on Africa's east coast. Skipjack are also excellent sport fish caught in a variety of ways, among them trolling feathers, or small hexheads within 25 feet of a boat's transom; jigging; and casting natural baits such as anchovies, sardines, or butterfish.

SLENDER TUNA *(Allothunnus fallai)*

Physical Characteristics

An oceanic species with a long, slender, and rounded body shape. There are no distinctive dark markings. The species has more gillrakers (approximately 75) on the first gill arch than other family members. Dorsal fins are close together, the first having 15 to 18 spines. It's bluish above and silver below. It's commonly reported in the Japanese longline fishery at between 26 and 38 inches.

Geographic Distribution

Found in the warmer ocean waters of the Southern Hemisphere, commonly between 20 and 50 degrees south latitude. One was taken in the early 1960s in Los Angeles Harbor.

SOUTHERN BLUEFIN *(Thunnus maccoyii)*

This very tough-fighting fish will, like its cousin the northern bluefin, run off a reel and dive deep when hooked.

Physical Characteristics

The southern bluefin has very short pectoral fins, much shorter than the head length. There are 23 to 31 gillrakers on the first arch. The pectoral fins are moderately long in large fish, spanning 22 to 31% of the fork length. In smaller fish even longer. In fish over 30cm in length the ventral surface of the liver is striated.

Coloring

Its upper body is black or a very dark blue, with a silvery white belly. A lateral iridescent blue band runs along the sides in live fish but fades after death. The first dorsal fin is a deep yellow, second dorsal and anal fins light yellow. Finlets are bright yellow edged with black.

Size

Southern bluefin reach 400 pounds. All-tackle record is 434.06 pounds in the Pacific, and in the Atlantic, (off Ocean City, MD) it is 374.66 pounds.

Geographic Distribution and Behavior

Found in the open oceans along the continental shelf, drop-offs, and in current lines. Sometimes found close to the coast if currents and bait conditions are favorable. The southern bluefin is common in the Atlantic, Pacific, and Indian Oceans, but absent from the Mediterranean.

Southern bluefins feed on ballyhoo, squid, pilchards, and other small fish along current lines and structural edges. Feeding occurs in daytime as well as at night, but early dawn is best for recreational anglers.

The fish are found on the surface to 250 yards in depth. Water temperatures and thermocline are the primary factors governing the vertical and horizontal distribution of the southern bluefin. Ideal temperatures are between 63 and 72 degree, but the fish are found from 55 to 84 degrees.

Juveniles and small adults are commonly found at the surface in groups or with other species such as yellowfins and skipjacks, often around floating objects.

Spawning occurs in the Pacific between 10 degrees north latitude and 10 degrees south latitude throughout the year, peaking from April through September in the Northern Hemisphere and January through March in the Southern Hemisphere. Mature fish can spawn twice a year, and females can lay between 3 and 6 million eggs each time.

The southern bluefin's main predators are large billfish and toothed whales.

Fishing Methods

Not surprisingly, Japan ranks first among countries taking southern bluefins, followed by South Korea. Longlines are the predominant method of commercial fishing. A new longline fishery now targets these and other tuna at depths to 300 yards. The fish are also being taken more by pole-and-line fishing in the northwestern Pacific. Their meat is highly prized in Japan for sashimi as a substitute for bluefin tuna.

STRIPED BONITO *(Sarda orientalis)*
Physical Characteristics

Upper jaw has 12 to 20 teeth, lower 10 to 17; 8 to 13 gillrakers on first arch; 17 to 19 spines on first dorsal fin. All-tackle record 23.43 pounds, off Mahe, Seychelles.

Geographic Distribution and Behavior

Widespread in the tropical and subtropical waters of the Indo-Pacific. In the western Pacific it will be found north to about 41 degrees latitude off Honshu, Japan. It's also found in northwestern and southwestern Australia, off Bali, and south of Java. Farther east striped bonito can be found around the Hawaiian Islands and America's Pacific Coast from California to Cabo San Lucas, west to the Galapagos Islands, and off Chile.

They school with other small tuna off the Indian coast from May through September, followed by smaller striped bonito in October and November. Off Sri Lanka they are found year-round. Striped bonito feed on clupeids, other fish, and crustaceans.

Fishing Methods

No specific commercial efforts exist, but the fish are commonly taken with other species when trolling, purse seining, pole-and-line fishing, and gill netting. They're also good sport fish on light tackle or a fly rod.

YELLOWFIN TUNA *(Thunnus albacares)*

Sometimes difficult to distinguish from the bigeye and bluefin. The yellowfin's flesh is light and often canned.

Physical Characteristics

Length of pectoral fin over 80% of head length. Finlets behind second dorsal and anal fins yellow with black margins; no white margin on caudal fin. Gillrakers 24 to 34: no striations on ventral surface of the liver; right lobe longer than central lobe (see drawing); all lobes somewhat pointed.

In large, mature fish, the second dorsal and anal fins sometimes become very long, and such fish are then easily distinguishable. These fish used to be called Allison tuna and were thought to be a different species from the yellowfin. Scientists now agree that all the world's yellowfin tuna belong to one species. Differences such as fin length or coloration are no more significant than a human's arm length or hair color.

Coloration

Yellowfins are the most brilliantly colored of the tuna, with a yellow stripe running laterally along their upper sides and a bright yellow appearance to much of their fins. The lower sides commonly have white spots with vertical stripes, even in large fish. The dorsal skin is dark blue, the ventral silvery-gray, the side golden. Young fish less than 51 inches long have chains of white spots. The first dorsal fin is lemon yellow, the second and anal fins yellow. Finlets are yellow with black edges but turn black shortly after death.

Geographic Distribution and Behavior

Atlantic and Pacific species, once thought to be different fish, are now known to be the same. All are found in subtropical and tropical waters around the world and limited to the upper 100 yards of water, concentrated by warm core eddies that spin off from the Gulf Stream then move toward land and water temperatures above 65 degrees.

Young fish form large schools with bigeye or skipjack tuna. The species is very nonselective in its feeding habits, eating other fish, crustaceans, squid—whatever is most available.

Yellowfins seem to roam over an area up to 10 miles wide each day, returning once or more to a particular spot. This spot is always something that attracts them, such as slope or underwater structure that may attract food, floating lumber, a dead whale. Why they are attracted to these objects is not known, although speculation is that yellowfins use these objects as an underwater "fix."

The fish are easily disrupted by currents, or anything that may cause changes in water temperature. They may suddenly disappear from one area only to turn up abruptly somewhere else.

Spawning takes place throughout the year in tropical waters, but is restricted to late spring and early summer in subtropical areas. The Pacific yellowfins that migrate across the equator may spawn twice each year. Each female spawns at least two batches of up to several million eggs each. These eggs remain in the warm surface layers of the water, never falling below the thermocline. When these fish are in the egg stage or very young they are preyed upon by many ocean fish, particularly larger yellowfins and white marlin. The fish reach sexual maturity at 1½ to 2½ years of age.

In the past decade or so, an unexplained new phenomenon has occurred with the yellowfin. Before 1979 these fish were found primarily in the Gulf Stream and as close to the East Coast as the continental shelf. However, beginning around 1979 surprised anglers began to catch yellowfins at the 30-fathom line; as recently as 1984 they were caught at the 20-fathom line. Obviously, something has drastically changed that has made these fish venture in closer and closer to our shores, but what? Many experts speculate that these fish have come in to feed off the abundant food resources that occur on the continental shelf. But why now? The shelf has always been an abundant food source. The most logical explanation would be that a water temperature barrier has been removed. It's now an accepted fact that the earth is undergoing a warming trend, and as this occurs, so will changes in water temperatures. A 1-or 2-degree variation in water temperature at the continental shelf wouldn't be a notable change, yet it could push the summer thermocline to a new depth and at the same time make the layer of warm surface water that much denser. This would allow yellowfins access to new areas such as the food-rich waters of the continental shelf and inshore.

Growth Rates

Yellowfins are the fastest growing tuna, reaching 7.5 pounds in 18 months and 90 pounds in three years. The largest fish to date is 388 lbs., 12ozs., caught off San Benedicto Island, Mexico, but fish of 400 pounds have been reported by purse seiners and longliners. Most fish caught on rod and reel are in the 30-to 150-pound range.

The maximum life span of the yellowfin is unknown but estimated at nine or ten years.

AGE (YEARS)	LENGTH (INCHES)	WEIGHT (POUNDS)
1	17–20	8–10
2	30–35	25–35
3	45–55	85–100
4	55–60	130–150
5	65–70	150–170
6	70+	180+

Migration

Tagging has revealed that these fish do not travel great distances. Much remains to be learned about their migrations, however. Most of our information about yellowfins comes from Pacific fish and research done with fish aggregation devices. The Woods Hole Oceanographic Institute and commercial longliners have also given us a general picture of the North Atlantic yellowfin's migration routes.

North Atlantic yellowfin migration is closely tied to the movements of the Gulf Stream from its point of origin in the Gulf of Mexico, around southern Florida, and northward to New England where it turns and crosses the Atlantic to northern Europe and then south to the Sargasso Sea. As the Gulf Stream passes the coast of Long Island, small pieces of warm water or warm core eddies break off, moving westward toward the continental shelf. These eddies bring warm water closer to shore, and with it tuna as well as other fish not normally found offshore, such as dolphin, marlin, or even sailfish.

During the winter months yellowfins seem to congregate along the southern edge of the Gulf Stream from Cape Hatteras to about 500 miles east. Here they find water temperatures above 68 degrees, as well as abundant food. When spring arrives the yellowfins disperse in all directions. They'll move north into the Gulf Stream, southwest toward Cape Hatteras, and south across the Sargasso Sea between Bermuda and the Bahamas. This is when they spawn. By the time summer arrives the stocks will have split into two groups, one off Bermuda and the other north and on the continental shelf as well as inshore from Cape Hatteras to New England.

As fall arrives and the inshore waters cool, yellowfins leave the inshore waters, moving along the continental slope and into the canyons where water depths range from 100 fathoms upward. There they will once again find water temperatures to their liking.

Many questions concerning the yellowfin still need to be answered. Do different stocks interbreed and interact with each other? When these fish spread out in the spring, just how far south do they go? Is the stock found off Bermuda a nonmigratory one? With the demand for yellowfins rising at alarming rates, we must learn more about these fish before we can effectively attempt to manage them.

Fishing Methods

The yellowfin is taken commercially in all the tropical regions of the world and especially in California, where it is the mainstay of that state's tuna fleet. The Japanese are now working populated ocean regions over the entire world in pursuit of these fish, and will deliver their catch to markets and canneries worldwide.

Live baiting and purse seining are most popular methods, with longlining gaining rapidly in popularity. Because these fish breed so profusely and grow the fastest of all the tuna species, they can and have recovered after having their stocks depleted. In 1981 the Japanese left the Gulf of Mexico after overfishing the yellowfins there; five years later the stocks had recovered. Flesh is light and marketed as such when canned.

PART 2

BEFORE LEAVING THE DOCK

4

THE
BOAT

During my years of fishing and knocking around boats, I've come to the conclusion that there is no one boat that meets all the standards necessary to be called a true tuna boat. About the closest that anyone has ever come to it was the Merritt Yard's 37-footer, built in the 1950s and 1960s. This fishing machine was used to fish off Cat Cay and Chub Cay, and Bimini during the spring bluefin run. In spots like the Bimini Trough, spotters in "oil rigs" (tuna towers) could actually see vast schools of bluefins ripping through on their journey north. They'd spent the winter in the Gulf of Mexico, had spawned, and were now in search of the abundant schools of bait found from New Jersey to Canada. This was the heyday of tuna fishing—a time when men and women such as the Farringtons, Lerners, Tommy Gifford, the Merritts, Ryboviches, Maytags, and a long list of others would spend April and May pursuing these great fish. The Merritt 37 was perfectly designed and built for this. Small enough to handle like a dream, yet big enough to deal with the often rough seas, she was powerful, laid out perfectly, easily handled, and a true tuna machine.

Capt. Clay Kyle ran these boats in the early days of tuna fishing. "Allen and Buddy Merritt built the first good tuna boats," he told me. "They were narrow and long hard-chine boats that ran like hell and had two engines, a fighting chair, V-berths, and not much else. Then John and Tommy [Rybovich] started building boats. The *Bahama Mama* was their first good tuna boat. She was 38 feet long and had two 200-horsepower motors. There were also lots of Chris-Crafts back then. Usually 35-footers with gas engines. They were a pretty boat, all varnished and teak decks. George Bass, who was one of the best tuna fishermen around, had a black boat called the *Sambo*. C. C. Anderson ran it. There were other good boats, too, like the Consolidateds and Norsemans."

Of course in the years since, the adage "bigger is better" has come to prevail, both because we often have to travel farther to find the bluefin and other offshore species, and because we are simply richer as a society and more prone to displays of ego such as big boats. I feel that anything over 48 to 50 feet is too big to handle effectively and efficiently. A good tuna boat must be able to back, spin, run down and in all ways keep up with a tuna, and I feel that the bigger sport-fishing boats just aren't as efficient in this as the 50-footers. Which isn't to say that any boat below 50 feet in length will not be a good tuna boat. Hull configuration, engines, cockpit layout, flying bridge layout, and visibility all play important roles, and in purchasing a boat for offshore fishing these factors all need to be taken into consideration.

Today many good boats for tuna fishing are built, including the old standards like Ryboviches and Merritts— boats whose features everybody has copied, such as modified or deep V—hulls, cockpit controls, efficient cockpit layouts, and powerful engines. While many

Merritt yard.

Rybovich taking shape.

excellent production and custom boats are built today that will do a fine job for the serious offshore angler, I don't feel that today any one make or model comes close to what the Merritt 37 was in its day.

Instead I feel it's important to try to incorporate as many features into your boat as is practical for safe and effective tuna fishing, while at the same time meeting your individual needs. It's no secret that all boats are compromises to some degree, and the ideal tuna boat is no exception.

COCKPIT

Look for a large and well-drained cockpit. It can never be too large. I think my own 31-foot Bertram's cockpit is perfect for one angler and one mate—anything more would be pushing it, but we often have two people wiring fish offshore. My fighting chair removes easily and breaks down to be stored forward or dockside if we want to do some stand-up fishing. If we're going trolling, there is still ample room with the 80-pound chair, as long as things stay organized. Once the fish is alongside the boat we may remove the seat and store it below for more working space in the cockpit.

The floor of the cockpit should be nonskid. Teak is good if you can afford it, with between 2 and 2½ feet of freeboard. The new fiberglass or West System-treated nonskid cockpits are great. After replacing my teak cockpit twice, I went to a West System. I love the safety of it as well as the simplicity in cleaning. And although it's white, I don't have any problems with glare.

Under the gunwales you should have all your gaffs, harpoon stick (if you use one), and tagging stick stored securely. I put a tennis ball on the point of each gaff so that legs don't get caught on it, and coil up the flying gaff lines, tucking them behind the gaff. Plenty of efficient storage space is also imperative, so if you can find a boat with tackle storage in the cockpit, that's a plus. Perhaps the best rod and tackle storage I've seen is on Henriques Boats, built in New Jersey by an experienced angler and boat-builder. Of course other boats are good, too, particularly downeast-style boats. And you can always customize your boat's cockpit to suit your needs. You'll quickly find that you can never have enough space for lines, lures, line, hooks, baits, and so on, but with proper planning and trial and error you can determine the best cockpit layout for your boat. Keep in mind that flush-mounted storage is your best bet in the cockpit if it's at all possible. It doesn't crowd the cockpit, and it eliminates any risk of getting caught on or hanging up on a protruding knob.

Flush-mounted or recessed rod holders that can hold gaffs, tagging sticks, tailropes, lines, and other offshore equipment should be evenly spaced around the sides of your cockpit's interior, the number of them depending on your cockpit's length and available space. Strive to have at least four to six on each side.

ROD HOLDERS

I have six rod holders mounted on the gunwales, including two striking rod holders closest to the stern on each side. I also have two vertical rod holders mounted on the transom that I often use for flat lines trolled close to the transom. In addition to those eight I sometimes use the two rod holders mounted on either side of the fighting chair, and there's at least one rail-mounted rod holder up on the bridge that I use for the center rigger. A trick I've learned to keep the rod butts from destroying the holders when you hook a tuna or other big fish is to drop a golf ball down inside the holder before inserting the butt. The rod will still fit in but when you hook up, the rod can swing freely, rather than tearing the pin out inside the holder. And you or the cockpit crew still have enough time to get to the rod and begin fighting the fish.

A Rybovich sport fishing boat.

SAFETY LINES

With a good rod-and-reel setup costing upward of $1,000, it's wise to always attach each rod to a safety line, whether you're fishing or just traveling to or from the fishing grounds. I've never had a rod go overboard, but a couple of close calls with inexperienced anglers have made me a believer. These lines are available in all offshore tackle stores, or catalogs, and are well worth their minimal cost. You can also make them yourself with some ⅜-inch, three-strand nylon line, Splice a small stainless or brass clip to one end. The other end should have a loop spliced into it to make it easier to fasten to the stanchion or cleat. The lengths will depend on the size of your cockpit and your rod placements, as well as where you anchor or tie them off. I use 15- and 25-foot lengths in my Bertram, each looped around the stanchion of my fighting-chair, but you can also attach them to a cockpit cleat. I like the fighting-chair stanchion because it gives me a little more versatility moving around the cockpit when I'm hooked up and fighting a fish, particularly on stand-up tackle. It also gives the rods a central point from which all of the lines can begin eliminating confusion—a very important consideration.

A Rybovich, the first true sport fishing boats, and the standard by which all modern sport fishing boats are judged.

Some anglers leave the safety line attached throughout a fight, which is a good idea if it isn't interfering with your ability to fight the fish. Others remove it when they're in the chair or harness. I try to leave mine in place at all times, especially with young or inexperienced anglers. Either way, invest in them and make sure you've always got one attached securely to each rod. It will give you peace of mind and eliminate a costly loss should something go wrong offshore.

CONTROLS

It is imperative that the helm station—whether it's on the flying bridge or inside—offer the captain a good view of the cockpit. When fighting a fish, he will need this view to determine the best strategies, often in split seconds.

POWER

Your engine choice is totally dependent on your budget. Obviously, diesels are best if you can afford them. They're more reliable, require less maintenance, have much less risk of fire or explosion, and run economically. They are very expensive initially, however. Gas motors are fine if maintained well. I have them in my Bertram and end up replacing them about every four seasons, just to be on the safe side. They run well, fast, and fairly economically in my boat—about 1 mile per gallon, which is pretty good. I'd love to convert to diesels, but the expense is just too much for me. In the larger boats diesels are now the norm, and rightly so.

CENTER CONSOLES

In recent years, as center-console designs have been refined, these boats have become true contenders for tuna fishing. They are fast, easily maneuverable, and give an angler a 360-degree fishing platform if set up properly. Their downside is of course comfort and room. But for the angler who wants a fairly versatile fishing platform and does not have a huge budget, the center console is a great choice. Ocean Master, SeaCraft, Mako Marine, and Regulator all make excellent boats in the 26- to 32-foot range—ideal for tuna fishing in good weather conditions. I've seen many of these center-console boats on tuna grounds such as Southwest Ledge, Butterfish Hole, and Stellwagen Bank in the past decade or so.

Most anglers use a rocket launcher setup mounted in conjunction with the seat behind the steering area. This allows anglers to stay close to the action and, in the event of a hookup, to get to the rods easily. I've also seen a fighting chair mounted in the forward section of the center-console boat, giving the captain a view of the action at all times, as well as aiding in operating the boat most efficiently when fighting a fish. The area behind the helm station can then be used for tackle, gaffs, tagging sticks, and the like until the time comes to boat or release the fish. In my estimation both are excellent choices.

The speed and agility of center consoles is excellent both for getting to the tuna grounds and when for maneuvering after you're hooked up and fighting a fish. They also enable you to pursue inshore species easily and without a full crew. You won't want to do many overnighters on one, but with the power options and fuel capacities available today, you won't need to. In favorable weather and with some good planning, you can turn a once-overnight trip into an easy day trip.

FUEL CAPACITY

Make sure you've got enough fuel to make it out to the fishing grounds and back—plus! Always take more fuel than you think you'll need in case

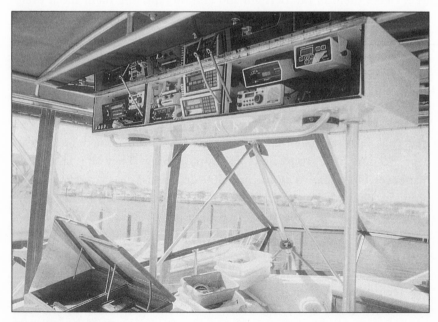

Good electronics layout.

you hook up a long-fighting fish, get lost, or run into foul weather. It happened to me once as I was coming back from Block Canyon. After getting caught in a horrendous windstorm, I ran out of fuel within 3 miles of Montauk Light. Not only was the 9-hour trip back a nightmare, but to add insult to injury, I had to call to get towed in. Know your motors and how much fuel they'll burn pushing your boat. Make sure you've got good fuel capacity, and invest in a FloScan gauge. It'll let you know how much you're burning all the time while allowing you to choose the most economical cruising speed for your boat and planning the optimal routes for your offshore trips.

ELECTRONICS

Electronics are another essential part of a good tuna boat, and with your life and your crew's lives dependent on them, don't cut corners. Electronics are essential for accurately navigating, finding the places where fish may be, and—most important—contacting others in an emergency. It's a good idea to have all electronic devices installed professionally if you can afford it rather than cutting corners and trying to do it yourself, unless of course you know what you're doing. You never want your electronics going down or not working properly when you're offshore. This would create an absolute nightmare for you and anyone on board. Ask around the dock or your club, and find out what company has a good reputation for installation and servicing, then establish a relationship with them.

Electronics should be placed where they can easily be accessed and scanned. You'll also want your alarm's lights and sounds to be easily noticed.

Must-haves on an offshore tuna boat are as follows: 2 VHF radios, at least one loran and/or GPS (Global Positioning System), surface temperature seawater gauge, radar, color or mono scope, digital depth finder, FloScan meter, EPIRB, and life raft. If you're fishing in the canyons, add a single-side band radio, plotter, and autopilot. All this is in addition to your U.S. Coast Guard-required equipment.

Electronics are frequently improved by manufacturers to make them more efficient—and also to get you to replace your existing equipment. The GPS is a perfect example. Just as we were all getting to be experts at using lorans, the GPS was introduced. It is a lot more accurate and dependable, though, and isn't affected by atmospheric conditions that disrupt normal loran use. Radar will help you get to your fishing spot in poor weather without running into another boat or obstacle. It will also help you locate fishing fleets offshore, which are great telltales of hot fishing spots. Or use a VHF radio that has a scan feature to program multiple channels and then listen in on action that may be happening in other spots. The effective range of a VHF is usually about 15 miles in good weather conditions, though, so a single-side band radio—which has an unlimited range—would be a good addition to the offshore boat.

The seawater temperature gauge is an integral part of the tuna boat. It allows you to find eddies, or bodies of water with contrasting water temperatures. These areas of water guide the movements of the tuna that prefer waters around 67 to 68 degrees.

The color sounder is another must on the tuna boat, and all anglers should become experts in its use. It will show you the bottom contours, locate schools of bait, and even "mark" a tuna feeding under your boat so you can adjust your lines when chunking. It should be matched with a powerful wide-angle transducer, which will give you a wider viewing area under the bridge.

If you have any questions, talk over your needs with an experienced electronics salesperson, who can direct you to the best equipment based on your fishing locations, type of boat, and methods of fishing. You can then make an educated purchase. Here on eastern Long Island we are fortunate to have Seatronics in Hampton Bay, which has a long record of working with anglers not only to design the best possible electronics package for their needs, but also to service them when necessary. Again, find out who has a good reputation for servicing in your area.

Finally, and perhaps most important, remember that anglers ultimately catch fish, not electronics. Familiarize yourself with the important aspects of fishing such as water temperatures, sea conditions, and bottom contours. Subscribe to and use surface temperature charts; they're an invaluable aid when used in conjunction with your electronic package. Educate yourself about electronics choices. This and your own refined intuitions will ensure hookups for you.

5

BOAT ACCESSORIES

GIMBAL BELTS/KIDNEY HARNESSES

When I was a kid fishing on my family's boat, the gimbal belts were nothing more than small leather cups mounted on a leather belt that fit around your waist, around your shoulders, or both. They were the most basic designs imaginable, and can still be found in some tackle stores and even on my boat today. Fortunately, these integral parts of stand-up tuna fishing have been refined into efficient and back-saving equipment.

While many good belts and harnesses are made, I use a system developed by Dennis Braid of Braid Products in California. It is a combination gimbal belt and back/kidney harness. I've had fantastic success landing fish while wearing it, and it can be adjusted to fit each angler efficiently. It's saved my back on more than one occasion. Its design makes it easy for you to take a break while battling a tuna—stretching, loosening up your hands, and regrouping while keeping the fish hooked up.

FIGHTING CHAIR

The fighting chair is an essential part of any serious fishing boat cockpit, particularly when you're fishing for large tuna or giants. A few years ago three of us went offshore looking for yellowfins to fight on stand-up rods.

We'd taken the fighting chair out of the boat the night before to give us more room, thinking we wouldn't need it for the 100-pound-plus yellowfins that we heard were around.

As luck would have it, we arrived at the fleet between Block Island and Montauk Point, and within 5 minutes of anchoring I was hooked up to the biggest tuna I've ever fought—on a 50-pound stand-up rod! We took turns fighting this fish for four hours, with one guy begging me to cut the line because he was so worn out. In the end we lost the fish because it chafed the leader, but only after backing on him for over 20 miles. If we'd had the chair in the boat, this story might have had a different ending.

Murray Brothers chair.

Your chair should match your boat—not in color, but in size. For instance, my Bertram has an 80-pound chair in it. A 130-pound chair would be too big for the boat, and take up valuable space. A sailfish chair might be perfect for center consoles or smaller boats, but it wouldn't make sense as the primary chair in a 44-foot or larger boat, which would easily fit a 130-pound or unlimited chair. It's also important to position your

Helm chairs.

chair properly when you're getting ready to install it: Make sure that your trolling rod tip clears your transom. This will ensure that when fighting a fish, you won't have to worry about your line chafing on the transom's covering boards, resulting in a lost fish. If you have a question about what size is practical for your boat, ask the manufacturer, but generally you should install the largest chair that will fit in your boat without taking up all your space.

BUCKET HARNESS

This is an integral part of the fighting-chair system. As its name implies, it's a well-padded bucket-shaped harness that the angler sits in when using the fighting chair. The rod is placed in the fighting chair's gimbal, and the rod-and-reel system is then attached to the bucket by two straps with snaps on each end that clip on the reel's eyes. The angler, chair, rod/reel, and bucket harness are now connected as one unit, and you use the bucket harness to slide back and forth in the chair as you attempt to gain line on the fish. Here the addition of some liquid dish soap is a real plus. Squirt a little from time to time on the fighting-chair seat. It will reduce any drag created in fighting the fish and help you slide, making it that much easier to bring the fish to the boat. This system also allows you to take a quick break in the midst of a battle to take a drink of water, massage hands, or just briefly pause without losing the rod and reel overboard, just as the stand-up harness system does. When used properly, this system will give you a huge advantage over the fish, particularly in conjunction with a knowledgeable captain and crew.

USING YOUR FIGHTING CHAIR

As anglers with experience know, fighting a fish from the chair is not a matter of macho strength as much as it is the ability to work together. With the proper crew, bringing a big tuna to the boat can be almost effortless. I know of one angler fishing the spring bluefin run off Hatteras who brought 52 fish in the 300- to 400-pound range to the boat to be tagged in one day! All because he was fortunate enough to have an experienced captain at the helm and a knowledgeable mate and wireperson in the cockpit. On the other side of the coin, I once saw a macho-type angler flipped backwards right out of the chair when his line broke as he tried to horse in a tuna.

ROCKET LAUNCHERS

These are perfect for the smaller boats such as center consoles, and also on larger boats for the light-tackle enthusiast. Rocket launchers allow excellent cockpit rod storage for all boats when you're traveling or trolling. They can be outfitted with a rigging tray, and some designs also feature drawers for tackle storage, giving the angler a central point for all needed equipment and accessories. They hold numerous rods of all types, including trolling, stand-up spinning, and fly rods, and allow you to have a baited rod set up and ready to go in the event that a fish is teased or baited up. I've used them extensively when light-tackle or fly fishing for offshore species. Keep a diverse selection of rods ready to go in the rod holders of the rocket launcher.

CENTER RIGGER

These are especially useful for trolling multiple rods. Most boats have one mounted between the outriggers on the flying bridge, cabin top, or tower. One well-known tuna angler in Shinnecock, Tred Barta, has been known to mount four of these on his flying bridge, in addition to the two out-riggers, so he could troll 11 rods. Tred does catch amazing numbers of tuna with this setup, including the elusive bigeyes. All his center riggers were mounted on a 31-foot cruiser-type boat that he often fished alone or with one other person. It must have made for all kinds of logistical headaches, but again he was usually successful.

On my Bertram my center rigger is mounted on the flying bridge. I use it to hold my farthest lure rig back well behind the rest of the trolling pattern. I also always put a lure with a Boone or Mold Craft teaser bird in front of the lure to make a big commotion. It often results in hookups and has made me a believer in rigging a center rigger this way. On larger boats center riggers can easily be mounted on the lower part of the tower and rigged so that they can be worked from the flying bridge.

FLAT LINES

Flat lines have become a must-have on my boat whenever I'm trolling for tuna. They prevent your lines from getting tangled around rod tips in foul weather, ensure that your lures track effectively, and hold your lures or baits in place up close to your boat's transom where you want them.

Mine are mounted on either side of my boat's transom, screwed into the rub rail with stainless screws. Here I can easily put my rod's lines through them, adjusting the lures' positions as needed. When we get a hookup on one, the person in the cockpit can see the line releasing right away. They can also be rigged through the cockpit scuppers. Attach a longer length of line to the clips, then pass it through the scupper and out the transom. Attach the free end to the cockpit cleat. You can now reach over and place your line through the clip.

GIN POLE/PULLEY SYSTEM

Gin poles were a part of every serious offshore boat until recently, when the simple block-and-tackle system used with the transom door came into being. Gin poles are made from wood or metal, mounted adjacent to or through the boat's gunwale, and fastened securely to the structure of the boat. They hold a block-and-tackle system that is used to hoist a tuna or other large game fish out of the water and into the cockpit. Then the fish can be lowered into the cockpit to be dressed or hung on the gin pole for all to see.

With so many boats now featuring a transom or tuna door, a block-and-tackle system mounted inside the cockpit on the same side as the door will accomplish the same thing much easier.

TRANSOM DOOR

The transom door gives the crew a huge advantage in bringing large fish into the cockpit. Because of its position close to the waterline, it's often much easier to bring in a fish after properly securing it than it used to be to hoist it over the side of the boat with a gin pole.

I've also seen rollers mounted on the boat's transom just under the transom door. Although these look odd on the transom of a sport-fishing boat and are a little unsightly, they definitely make bringing in a fish easier.

FISH BOXES

If your cockpit has enough room underneath, fish boxes are an invaluable addition to a boat. I ran a boat at one time for a famous piano-playing rock star who had the most amazing 46-foot downeast-hull sport-fishing boat built I've ever been on. In addition to handling like a dream, this boat's cockpit was big enough to hold five people, including the angler in a Murray Brothers 130-pound chair, with no one getting in the way. I'm still amazed at that boat's room and the ease that fighting fish took on in it. Its design secret was the amazing fish boxes built under the cockpit. One night we boated and kept 15 good-sized tuna from 60 to 150 pounds in Block Canyon, and all came back to Montauk in excellent shape.

Good fish boxes are usually insulated and have a drain plug so that melted ice and seawater can be drained into the bilge and pumped overboard. I always mix ice and seawater to keep my tuna in, whether I put them in the fish box or cooler. It keeps the fish fresh while not dramatically changing the flavor of the meat, as fresh water alone would do.

BAIT WELL

This is another must-have for serious sport-fishing boats. Bait wells allow you to keep baits alive until you're ready to use them, and live baits are better than any other when you're live lining or kite fishing for tuna. These smart fish will always choose a fresh bait over an older one, and offering them a live bait will always give you the edge. Many variations on live boxes are available, from the state-of-the art types that come as standard equipment on new sport-fishing boats to the most basic types you rig yourself.

If your well is to be installed on a more or less permanent basis, you can purchase one from any of the manufacturers that specialize in these systems. I use a well system made by the Caddy Company of Central Islip, New York. It fits under the cockpit in a bilge hatch, and has paid for itself time and again in catches of fish. It is durable enough to take a beating on those days when the weather is less than perfect, but it has yet to break up after many seasons of use. It also keeps bunker, snapper blues, and other bait alive until we can get to the tuna grounds—sometimes a two-hour-plus run. Murray Brothers of Palm Beach also sells a very efficient system. The tank is doughnut shaped and designed to be slipped over the fighting chair's stanchion in either a temporary or a permanent mount. Mounted on the cockpit floor, it's out of the way of any fishing activity and readily accessible.

Building a Live Well

MATERIALS
- 1-gallon plastic garbage pail
- Small bilge or saltwater washdown pump with a 500-gallon-per-hour capacity
- 25 feet of ½-inch or ⅝-inch hose
- PL 5200 adhesive

1. Cut a hole 2 or 3 inches from the top edge of the garbage pail so that excess water can drain out. Then attach the bilge hose outlet backward with some PL 5200 adhesive. You'll later attach a piece of hose to this.
2. Place the bilge pump securely in the pail and put it all where it will be out of the way of the fishing action—either somewhere in the cockpit or on a swim platform.
3. Run the length of hose from the outflow outlet of the pump into the pail. If you have any excess hose, coil it up in the bottom of the pail. The force of the water entering the well will keep all the water flowing in a circular and upward motion, ensuring a fresh supply of water at all times. This is vital in keeping some of the less hardy baits such as bunkers alive.
4. In order to keep any excess water from the bait well from spilling out due to pounding or the motion of the boat, secure the lid to the top of the pail with handles, if available, and/or with a bungee cord.

ANCHOR RETRIEVAL SYSTEMS

When chunking inshore, I always anchor up on loran numbers I've entered in my logs that have resulted in productive days of fishing. I have two different anchor line setups that I keep in my boat's rope locker. The first is 300 feet of anchor line that I use for depths from 175 to 200 feet. The second is an additional 300 feet of add-on line that I use for deeper waters. I use ½-inch line, but you should choose your line (and anchor) based on your boat's length and weight. My line is stored coiled in the orange plastic baskets used by commercial anglers. I always wash it off and let it dry on the dock after using it.

The anchor retrieval system is an invaluable addition to your boat, allowing you not only to retrieve your line easily but also to get off your anchor effortlessly when you hook up, and to retie to it after boating your fish. It can be made for about $100, but will save you that much easily in work and aggravation the first time you use it. The system will last for years and save your back, too.

It's a simple rig made from one of the large orange-colored float balls first used by Scandinavian commercial anglers, with a short length of ½-inch line eye-spliced to the hole on its bottom. At the trailing end of the ½-inch line attach a stainless or brass snap, again with an eye splice. This snap will attach to a stainless ring that goes over your anchor line and will position the ball above the anchor line on the surface. At the end of your anchor line you can attach a lobster-pot-type float; I use one of the antenna buoys seen on moorings. (The reason will become obvious soon.) All these parts are easily available from places such as West Marine, Outer Banks, Reliable Gaffs, and Fisherman's Paradise.

To use the rig, simply hook the ring over the anchor line and drop your anchor overboard. Then slowly back away from the anchor as the line plays out and the anchor takes hold. The ball will remain on the surface as the line passes through the ring. When you are securely anchored and have the proper amount of line out, tie the line off to your bow cleat with the antenna buoy attached to the very end of the line, and placed on the boat's deck.

When you hook up and the engines are running, simply run up to the bow and untie the anchor line, throw the buoy overboard, and begin to fight your fish. Then when you're done, come back to your anchor line, pick up the antenna buoy, and retie your anchor line until next time. Simple yet very effective.

At the end of the day when you have your fish in the cooler and others swimming around with tags in them, it's just as easy to retrieve your long lengths of anchor line effortlessly. After taking a compass heading of the anchor's position, I take the end of the line and tie it off to a cockpit cleat. Then I slowly turn the boat out and about 90 degrees away from the anchor for 25 to 30 feet, then again turn to the compass heading of the anchor and slowly run the course. The anchor line will now pass through the ring on the line until the ball is directly above my anchor. At this point the ball assists me in "lifting" my anchor off the bottom until it comes to the surface and reaches the ball. I know when this happens because the ball starts to be pulled through the water behind the boat as the anchor's shanks attach to the ring. At this point I simply put the boat into neutral and begin to retrieve the line into the baskets or cockpit by hand. It's a lot easier than trying to "hump" the line in myself.

6

TACKLE AND EQUIPMENT

RODS

When you're choosing a rod, a basic necessity is to make sure it meets all IGFA requirements. These minimum requirements identify the pound class of the rod, which should be matched with an identical reel class. In other words, a 30-pound rod should have a 30-pound reel and line test, a 50-pound rod needs a 50-pound reel and test, and so on. This gives your rod system balance and will also make it easier for you should you apply for a world record someday.

Generally you should be able to handle a tuna three times as heavy as your line class. In other words, a 30-pound-class setup should easily handle a tuna of around 90 pounds, and so on. This is just a general rule of thumb, and experienced anglers can raise that ratio much higher by using good technique, adjustable drag settings, harnesses, belts, high-grade line, and an experienced captain and mates. Another rule of thumb is to use 30-, 50-, and 80-pound setups for yellowfins and medium bluefins, 80- and 130-pound for bigeyes, and 30- to 50-pound class for albacore.

The rod's butt section should be no longer than 27 inches, and the tip section 40 inches. Look over the rod before you buy it to make sure it states somewhere that it meets IGFA requirements. Don't scrimp on price and end up with a low-quality rod. By spending the extra money on a good brand-name rod or even a custom-built one, you will be ensuring the best performance when battling a tuna. When maintained properly, it will last a lifetime.

Trolling Rods

Most traditional trolling rods are 6 to 7 feet in length, with a stiff action and an aluminum or wooden butt. My preference is aluminum, but this is simply from an aesthetic and maintenance standpoint. Wooden butts are just as good. The rod's foregrips are best when made from soft foam or cork. I prefer cork, but many of my rods also have foam, particularly the stand-up rods. Guides are conventional or roller, and here my clear choice is roller guides. They put much less friction or stress on the line and in general ensure a smoother fight. Friends of mine use the conventional guides, though, and like them, particularly now because they come with a Teflon coating, eliminating the chances of nicks or imperfections that will damage lines. Just make sure your rod has enough guides to ensure an even distribution of stress. Your rod should bend evenly from the butt to the tip. This will help a lot in setting the hook when the time comes.

Trolling rods should not be used when you're standing up and fighting a fish, and especially not when you're trying to work a deep-sounding fish to the surface; they'll put undue strain on your lower back. They are very efficient on a surface-running fish or when used in conjunction with an experienced captain and a fighting chair, but tuna are not surface-running fish, so avoid using them in a stand-up situation. On the other hand, when used from a chair by a knowledgeable angler and boat crew, they can put more pressure on a fish than any other type of rod, resulting in a successful catch.

Stand-Up Rods

West Coast or stand-up rods were first used on the long-range party boats that fish from San Diego and other ports in search of tuna. They were designed to let you fish without a chair but not destroy your back.

Stand-up rods are generally from 5 to 6 feet long, with the blank extending through the butt. The butt is shorter than a trolling rod's and the foregrip much longer, giving you an advantage in adjusting hand positions. Guides are more closely spaced than on trolling rods, and again come in conventional or roller types. My preference is roller guides, but the first stand-up rods that I had built by Altenkirch's in Hampton Bays in

1987 have conventional Teflon-coated guides with a roller tip. They have never given me trouble, and we have fought countless tuna on them. By the way, they were the first stand-up rods that Hank built at the world-famous Altenkirch's and, like all his quality rods, still look brand-new today.

Stand-up rods are a poor choice for trolling, and completely useless in a fighting chair. Their short length allows the line to chafe on the boat's covering boards, risking a break-off, and from the chair a stand-up rod is an impossible tool for turning a green running fish. For chunking, however, or when used in the stand-up position after hooking a trolled lure, they are phenomenal as long as you're in relatively good shape and know the proper technique.

The rod and reel you use for stand-up fishing should always be of the same class—a 30-pound reel on a 30-pound rod, and so on. Both stand-up and trolling rods are more than acceptable; just don't try to use a trolling rod for stand-up fishing or vice versa.

Bent Butt Rods

Guides
As I've said, I prefer roller guides and tips on all my rods. It's my feeling that they reduce friction better than the standard type do, and are less apt to damage line if impaired in any way.

REELS
Prior to 1970 most offshore anglers used the star-drag reels—reels with a star-type adjuster behind the reel handle that allows you to increase or decrease the drag to suit the fish. Today the lever-action drag-setting reels made by companies such as Fin-Nor, Penn, and Shimano are rapidly gaining in popularity. Drag washers are also being redesigned and refaced to increase surface-area contact, resulting in smooth operation under stress as well as a longer-lasting washer.

For tuna fishing I prefer the lever-drag reels to the older but still useful star drags. I keep a couple of backup star-drag reels mounted on trolling rods in my rod storage locker aboard the boat, and use them for jigging or spooning tuna at times. Still, to me there's no question that lever drags feature a more refined and smoother drag system, are more reliable than the

Tuna reel from Accurate Fishing Products.

star-drag system, and certainly are much easier to adjust while fighting a
tuna. During a tuna's initial hard run, the drag washers on a star-drag reel
tend to heat up, causing the drag setting to change. You must then direct
some of your attention to reel adjustments rather than fighting the fish—
something you should try to avoid. Star-drag reels are also notorious for
binding up at the least-opportune moment. This will inevitably result in a
broken-off fish. This isn't an issue with a properly cared for lever-drag reel.
You can easily adjust drag settings and, because of the drag construction,
don't have to worry about jerking or your spool freezing up.

There's nothing wrong with star-drag reels—many record fish have
been caught on them through the years, and more will be in the future—
but for overall reliability, smooth action, and avoiding lockups and jerks,
lever drags are far superior. Penn Internationals and Fin-Nors were at one
time the standards for offshore fishing reels, but in recent years Shimano,
Daiwa, and Abu-Garcia have also come out with very good alternatives.
They offer the lever-drag systems, wide spools for extra line capacity, and
two speed options on some models.

Lever-drag reels are classed or sized by the pound-test line they were
built to handle. Recognized IGFA classes are 12, 20, 30, 50, 80, and 130.
Reels in the 30- to 130-pound class are also available in the wide-spool
version, which allows you to put up to 40 percent more line on your reel
and also safely put one size heavier line on the reel. Thus a 30-pound reel

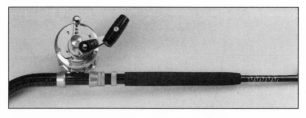

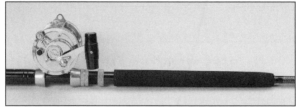

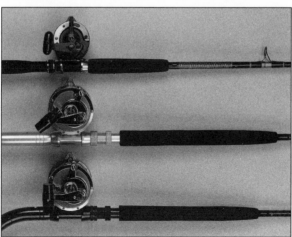

A selection of Penn and Shimano tuna reels. Courtesy Stalker Outfitters.

could hold 50-pound test, and so on. Putting a heavier line on your reel is appealing, but it cuts down on your reel's retrieval rate, so be careful.

Two-speed reels are now also gaining in popularity, particularly for fighting large tuna or billfish. The standard high-speed retrieve is great for working a fish in to the boat; as the tuna or billfish begins to dive, the lower gear ratio is excellent for hoisting it back to the surface. Two-speed reels are excellent when used with stand-up rods, and give you the advantage on lighter tackle such as 30- and 50-pound test.

Overall, I think the two-speed 50-pound wide-spool reel is the best choice. It can be used on trolling rods and stand-up setups, in both large and smaller sport-fishing boats. In my Bertram, which is 31 feet long and has adequate cockpit space, these reels have whipped yellowfins and bigeyes over 200 pounds on both stand-up and trolling rods.

REEL MAINTENANCE TIPS

- After every fishing trip, even if you plan on fishing the next day, slack off completely on your reel's drag system before putting it away. This applies to all reel types. It will add life to your drag washers as well as ensuring that your reel doesn't lock up at the wrong time. You should also do this when you put your reels away for the nonfishing months.
- Change your drag washers at least annually—more if you fish a lot or if a wide selection of people use your reels.

Setting the Drag

Let's assume that you have the proper combination of rod and reel, with the best drag system and guides available. Your next step is to set the drag on your reel. You'll need a drag scale, which is available at any of the better tackle stores. These are generally made from brass and will last a lifetime if properly cared for.

A rule-of-thumb formula is to set the reel's drag at one-third of the line's breaking strength while in the strike position, and half its breaking strength at the full position. For instance, with 30-pound-test line you'd set the drag at 10 pounds; with 50-pound test set at approximately 17 pounds; with 130-pound-test set at approximately 43 pounds. To set a drag accurately, have someone hold the rod securely (or place it in a rod holder). Now rig the line through the guides and out the tip, tying a heavy snap swivel to the free end. Push the lever to the strike setting and attach the drag scale's hooked end to the swivel. Pulling on the scale and line, adjust the preset drag knob on the side of the reel until you've registered the proper setting. Then move the lever forward to the full position and repeat the process until you've reached about 50 percent of the line's breaking strength. Both settings are now preset, but you should still check them frequently, especially after catching a fish or before your next trip offshore.

LINES

Dacron

Dacron is a synthetic line made by braiding or twisting a number of fine strands together. It is generally stiffer or less forgiving than monofilament and will therefore set the hook better. Yet because of its stiffness, you'll need more skill to hook fish. It doesn't stretch, so the inexperienced angler may end up losing fish more often than not. I know I have. It does have three good advantages, though: It incorporates great strength into a relatively small diameter, you can get more of it onto a reel spool than you can of mono, and it has less resistance when pulled through the water. The latter is a crucial characteristic, because when a big fish pulls a lot of line from a reel during a fight, it creates an enormous amount of water drag, which can and does prematurely tire out both you and the fish. It also increases the possibility of the line breaking.

Dacron line is my first choice when I'm fishing for the powerful giant bluefins and bigeyes. Here's why: A few years ago, while fishing off Cape Cod, I hooked and boated a bluefin that turned out to weigh 1,065 pounds on 130-pound-test Dacron line after a three-hour battle. That in itself is amazing enough, but after I got back to the dock I was approached by the owner of a boat that was in the fleet with us chunking. In a nice manner he showed me a piece of ⅜-inch nylon anchor line that looked like someone had cut it cleanly with a sharp knife, and told me that during my hookup and the fish's initial run, my Dacron line had severed his anchor line. At first I couldn't believe that this could happen, but after asking around I found that it could. This made me a true believer in Dacron line for chunking bluefins. After the boat owner left with some cash in his pocket for a new anchor line, I checked my reel's line and couldn't find any sign of defects!

Monofilament

Monofilament line is just what its name implies, a single-strand line made from synthetic materials by a process known as extrusion. In this case a material is forced out of very fine holes, depending on the pound-test being made. Because the material is synthetic, monofilament lines are also impervious to water and therefore won't rot, mildew, or swell when wet. They incorporate great strength into a small diameter, stretch when under the stress of a tuna's fight, and are more forgiving than Dacron. They're thus a much better choice for the inexperienced angler, and used generally by charter boats. It's also much easier to spot defects, nicks, or abrasions in monofilament, which can save you a lot of heartache down the road.

LINE MAINTENANCE

Lines should be checked regularly for imperfections. If you fish only a few times a year, you can get away with changing your line annually. However, if you're like most tuna anglers and spend each free day offshore trolling, you should change your line at least once during the season and more if necessary. Granted, this can get expensive, but it's still a smaller price to pay than is a lost trophy fish. Just make sure you dispose of the line properly, especially in the case of monofilament. Wrap it up in a bag and take it to a recycling center or your tackle store or marina, many of which now will accept old line. This way you won't bring any unnecessary problems to innocent wildlife such as seagulls or fish.

What color line to use, whether monofilament or Dacron, is another one of those details that can be debated endlessly. I'll take the easy road out and recommend that this decision is better left up to the individual. I will say, however, that I use smoky blue and gray monofilament lines, and green and black Dacron lines.

LEADERS

Leaders are as important in tuna fishing as they are in all other types of angling. Wire was once the material of choice for chunking tunas, and even for daisy chains and lure rigging. Now with monofilament a proven winner and coming in such a diverse range of pound-tests, colors, and diameters, wire is rarely used. The last season I used wire in my rigs was in 1983, and over the years I've learned to rely more on mono leaders. It has produced more fish for me.

While wire certainly offers an advantage in strength, it does crimp easily, weakening it, and also is much more visible to the often leader-shy tuna. All my lures are now rigged with mono leaders ranging from 8 to 15 feet in length. While the IGFA allows leaders over the 20-pound class to be 30 feet long, I feel this is much too long to be effectively handled from my boat. Shorter lengths give the cockpit person an added advantage in handling a fish and bringing it to gaff or alongside to be tagged. Each boat and crew is different, of course, so don't be afraid to experiment with length.

I generally use 100- to 200-pound test on my smaller lures, and up to 300-pound on my larger lures. Many companies such as Ande, Maxima, Hi-Seas, and Jinkai make leader material in coiled lengths or spools. The spools store easily in the already-cramped tackle boxes aboard my boat, which keeps them out of the sunlight so they won't become tangle-prone or dried out.

On my lure leaders I always crimp a loop or thimble in place on the end. This easily connects to the rod line by a snap swivel. On chunking rigs I use the same ends, plus an occasional swivel. Regardless, when a fish is successfully battled and brought alongside the boat, reel your line up to just before the snap swivel, and keep your rod tip pointed in the air. This will take up slack, and greatly help the person in the cockpit who's going to leader the fish.

End Loops

You need a way to attach your leader easily to the snap swivel at the end of the reel line. The four best ways I've found to do this are to form a loop using the offshore loop knot, a stainless thimble, coil chafing gear, or tubular chafing gear.

The two simplest of these are the stainless thimble and the chafing tube held in place with a crimp, but my favorite is the offshore loop knot, again held in place with a crimp. The coil chafing gear also works very well and should not be ruled out.

It's important to check these loops throughout the season for nicks, wear, or imperfections. If any show up, don't take a chance; just rerig them. This will eliminate any chance of a lost fish.

CRIMPS

In order to rig lures, attach hooks to lines, or connect leaders to your line, you need a strong, fast, and reliable way to form loops. Crimping is by far the best method. Use aluminum or copper crimps made by Sevenstrand, Hi-Seas, or Jinkai. Crimps come in a large assortment of sizes to fit all line tests. I've found that by using a crimp with a diameter one size larger than my line, I get the best fit and strength. For instance, a 200-pound conventional leader has a diameter of 1.3 millimeters, so use a 1.4-millimeter crimp.

Crimps also come in three shapes: oval, formed copper, and round. The round is used primarily for rigging daisy chains to keep squid or egg sinkers in place, and the oval and formed copper for rigging purposes. I check my crimps often to make sure that they're in good shape and not beginning to deteriorate from use, salt water, heat, or all of the above. If needed, snip off the connection and quickly rerig. It only takes a few minutes, and is well worth it for the security of knowing your rig will not fail.

Your choice of crimping tool is crucial to strong connections. The best types are the bench-mounted kind you see used in tackle stores. They cost about $150 to $200 but are worth it if you're serious about your fishing. They apply even pressure to the entire crimp when used, ensuring a complete connection, and will not damage the crimp or line as the less expensive tools can if used improperly.

These less expensive crimping tools are like a pair of electrician's wire-stripping pliers or a pair of cutting pliers. They should be used with care so as not to damage and weaken your line. You can usually see this happen if it does, and simply rerig more carefully. Just be sure that when crimping with these pliers, you match the size and style of the crimp to the opening. Also, because the Hi-Seas and Jinkai crimps are distinctively different, you should use the same manufacturer's crimping tool with their crimps.

HOOKS

Overwhelmingly, my two choices of tuna fishing hooks are the Mustad and Gamakatsu brands. I use sizes ranging from 5/0 to 12/0. The 5/0s are for smaller yellowfins, and the 12/0s are for giant bluefins, albeit rarely.

Use small hooks when live baiting to ensure the least amount of damage to the bait and thus the longest productive period in the water. My choice is either the Mustad 94150 in sizes from 4/0 to 8/0, or the razor-sharp Gamakatsu hooks now a part of all smart anglers' arsenals. Mustad 7734, 7699, and 7731 hooks are also excellent. Use the smaller-sized hooks with snappers and the larger with bunkers.

GAFFS

Gaff Handles

Today aluminum and fiberglass are the two most popular gaff handle materials. Both have pros and cons. Generally aluminum handles are more rigid and lighter, while fiberglass is stronger, heavier, and more flexible. However, the offshore tuna boats in California use gaffs with bamboo handles because they are light, flexible, available in long lengths, immune to salt water, and inexpensive. These guys gaff thousands of fish each year from boats high off the water, and they don't want a gaff that will wear them out right away. While the bamboo handles may not last long, they save the gaffer's arms and backs.

Whatever you do, choose a gaff that is strong and not a bargain-basement brand. I learned this the hard way once on my boat. We were chunking off Block Island and hooked a 150-pound yellowfin that was brought to the boat in about 20 minutes. Shorthanded that day, I jumped off the bridge and grabbed a straight gaff set out on an engine cover. I gaffed the fish, and, resting the gaff handle on the boat's gunwale for better leverage, watched it as first it bent downward, and then snapped! With this the fish took off ˙for deeper water again, half of the gaff still in it. Luckily the angler had his stuff together and had backed off the drag so the fish could run. About 10 minutes later the fish was up swimming in circles, the broken gaff reflecting in the water. We

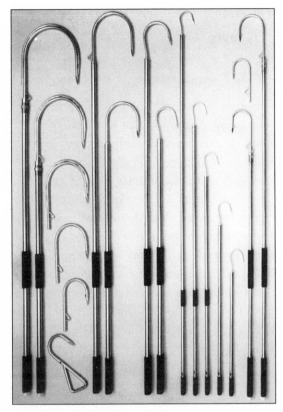

Gaffs for tuna. The "flying gaff" is at right.

soon had it alongside the boat again, and this time put a good gaff in it and brought the fish into the boat.

Length of gaff handles really depends only on the size of the boat; a 5-foot gaff is more than adequate for the average small boat, where a long gaff will only restrict maneuverability. If the boat's gunwales are high, though, a longer gaff may be your choice. Remember that IGFA regulations for taking fish specify that the overall length of the gaff handle and hook not exceed 8 feet.

Gaff Hooks

Most gaffs feature stainless steel hooks because they won't rust. Unless the steel is heat-treated, however, they could bend on you, so beware. There is also a high-carbon steel hook that won't bend; unless it's properly cared for, though, rusting will be an issue. Some companies are now using air-

craft-grade stainless steel. These hooks have just the right amount of for-
giveness in their action and won't break like some of the lower-grade
heat-treated stainless hooks.

Straight Gaffs

The most commonly used gaffs are straight gaffs in which the hook is
permanently affixed to the handle or pole. They come in a wide assortment of sizes for uses ranging from surfcasters pulling bass up on the
beach to 14-inch reinforced gaffs with 8-foot handles or longer for giant
bluefins. The most common straight gaff is one with a 3-foot handle and
4½-inch hook. I carry one of these on my boat and now use it for gaffing
everything from bluefish to small school tunas. It also works well for
steering tuna to the side of the boat to be gaffed, or tagged and released.
There are now gaffs being made especially for tuna fishing that feature a
4-, 5-, or 7-inch hook, a 6- to 8-foot overall length, and a ½-inch length
of nylon line. You use them as you would a flying gaff, with one difference: The hook does not release. As long as you use good judgment and
don't gaff a green fish, these gaffs can be used effectively for everything
from schoolies to giants.

Flying Gaffs

Flying gaffs are simply gaffs with a detachable hook. Welded to this hook
is an eye to which is attached a line no more than 30 feet long (the maximum allowed by the IGFA). The lines are usually ⅜ or ½-inch in diameter, and their free ends are tied off to one of the cockpit cleats or snapped
to a collar around the stanchion of a fighting chair. This line then helps
ensure that the fish will not get free after gaffing.

   A common problem with flying gaffs is attaching the hook to the
handle so that you are able to sink the hook into the fish while not interfering with its release. Manufacturers have come up with various ways of
doing this, including twist-lock configurations and using a piece of line
to secure the hook to the handle. I like the latter method, which allows
the hook to be installed in the handle easily but also securely enough for
proper gaffing. I use 20-pound-test Dacron line for this, wrapping it a few
times through the ring on the hook and cleat on the handle. When the
fish is gaffed, the line breaks under the stress and separates the handle
from the hook. Be careful, though: Using too heavy a line will result in a
gaffing nightmare. Try it out dockside first to get the right combination
down for you.

Masking tape also works well for this. Again, make a few wraps around the line and handle at the head of the gaff, and several more wraps down the handle to hold the line in place. (This is also a good idea when you're using the line to secure the hook to the handle.) Be sure to use masking tape, not electrical or duct tape. Both are much tougher and may not release for you.

Because even ⅜ and ½-inch line will take punishment from the powerful tuna, nylon line is preferred over all other types because it is more flexible, easier and safer to handle, and easier to replace. The flexibility or stretch helps keep the gaff's hook embedded in the fish without ripping or tearing apart the meat should the fish try to get away.

Making a Stanchion Collar
On my boat I've spliced a short length of ½-inch nylon line with a stainless ring attached around the base of my fighting chair. This acts as a kind of collar to which I can then quickly hook my gaff line to with the aid of a snap hook that I've spliced to the end of 20 feet of gaff line (the perfect length for my boat). Because the length of line will vary with each boat depending on the size of the cockpit, the length of the gaff's handle, and the height of the freeboard, set up your gaffing systems well beforehand at the dock to ensure the maximum efficiency.

TAILROPES
Years ago in the Wild West, a cowboy's most important tool (other than his six-shooter) had to be his lariat. He used it to lasso cattle, wild animals, bad guys, and even saloon girls. Today, as any experienced offshore angler will tell you, one of the most important pieces of equipment in the boat is a tool very much like the cowboy's lariat—the tailrope. Proof that the more things change, the more they remain the same!

The angler uses his tailrope in order to "lasso" and gain control of the fish, usually but not always after gaffing. Securing the tail of the fish as it's brought alongside the boat almost completely disables the fish, allowing the angler and the crew to subdue it and drastically reducing any chance of losing it.

An added advantage of the tailrope that many tag-and-release anglers are discovering is that when used without a gaff, the tailrope disables and secures the fish without causing injuries. This lets the fish be safely released.

Types of Tailropes

A tailrope in its most basic form could be nothing more than a 15- or 20-foot length of ⅜ or ½-inch dock line with its free end passed through the eye-spliced loop. This simple tailrope is most effective after the fish is secured with a gaff and a more conventional tailrope, but it can be used by itself in any case. One drawback is that because rope tends to float, it's hard to fit the loop around the fish's tail while it's in the water.

A more refined version that I favor is the tailrope made by Pompanette. It's comprised of a 10-foot section of ³⁄₁₆-inch braided nylon line with a stainless-steel cable inserted the entire length and a galvanized clip attached to the end. Connected to this is another 8 feet of ⁷⁄₁₆-inch nylon line with an eye splice at the end. The weighted cable end is the piece that secures the fish, and because it's weighted, it's much easier to maneuver and fit over the fish's tail when it's leadered alongside the boat. This is a real asset, particularly when you're trying to subdue a fish in choppy seas. After the fish is successfully tailroped, it should be secured to be brought into the boat.

FISH BAGS AND COOLERS

Since you'll want to ensure that the fish you take home will remain fresh, a good cooler or fish bag is a real necessity in any tuna boat. I remember seeing a guy pull into a marina in Montauk a few years back in a big, new sport-fishing boat. He was pretty full of himself after a successful day of fishing, gold chains sparkling in the afternoon sun as he backed into the fuel dock. "I've got a load of yellowfins to sell," he announced so that everyone at the next marina knew, too. He sure did have a load. Thirteen of them baked in the sun, lying scattered around his cockpit looking like pods from *Invasion of the Body Snatchers*. Of course he didn't get one cent for them, and more important, he wasted about 1,000 pounds of fish, something that could have been prevented with just a little education.

Canyon Products makes the best fish bags I've ever seen. They're durable, they're well insulated, and—most important—they work. They come in various sizes, and each boat should have one onboard. I keep mine in my freezer at home until I go fishing. Then I pack it with shaved ice and put it down below the deck, out of the sun. It always keeps my tuna fresh until I get back to the dock, even on overnight trips.

Coolers are excellent for keeping smaller tuna and baits fresh, too. SSI, Igloo, Coleman, and Gott all make excellent ones, in a wide range of sizes. The color of choice should be white, which will keep the ice inside frozen longer. Temper your cooler if you can before you go fishing by putting it in a freezer or walk-in, or filling it with ice. This will help keep everything inside fresh. I use the large SSI cooler in my boat, and have seen it keep ice for over three days. You can easily put a 50-pound yellowfin in it, where it will remain fresh until you're ready to dress it. It's also a good idea to secure your coolers in place so that in rough seas they're not sliding or banging around inside the boat. Lash them down with dock lines or bungee cords, or establish a permanent place for them where they can be easily tied or fastened in place.

PART 3

FISHING FOR TUNA

7

FINDING THE TUNA

Structure, water temperature, and food: These are the three things to look for when you're looking for tuna. Bottom structure and contours are important because they attract bait that tuna come in search of. Pretty basic stuff, but true. Some structure, such as the gradual drop-offs on the way to the continental shelf, are gradual—each in increments of 10 fathoms or so. Others, like the edge of the continental shelf itself, are a lot more dramatic. They drop off like an underwater wall.

The best way to find these spots is with your GPS or loran and a bottom contour chart (put out by numerous private companies and available at tackle stores and catalog houses). These charts not only show you the drop-offs in particular areas but also give you the coordinates to help you get right on them. They're also all laminated in plastic that gives them a very long life if you keep them out of the sun. The National Oceanic and Atmospheric Administration (NOAA) also puts out good charts of bottom contours, but these are printed on paper. Unless you put them into a plastic sleeve or keep them under a cover, they won't hold up well. I use the laminated charts, tracing various drop-offs on them with colored Magic Markers.

WATER TEMPERATURES

Water temperatures might be the single most important factor in a tuna's life. Longliners and other commercial fishing vessels have used water temperatures to find tuna for years now, and no boat should be without a good surface temperature gauge such as the Dytek model. Working warm eddies will often make the difference in a day's fishing. These eddies can be a few square miles in size, or they can be hundreds. Basically I look for changes in the water's color to locate eddies. Inshore waters are greenish in color, canyon waters a rich, beautiful blue.

Eddies always spin in a clockwise direction, and there is much debate as to just which parts of them are best for fishing. Some anglers like the northeast corner, because of the great changes in water temperatures found there, while others prefer the south and southwest corners because they pull the warmer water in. I'm not sure it makes a difference, although I know many will disagree. I think it's more important to find and fish those areas that attract the tuna, working different areas of them until you hook up, then continuing to work them.

To find eddies, you can search blindly while keeping an eye on your surface temperature gauge, or you can make your life (not to mention your fuel bill) a lot easier by using a company that through satellite imaging can identify good spots for you to travel to. The one I have used with great success for years is Roffer's Ocean Fishing Forecasting Service in Miami, Florida. Run by Mitchell Roffer, Ph.D., a graduate of the University of Miami's Rosenstiel School of Marine and Atmospheric Science, Roffer's provides the angler with comprehensive fishing forecasting analyses. Data are gathered from satellites, weather buoys, and other ships in order to define such things as water temperatures, bottom structure, and currents. This allows Roffer's to identify areas of the oceans where baitfish congregate and where tuna and other offshore species will be, too.

By combining information on water temperatures, which are so crucial to the daily life of tuna; water motion, stability, and shape; and orientation of local currents, Roffer's is able to genearlly forecast the location of offshore species. Add water color, location and movement of eddies, bottom topography, and other features and Roffer's can pinpoint specific regions where tuna and other offshore species will be. You can go directly to a good-looking area rather than wasting time, fuel, and money searching for fish.

You can subscribe to Roffers' service for the season, or call and use it on an as-needed basis. Mitch and his staff will fax you the latest satellite images, complete with loran and GPS numbers, as well as giving you a brief history about who's caught what where in your areas. He's a wonderful person, extremely helpful, and his valuable service really does work.

MORE THINGS TO LOOK FOR

Whales and porpoises need huge quantities of food each day, and spend their days either looking for schools of baitfish or eating what they've found. If you see either creature working an area, there may be tuna around, too.

Commercial draggers working an area can also result in feeding tuna. Years ago we used to look for Russian trawlers, then follow them until they hauled back their nets. When we trolled by we'd occasionally spot yellowfins or giant bluefins feeding on the surface as the net's overflow fell into the water. This led at times to hookups with giants when nothing else was working.

Birds, weed lines, and rips are more signs of tuna. Keep an eye out for the petrels nicknamed Mother Carey's chickens or tuna birds. They're the little brown birds that seem to dance on the water's surface, looking for or feeding on small bits of leftover baitfish that tuna have devoured.

Rips are the meeting places of two currents from opposite directions, and they can produce fish. Baitfish can get caught up in them and attract feeding tuna or billfish. Weed lines—always been hot spots for finding fish—may be formed as the result of mild rips. They give cover to little baitfish, which hide under and inside them. If you sight one as you troll, always give it a shot. Offshore lobster-pot buoys do the same thing on a smaller scale, but in addition to the well-known dolphin, I've seen tuna and white marlin come zooming out from underneath one.

COLOR SCOPES

This is an imperative piece of equipment on any tuna boat. Color scopes will show you clearly not only bottom structure but also schools of baitfish and tuna, and every individual tuna when chunking.

Color scope technology has now evolved to the point that you can interface your scope with all your electronics. When you pass over a particularly hot-looking spot, you can save its numbers. This allows you to work the area over and over again in search of fish. A few years ago we hooked up a tuna off Montauk. I immediately hit my Dytek to get the numbers and, after tagging and releasing the fish, went back to the same spot and hooked up again. We did this four times before the action stopped. When you're chunking, the color scope allows you to adjust your baits for a better presentation after you spot a tuna or school. If the fish move to different depths as they feed, you can follow them. Schools of bait or tuna show up as large colored spots, while individual fish or smaller schools appear as smaller spots.

Color scopes can also show you the underwater thermoclines that are so important to tuna's movements. These are areas where the warmer and thinner layers of water meet the colder and denser layers. Thermoclines rise and fall with underwater currents. If you find an upper-level thermocline, fish it: It may push tuna closer to the surface within range of your baits or lures.

8

SELECTING
AND
USING LURES

LURE TYPES

For many offshore anglers, trolling lures is *the* way to fish for tuna, and in the past decade infinite numbers of lure types, shapes, and styles have been developed using plastic-type materials to accommodate every possible theory about what tuna want. Shopping for lures for me today is no different than toy shopping at F.A.O. Schwartz with my grandmother when I was a youngster. I still feel the same way when I walk into Altenkirch's, Capitol Tackle, or Murray Brothers, or look through the catalogs offered by Stalker Outfitters, Finest Kind, Capt. Harry's, and a long list of others.

Which type of lure is best? I don't think there's any real answer to that. Some—the Green Machine, jetheads, door knobs, C&H Stubbies, and Mold Craft soft heads—produce consistently. But so do Sevenstrand Tuna Clones, Boone Sea Minnows, and Murray Brothers lures. For this reason I feel that it's a good idea to mix your lures up at all times, keeping a log of which ones produce under varying weather and sea conditions.

I use eight basic types of lures for trolling tuna: jetheads, bullet heads, flat heads, door knobs, cupped heads, yap heads, kona heads, and angled heads. The action of a lure will depend on its weight, head type, size, and skirt type and length, as well as your boat and trolling speeds, so don't be afraid to experiment. Each boat has its best trolling speed under each sea condition.

LURE RIGGING TIP

The most important thing to remember about using lures is that they must all be weighted. A lure must swim straight and under the water's surface if you're to realize the maximum ratio of hookups to strikes. Over the years I've noticed that when tuna strike a lure, they crash at it, throwing water all over the place. Before I began to weight my lures, this crashing resulted more times than I like to admit in a missed strike. When a tuna hits, it pushes up a wall of water in front of it similar to a bow wave. With an unweighted lure in the fish's path, this bow wave actually pushes the light lure away from the open mouth. This didn't seem to happen with the heavier jetheads, I noticed, so I tried weighing down my other lures a bit with 2- and 3-ounce egg-shaped lead sinkers placed up toward the lure's head and held there with a simple crimping sleeve. It made the lures run straighter and track better, as well as stay under the surface, particularly those lures that were run off an outrigger. And it made a difference right away in my hookup ratio.

I've fished both baits and lures for the smaller species of tuna but have had my greatest success with the artificials, even in foreign waters where artificials are scarce and naturals are the bait of choice. For species other than bluefin tuna, plastic lures are by far my favorites, for a number of reasons. They allow you to fish a much greater area each day, because you don't have to rerig and reset them like you do natural baits. They also come in a much wider variety of styles and colors than naturals do, and they're much more forgiving for the inexperienced angler.

With artificials there's no need to drop back or to count to 10 before you set the hook. And the damn things really do catch tuna, and lots of them. There are many different sizes, styles, and types of lures available; the experienced tuna angler should stock a wide variety for differing fishing conditions.

The most important thing to remember about trolling lures for tuna is that they must be straight running. By this I mean that they should stay in the water rather than jumping out from time to time. Avoid any lures that skip or jump along the water's surface; they will reduce your hookup percentage drastically.

- **Jetheads** have heavy metal heads with holes in them to let water pass through with great force, creating a trail of bubbles or "smoke" in its path. This is something I think tuna are particularly attracted to. They come in three different sizes: 200, 300, and 400; the larger 14-inch lures are 200s, and the smallest 10-inchers are the 400s. These versatile lures can be fished anywhere in a pat-

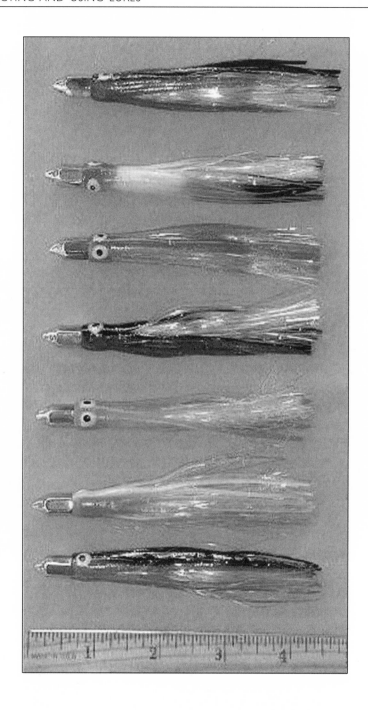

Hexhead tuna lures.

tern, because they stay well under the surface whether in close to the transom or far back off the center rigger in a rough sea. They are particularly effective on bigeyes at dawn or shortly thereafter, but I've taken all types of tuna on them with the exception of giant bluefins.

- **Bullet heads** include the Psychobead and Green Machine types. The Green Machine, manufactured by Sevenstrand, is the most consistently producing lure that I've ever fished, and no trolling rig should ever be without one. These lures feature a rounded or pointed nose that allows them to travel through the water effortlessly. Because of their shape and ease of travel through the water, they can be placed anywhere in the trolling pattern.

- The **kona heads** I use are not the larger, splashier types used primarily for billfish, but the smaller and medium-sized types with a head no more than ¾ inch in diameter and featuring a dished-out face. These lures are so effective because of the commotion that their faces create. They'll spray or spit water periodically as they slide down the face of a wave, attracting the attention of nearby tuna.

- The **yap lure** was developed and first used off Hawaii. It runs very straight, pushing a lot of water as it goes. When it turns and dips below the surface, the head shape pulls a pocket of air with it, along with a stream of bubbles that tuna love.

- **Flat head lures** are similar to yap lures, and also good tuna producers. They take huge amounts of air with them as they dip below the water, streaming bubbles behind.

- **Angled head lures** splash a lot more water on the surface before diving and leave a stream of bubbles.

- **Cupped face lures** push a lot of water and swim erratically from side to side on the surface before again darting below with a big bubble stream. They, too, are good tuna lures, and can be trolled effectively in big seas when you must troll slower.

- The **door knob lures** made by Area Rule Engineering are among my favorites. They come in many sizes and a wide range of effective colors. Their aerodynamic head shape allows them to stay in tight patterns very well at higher speeds, and it makes plenty of bubbles to attract inquisitive tuna.

Jethead tuna lures.

Keep in mind that even as this is being written, new lures are being introduced and older models phased out. For this reason it's important to stay up to date on new developments in lure designs and features.

LURE COLORS

What lure colors to use is another perplexing problem for tuna anglers, especially with such a wide selection offered. An old tuna captain in Montauk once told me that "it doesn't matter what lure color you use, as long as it's green." He was right as far as I'm concerned. I think every trolling rig should have at least one Green Machine in it, and green lures do catch a lot of fish here in the Northeast. Then again, everybody I know fishes at least a couple of green-combination lures in their rigs.

I've also noticed that different-colored or patterned lures seem to produce better in different parts of the world. For example, a friend of mine who lives in the Cayman Islands buys a particular type of pink-and-white lure a few dozen at a time from a Florida manufacturer, while a friend in Venezuela swears by yellow-and-orange-skirted lures. It's my feeling that the role color plays in lure fishing can be argued indefinitely without explicit proof of any one theory. A man who has caught a giant on a particular-colored lure will argue till he drops that his is the color of choice.

Still, studies now seem to indicate that the darker shades, such as black and purple, permeate farther through cobalt depths, while red is the least visible under water. To support that conjecture, there are indications that fish can only distinguish *shades* of colors rather than the actual colors themselves. (How they've decided this I'll never understand, but that's what I'm told.) So who knows? All I can say for certain is that here in the Northeast I've had considerable luck with green and green-combination lures for tuna. My preferences are green, green/yellow (when dolphin are around), green/yellow/orange, and green/white. Other lures that seem to produce well for me are blue/white when flying fish are in the area, clear with speckled skirts when there are squid around, and black/purple when schools of skipjacks or bonito are prevalent. In addition, I think it's a good idea to always troll one oddball color in the pattern, placed in any position. I feel that this can stimulate a lone fish in the area to hit.

A very general rule of thumb to follow is that lighter-colored lures seem to produce well on sunny, bright days, while darker-colored lures work better on cloudy days. Therefore black/purple will and does work well early in the morning and late in the afternoon, with pinks or oranges good on sunny days from 11 A.M. through 2 P.M. One more important thing to remember is to mix up shades in your rig. There are always going to be days when a particular color works better than all the others.

LURE WEIGHTS AND SIZES

Once again, there are no rigid rules when you're choosing a lure weight or size. I feel it's better to mix up your sizes and weights. On calm days you can get away with smaller, lighter lures, and on rough days try the opposite. Generally I'll put the smaller jetheads, hexheads, or Tuna Clones close to the transom in the prop wash. I've had a lot of hookups with this placement. But I've also had smaller lures work off flat lines and outriggers.

The very big lures that work well on marlins aren't good for tuna fishing. I do at times put one larger lure on my center rigger, way back with a teaser bird in front of it. It makes a hell of a commotion and gets hookups, too, but generally the bigger lures have no place in a trolling rig for tuna. I feel that medium-sized and smaller lures are best, and they work well together in a trolling pattern. One big lure in a rig can raise hell with the rest of the pattern if it's not placed and trolled properly. But don't forget—elephants do eat peanuts!

SINGLE-HOOK LURE RIGS

Smaller lures such as the C&H Little Stubby, Sevenstrand's Tuna Clones, hexheads, jetheads, and the new mini Green Machine are all good lures for tuna trolling. But because of their size, it is impractical to rig these lures with two hooks. For this reason, tuna anglers should familiarize themselves with the single-hook rig.

I like to use either the Mustad 7691S single hook or the Mustad 7982HS Siamese double hook in my lures. They are both stainless-steel hooks, which keeps rust stains off your lure's skirt. Single hooks also make it easier to release your fish, particularly if you file down or snip off the barbs.

I rig mine in three different ways using cable or mono leaders ranging from 150- to 400-pound test. The first method uses beads on the leader under the skirt that add color and action to the lure. Most of my lures are rigged this way. Using beads also gives your leader protection against nicks and chafes, and keeps the hook positioned where you want it in the skirt.

To rig it, simply cut the leader material to the desired length, plus a couple of inches as a safety buffer for connections and end loops. Slide your crimps onto the leader and fasten the hook in place, being careful not to damage the leader. Then add the desired number of beads and colors that you need to place the hook in the correct position. To check, simply put the end of the leader through the back of the lure's head and position it. When you've got enough beads in place, add one or two more crimps and form your offshore loop or stainless thimble to the leader's end.

The single- or Siamese-hook rig is very easy and works well in the lures with very short skirts such as the smaller hexheads or jetheads. First pass the leader through the front of the lure's head and out the skirt. Now add your crimps and any chafing tubing, passing the leader end through the hook. Form your loop, and position the hook where you want it inside the lure skirt. Then pass the leader end through the crimps again, and crimp into place. Tim off any excess leader material, and form your end loop on the other end of the leader.

A variation on this rig is the shrink-wrap or tape rig. Follow the previous steps, but wrap the rig in colored tape or shrink wrap. This will stiffen up the hook and hold it in place.

DOUBLE-HOOK RIGS

I use double-hook rigs on larger, longer-skirted lures. They offer a chance at a higher hookup percentage.

SPOON-FEEDING TUNA

A few times each season, it seems, you'll be running to a set of numbers and come across a school of tuna crashing baits on the surface, turning the water a foamy white. In between screaming and adrenaline pumping, my instinct is to slow down, toss out a few lures, and begin trolling around the school, waiting for the hookup that usually never happens. To say this is a letdown is an understatement at the very least. However, out of sheer frustration, I've discovered a method in the past few years that does result in hookups to these feeding fish—spoons.

It first happened with a crippled alewife lure that I had rigged for bluefishing on a rod below. Casting the spoon into the tuna school and cranking, I almost immediately hooked a tuna that in no time at all stripped my reel. So much for that fish, but I subsequently invested in some larger crippled alewives and Huntington Drone Spoons, which can at times make the difference on finicky feeding tuna. These flashy lures, which snap right to your rod's line, can be fished with or without a leader. They are very versatile, can be fished at almost any depth, and give off a seductive flash that tuna cannot seem to resist. I use the 2½ or 3½ spoons for school bluefins and yellowfins, rigged with 100- to 200-pound-test mono leaders.

Since feeding tuna schools are always moving after the fleeing baitfish, try to get your boat upwind and upcurrent from them—or even alongside—and flip the spoon or jig into their midst. Then, with the boat moving slowly forward, jig the spoons so that they jump out of the water, creating a commotion. If this doesn't work, try letting the jig or spoon drop deeper down, and then retrieve it in a jerking motion. You'll often catch a deeper-feeding fish. Drail sinkers or planers can also be added to get the spoons down deep.

When fish first show up in an area and are moving around quickly looking for bait to feed on, these spoons really make a difference. Then as time goes by and the fish settle in, traditional trolling methods will become effective again. Don't put your spoons away, though; use trolling drails or planers to get them deeper. Drails are torpedo-shaped leads that you rig about 10 feet ahead of the spoons. The added weight keeps them several feet below the surface for better trolling. However, many believe that the drails themselves may spook the tuna. I don't feel that this is a consideration, but nevertheless I now use a large 2-, 4-, or 8-ounce egg sinker rigged to the front of the spoons. It changes the spoons' action a bit but still produces fish. I rig mine right on the 10- to 15-foot leader just above the loop, using plastic chafing tube material and a crimp.

On days when you're marking tuna much more than a few feet below the surface, you may need the added help of planers to get your spoons down to the fish. I use the Drone 2 and 3 planers, fishing them right along with my regular tackle with no problems. They'll get your spoons down to about 50 feet, depending on your trolling speed, and can be used in a rig of lures without any risk of tangling. The downside (if it is one) to using the planers is the long 25-foot leaders necessary to rig them properly. Two are needed, requiring the cockpit man to handline a hooked fish up to the boat. Leader material should be 150-pound-test mono in two sections, as mentioned, joined by a barrel swivel. Don't be discouraged by the extra effort, and don't shorten the leader lengths—that will result in fewer hookups. Using spoons and spoons with planers really will put fish in your boat.

The bottom line is that spoons do work. Keep a few different sizes of them ready to go in your boat, and try them next time you come across a school of finicky tuna.

9

CHUNKING AND CHUMMING

During the 1960s, 1970s, and 1980s, offshore anglers pretty much perfected the technique of drifting for swordfish at night in the Northeast canyons. They'd travel anywhere from 65 to 100 miles offshore to such places as Hudson, Block, and Atlantis Canyons, or the Aquarium and the Dip. They then set up near or on the 100-fathom curve. Lines were set out with large hooked squid baits, each one illuminated with a cyalume light stick, and positioned at varying depths ranging from 120 feet on down. These boats then drifted throughout the night, ladling chum overboard or placing a chum bucket over the side to set up an oily scented slick on and below the water's surface. From time to time as an added enticement, chunks of cut-up baitfish such as bunker, squid, mackerel, or butterfish would be tossed overboard in the hope of getting swordfish to take one of the baited hooks. This technique worked quite well for the elusive swordfish as well as the occasional shark. More significant, however, was that surprised anglers found themselves catching large quantities of yellowfin and bigeye tuna.

A rigged butterfish ready for casting. Courtesy Milt Rosko.

Typical baits for tuna. Courtesy Milt Rosko.

Before long word of these "bonus" catches spread and more and more anglers made the trip to the canyons, particularly after the dramatic rise in tuna prices following the 1984 season and the decline of the inshore tuna fishery in 1988.

Initially drifting was the method used, and in some cases it's still the first choice. This technique allows you to fish a much larger area over the greatest possible amount of bottom structure and thus increase your chances of catching a mixed bag of fish species in one trip. The success of this technique depends a great deal on wind direction and tides, and it can be dangerous at night if you should inadvertently drift into a shipping lane. Sea anchors can be used to slow down your boat's drift but you must still keep a sharp eye out for your location and any traffic in the area.

Soon these canyon anglers began experimenting with chunking from stationary boats. Because of their 600-foot-plus depths, anchoring up in the canyons was at first out of the question; it would require great lengths of anchor line and hence additional cost. What the anglers learned, however, was that offshore lobster anglers were setting their strings (trawls) of pots in the same areas where tuna were being caught. Not only were these trawls in ideal tuna fishing grounds, but the masts that marked the strings of pots offered an excellent place to tie boats to.

TYING UP TO A HIGH FLIER

The Northeast's offshore canyons are known for abundant congregations of baitfish due to the bottom's changing structure. With underwater drop-offs and ledges, as well as collaborative ocean currents, masses of sand eels, squid, whiting, ling, and other baitfish are found, in turn attracting the various species of tuna that offshore anglers find so appealing.

To pursue these tuna, many anglers tie up to the high fliers that mark the offshore lobster trawls. This has caused increased friction between the commercial lobstermen and recreational anglers, because improperly tying up to a high flier can cause tremendous damage to expensive pots, lines, and buoys. As recreational anglers we must make the extra effort to get permission from a lobsterman before we tie up to his pots, and then tie up properly. I've found many times that when I ask one of these guys for permission to tie up to his pots, he'll have no problem with it, even directing me to a specific set and suggesting how best to tie up. Here's what I've learned.

The most important consideration when you're tying up is to use plenty of line. Most damage to pots is caused by the up-and-down motion of the boat in the waves, which in turn lifts and drops the pots on the ocean's floor, pounding and tangling them. Additionally, no lobster will enter a pot that's bouncing off the bottom. A 200- to 300-foot length of line, on the other hand, will cut down greatly on the strain put on the trawl, thus reducing any chances of damage. Cut down on the strain even more by adding an anchor ball.

Never tie directly to the pole itself. This can cause the float that supports the pole to ride up it, leaving the marker flag or radar reflector below the water's surface and impossible to find once you leave. Instead, tie your line below the counterweight, or even directly to the buoy line itself. Also, always tie on the downtide side of the marker. Tying on the uptide side would cause your boat to drift back over the entire length of pots, dragging them across the bottom. A good way to determine the current's drift is to simply take your boat out of gear. Then you can approach the high flier from downcurrent.

The lobster anglers were less than pleased with their new tenants. It seems that the anglers tying up to these pots were not using enough line or scope to secure their boats; as a result wave action was lifting and dropping the boats, causing the strings of lobster pots along the bottom to break up from the pounding action. In other cases the mast identifying the pots was lost entirely due to neglect or carelessness on the part of the sport fishermen when tying or untying their boats. Because these trawls of pots represent a sizable investment and the livelihood for the lobstermen, it's not hard to see why tempers flared at times.

Initially some of the lobstermen tried leaving the proper lengths of line tied to the masts for offshore anglers. Unfortunately, this benevolent act was interpreted by many not as a peace offering, but as a way to sabotage the tuna angler's boat by wrapping lines around the props and shafts. Complaints by lobstermen to the Coast Guard continued, and during the 1989 season things really came to a head. That summer the Coast Guard began sending cutters to the canyons to protect the trawls of offshore pots. I had one cutter come alongside me at night while I was tied up and ask if I had permission to be tied up to "private property." When I answered that I hadn't, I was instructed to "get off the pot immediately." As a result some anglers actually went out and bought the 3,000 feet of line necessary to anchor up in spots such as the Fishtails. One enterprising fisherman set up his own mooring 65 miles offshore, complete with a NO TRESPASSING sign! This seems to have alleviated the problems that face commercial and sport anglers, at least for now. If things are to be amicably and entirely resolved in the future, however, both sides need to sit down together and work out a compromise.

CHUNKING

Chunking itself is no more than chumming with cut-up pieces of baitfish instead of ground chum. It's perhaps a small distinction, but it becomes very meaningful when you're trying to attract tuna without attracting sharks. You see, sharks are motivated by scent alone, while smell, sight, and the need to eat motivate tuna.

The actual technique of chunking is very simple: You throw pieces of dead fish overboard upcurrent in order to lure tuna by stimulating their senses of smell and sight. Repeat this over and over throughout the day or night, each time waiting until the previous pieces have drifted from sight. This will create a food and scent line and hopefully bring the fish to your boat. Some captains feel that throwing massive amounts of chunks overboard is better than throwing, say, three to six pieces over at a time, and I'm sure this has benefits, too. My practice is that after setting up, I scatter several good-sized handfuls of chunks overboard all around my boat, then after I settle down I throw five or six chunks at a time. I feel that this way I'm not simply feeding any tuna that may be in the area, but instead arousing and hopefully maintaining their curiosity. I want to offer them just enough to hold their interest and desire.

Chunking must be adjusted to the strength of the currents as well as the quantity of fish at hand. In other words, the rate at which you disperse chunks depends to a great deal on just how fast the current is moving. There's no sense in continuing to chunk if all you're doing is keeping the tuna around someone's boat 1,500 feet away—that is, unless someone upcurrent is doing the same for you. Your goal, again, is to put out just enough bait to attract and entice the tuna but not so much that you satisfy their feeding needs. If you see tuna around your boat or suspect that they might be in the area, heavier chunking may be in order to keep them around. Remember, tuna must eat great amounts of food each day, and they must also continue to move in order to breathe. This should explain why chunking is such a successful method of attracting tuna.

When chunking offshore for tuna, you'll use an absolute minimum of one box of fresh baitfish per day trip, and two to three boxes overnight

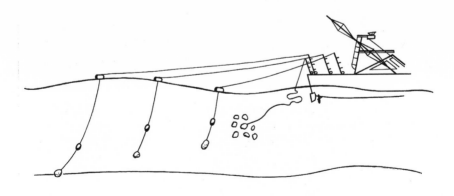

Chunking pattern. Chunking must be adjusted based on the strength of the current and the number of fish at hand.

canyon fishing. These baits should always be fresh if possible. Frozen baits just don't work as well. They lose their firm texture, scent, and taste, and tuna generally turn up their noses at them. I cut my baits up into two or three pieces, depending on their size. I usually put a block of frozen chum overboard as well. This gives you even more scent and many times can make the difference between going home with a fish in the cooler and going home empty-handed.

Once you've started to chunk, someone should keep an eye out at all times for signs of tuna. Do this visually by watching the chunks of bait and if you can by having someone simultaneously watching the color scope. Giants will show up as individual long scratches on the paper or screen, and the smaller schoolies will appear simply as smaller versions of the same. Seeing tuna swim through your slick is a beautiful and exciting moment, and in most cases it means your chances of a hookup just improved dramatically.

Some species of fish just lie back and wait for food to be put in front of them, but tuna must keep moving. This is where a color scope becomes a great asset. You can use it to easily determine the depths at which the fish are feeding, then position your baits at these depths to increase your chances of hooking up. You may also want to alter your chunking technique now to make your hooked baits more enticing and to bring the tuna

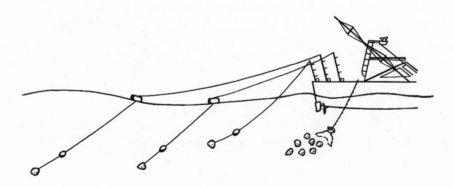

Chunking pattern for a heavy current.

in closer to your boat. Don't worry about them being boat- or noise-shy. When you've got tuna in your slick, they're usually more concerned with feeding than anything else. Watch an individual fish. It will begin to follow a regular pattern as it moves back and forth through the slick, picking up its food while continuing forward before turning to circle around for another pass. You should make yourself aware of this pattern: It will help you determine where to place your baits for the best chance of a hookup.

BASHFUL TUNA

In most cases boats and noise don't bother tuna, but they can be notoriously hook-shy at times. Even while feeding at high speed I've seen tuna swim up to and refuse a bait that had a hook in it. There is much speculation as to why this happens. Some think it's because a hooked bait is heavier and hence falls through the water faster than an unhooked piece, making it stand out from the rest. You can sometimes overcome this by careful observation of the tuna's swimming pattern as well as observing the rate at which bait chunks fall through the water. Then determine just how long you must wait before dropping the hooked chunk overboard. You want it to join the other baits as near the point where the tuna has been feeding as possible. If necessary, you can adjust the bait's sinking rate by inserting a piece of Styrofoam or other flotation in it.

Some feel that tuna are alerted by leader material or fishing line. Another theory that I first heard years ago and that I believe makes sense is that the tuna can actually "feel" the heat of the hook in the bait. This heat is transferred to the hook by the angler's hands while baiting. The hook retains this warmth for some time afterward, alerting the tuna— which as mentioned earlier is extremely sensitive to changes in heat.

CHUNKING RIGS

If you hook a tuna while chunking, it gains a great advantage after a particularly long fight (say, 30 minutes or more). The reason for this is that when hooked, the tuna must continue to open and close its mouth in order to breathe. The leader or line material begins to chafe from rubbing on the fish's interior mouth, resulting all too often in a prematurely lost fish.

To keep the advantage in the cockpit, anglers have developed chunking rigs.

The Mousetrap Rig

Jim Taylor, an expert angler from Hampton Bays, New York, who owned Blue Water Tackle Store, developed this setup, which eliminates the chafing problem completely when rigged and fished properly. Called the Mousetrap Rig for reasons that will soon become obvious, the effectiveness of this rig lies in its 7-inch piece of stainless cable, as well as its ability to allow you to use a lighter leader on those days when the fish are leader-shy.

The design and components of this rig are remarkably simple. On one end of the cable is the hook, in any size you choose, which is crimped on with a size B crimp for 270 cable or a size A crimp for 480 cable. At the other end is crimped on a welded steel ring that will be attached to the rod's leader or line with either a suitable knot or a snap swivel. This entire rig is then hidden inside the bait's stomach with the help of a rigging needle.

Chunk the rig overboard with the other baits (to keep it from looking like a hook bait). When a tuna takes the rigged bait you simply set the hook, which then straightens out the rig, leaving the fish with a piece of durable stainless cable protruding from its mouth and the monofilament leader or line 7 inches away. This will effectively eliminate any chance of a lost fish due to chafing.

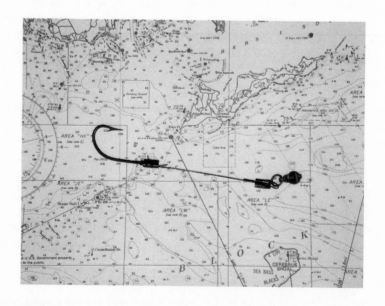

Mousetrap rig.

Taylor created many different variations of this rig, using a Mustad 7698B hook sized from 5/0 to 12/0 with either 270- or 480-pound cable; a 9174 Mustad in sizes ranging from 7/0 to 9/0 with 270-pound cable; and, in what seems to be the most effective combination, the razor-sharp superior-strength Gamakatsu tuna hooks in sizes 7/0 to 11/0 all rigged with 270-pound cable. It should be noted that these cables actually have a breaking strength of twice their rated capacity, making them ideal for anything from medium- to giant-sized tuna. The 5/0 and 9/0 hook sizes are recommended for chunking yellowfins, while the larger sizes are good for midsized and giant bluefins.

Leader strengths for the rig should vary depending on just how leader-shy the fish are on any particular day, but recommended strengths are from 130-pound test down. You can use heavier leader material if the fish aren't finicky that day, or when you're targeting giant bluefins. You should use at least 10 feet of leader material, however, and blacken it with a high-grade black Magic Marker to make it that much more invisible to the fish.

To rig the mousetrap rig properly, you'll need a 9-inch open-eye rigging needle, waxed dental floss or cotton thread (cotton thread is softer and doesn't cut into baits' mouths), and a sewing needle.

INSTRUCTIONS

1. Attach the line directly to the ring of the mousetrap; do not use a leader. The best connections are a thimble and a crimp for heavier lines, and a palomar knot on lighter lines. You can also camouflage the line now if you wish by marking it with a waterproof pen. Have a long-shank open-eye needle and a bait-rigging needle with cotton rigging line ready.

2. Insert the point of the hook (barb down) into the mouth of the butterfish. Rotate the hook in a downward motion, working the entire hook into the throat. Do not puncture the skin or exit the gill opening.

3. With the hook inside the throat, push on the cable so the hook falls into the body cavity.

4. Insert the open-eye needle into the mouth and push the point through the split into the tail. Hook the ring onto the eye of the needle.

5. Pull the needle from its point, and the ring and cable will enter the butterfish's mouth. Keep pulling, and pinch the cable as you go in order to guide it into the mouth.

6. Pull all the cable into the mouth until only the line is seen exiting. Be careful not to pull the ring and eye all the way through the butterfish.

7. Now you should be able to see the outline of the needle's ring and eye under the skin of the butterfish. Unhook the ring from the eye and pull the needle out through the tail.

8. Sew the mouth closed with cotton rigging line or floss. This will keep the rig inside the butterfish.

9. The finished mousetrap rig as it should look.

Tuna Bullet Rig

This is another rig developed by Jim Taylor that not only is innovative but again diminishes the chances of losing a tuna due to chafed leaders. It works particularly well on lighter-test leaders, which will break much quicker than the heavier ones. I've used it on heavy leaders, too, though, when fishing for giants. I've had great success.

The rig takes its name from its simple working principle: It slides down your fishing line and into the unsuspecting tuna's mouth. As you'll see, this eliminates any chance of chafed line from the tuna opening and closing its mouth. The rig's primary components are an 18-inch length of ¼-inch (outside diameter) nylon tubing (black is my preference), and an oval- or bullet-shaped lead weight of 15, 24, or 32 ounces (depending on

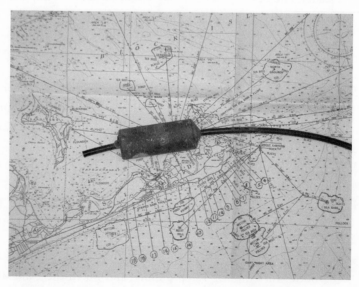

Tuna bullet rig.

tides and currents) with a hole through it that allows it to fit snugly over the tubing.

Over many years of experimentation I've come to use a more streamlined lead weight, which I feel encounters less resistance in the water and travels down the line (and into the tuna's mouth) faster. I also insert a small snap swivel in the top of the lead weight so that I can hook it into place on my rod tip until ready to use. More on that later.

Here's another tip that ensures smooth operation: Tie your hook directly to your fishing line rather than using a leader. This will prevent any hang-ups while the rig is on its way into the tuna's mouth. If you do use a leader use a blood or surgeon's knot to safely connect the two, and trim it as closely as possible so that the rig doesn't hang up. Then check to make sure that the knot is small enough that the rig travels over it smoothly before you actually begin fishing. Using a swivel will cause the rig to hang up.

SETTING UP THE TUNA BULLET RIG

The Tuna Bullet can be set up in a couple of different ways, depending on your chosen fishing method. If I'm chunking, I use two setups. The first is to attach the rig 15 to 20 feet above the hook by looping the line a few times, and holding the rig in place with a size 64 rubber band (see photo). This allows the rig to act as a weight when you're chunking, keeping your line down in the currents at the desired depths. Then when the tuna strikes, the stress on the line will automatically release the rig and allow it to drop into the fish's mouth.

The second method is to attach the rig to the rod's tip with the snap swivel, a piece of dental floss, or some other lightweight line. When the fish is hooked up, manually release the rig and let it go! This method also works very well when you have fish swimming in your chunking line or are working your baits. I also use it occasionally when I'm trolling for bigeyes and other tuna. When the fish strikes, you or the mate releases the rig before beginning to fight the fish.

The Tuna Bullet Rig is another proven innovation of Jim Taylor that has greatly increased the percentage of fish I bring to boatside to be tagged.

CHUMMING

I used to think that chumming and chunking were techniques used almost exclusively here in the Northeast, until I began to travel around the world a bit and see other anglers. Many embrace some sort of chumming to raise and hold fish.

During a typical day of shark fishing, most anglers will use two to three large containers of frozen chum (ground fish) to form and maintain a chum slick. The chum is either put into some sort of a container where it is allowed to disperse on its own, or it's ladled overboard manually in intervals of about 30 seconds. Either way the result is the same: As the boat drifts downwind and the chum is dispersed, a slick forms, which may cover miles of ocean as the day goes on. The scent of the slick as well as any small pieces of bait usually attracts fish from miles around. Sure, there are other considerations—location, bottom structure, water temperature—but basically a chum slick attracts game fish by its scent.

Chum bags and containers are available from any good offshore tackle store, or you can make your own with little effort. I've got two different chum containers, the first a large onion bag that I use primarily inshore when chumming for bluefish or little tunny. I put the frozen chum in it, tie it off, and hang it overboard, where the chum is dispersed throughout the fishing day. You can regulate the flow of chum by adjusting the depth at which you set the chum bag. For instance, completely submerge the bag and the chum will disperse much faster than it would if you submerged only a third of it. This will depend again on the wind and sea conditions, as well as how many fish are in the area. I generally chum heavily at first to attract the fish, then back off just enough to hold them once they are around the boat. This method works very well for light-tackle casting inshore. I've used it over and over again while casting for blues and little tunny with great success.

The chum container I use offshore is a 5-gallon plastic spackle bucket with two dozen ¾-inch holes drilled throughout the sides and six 1-inch holes on the bottom. The smaller holes permit seawater to flush through the bucket, while the larger holes on the bottom let the chum disperse as it thaws. These buckets are perfect for offshore fishing, because they're durable and the perfect size and shape to accept frozen chum. Their durability is especially important; I've often had blue sharks come right up and attack my chum pail. It has always held up.

Simply adjusting the container's depth in the water can regulate the rate of the chum's dispersal. Some captains, including myself, carefully cut up chunks of baitfish and toss them overboard into the slick. This increases the temptation for any game fish that may have found its way into the slick and, if done properly, can greatly help you get a fish to take one of your rigged baits.

There are two different schools of thought about the amount of chum and chunks to put overboard. Some feel that it's better to use chum sparingly, while others feel that more is better. I've seen draggers with holds full of bait anchored up on the tuna grounds and literally shoveling butterfish, squid, and other bait overboard. Both methods result in hooked fish. My feeling is that you should always choose the amount of chum to use based on the species of fish you're after and the sea conditions that day. When you're shark fishing, for instance, you should use less chum and chunks than when you're tuna fishing. Although sharks are incredible predators, they're not the eating machines that a bluefin or yellowfin tuna are. So a shark has to be enticed a little more into taking a bait than the tuna, which may eat up to 10 percent of its body weight each day.

CHUNKING AND CHUMMING TIPS

Both chumming and chunking are essential parts of offshore and inshore fishing worldwide, and both require more knowledge and refinement than just throwing pieces of bait overboard. Sadly, many anglers aren't aware of this and hence lessen their chances of successfully hooking fish. The following tips should help you:

- Fresh baitfish will always attract tuna better than frozen.
- Hanging frozen blocks of ground chum overboard in a perforated bucket or mesh onion bag works well because only a small amount of chum is released, depending on how deep you set your chum bag or pot. The resulting scent is released as the chum melts, attracting fish.
- Squirting menhaden oil or one of the new fish attractants on the water's surface will spread an enticing scent quickly.
- When you're chunking for tuna, a good rule of thumb is to throw a few pieces of fish overboard and then wait until they sink from sight before tossing out any more.
- Always chum or chunk steadily. Never leave a gap in your chum or chunk line, not even when you're hooked up, if you can avoid it. If you do hook up and find it necessary to move, throw a buoy overboard to mark the end of your chum slick. After boating the fish you can return to your spot easily and begin chumming again without interrupting your chum slick.
- If a fish comes into your chum slick eating chum pieces but refusing your baits, try putting a small piece of chum on your hook and letting it sink at the same rate as the chunks. This can be done many times if you add a small piece of Styrofoam to the bait first.
- Finally, never throw your chum containers overboard. Bring them back to the dock and dispose of them properly.

Through reading, dockside chatter, and experience, the various chumming and chunking techniques will start to pay off for you in boated fish.

CATCHING AND PREPARING YOUR BAITS

Now that you've attracted tuna to your slick of chunks or chum, and your rig is ready and waiting, it's time to toss the fish your baited hook. Bait will always be one of your primary expenses when tuna fishing. On just a day trip for tuna you can spend upward of $200 for bait if you have to buy it; on an overnight canyon trip you'll spend much more. Because of the tuna's huge appetite, you've got to have plenty of fresh bait aboard at all times. It's always better to bring more than you think you'll need rather than run short. Anything other than fresh bait is just a waste of money and your time. For this reason, invest in a good freezer to keep your baits in; the cost of it will come back to you in just one season. Also familiarize yourself with catching, preparing, and storing your baits properly so that as few as possible are wasted.

Much of my spring is spent not only getting my boat ready but also fishing for bait or buying it from local trap fishermen, who many times really make the difference in getting good fresh baits. Squid, bunker, mackerel, sand eels, butterfish, and herring are all excellent baits and should be gathered for the upcoming seasons. Mackerel and squid are best for rigging daisy chains or trolling, as you'll see, and the rest are all excellent chunking and chumming baits for tuna.

Beginning in April we fish for mackerel as they migrate through the area on their way north. We catch as many as we can, as quickly as we can, because the migration is over so soon. We then prepare and quick-freeze them for use later in the season. Handle the mackerel carefully when you catch them so that their mouths and tails are not ripped or their bodies damaged. Otherwise they won't make good tuna baits. (Do use them for a chum mixture or shark baits instead of throwing them away.) Place the mackerel in an iced cooler with a mixture of kosher salt and crushed ice in a slurry of salt water. This will preserve them in the best possible way for later in the season.

I catch squid in early to mid-May from docks and piers at night. Squidding has become so popular that hundreds of people can be found some nights "jigging" squid under the lights at a commercial fish dock nearby. Koreans drive out from New York City just to catch them, and can be found cooking them fresh on small propane stoves on the dock. On a good night you can catch a couple of spackle buckets full of squid in no time. It has really turned into a favorite pastime for my two boys.

You can buy other baits from commercial anglers if you make arrangements beforehand. They will often give you the fresh baits in their tubs; take them home to wrap and freeze, and be sure to return the tub. I have two friends who tend fish traps, and I arrange with them prior to each season to purchase various baits. I store my squid in individual large freezer bags four to six to a package; herring, butterfish, bunker, and sand eels go into plastic spackle-type buckets with lids. Again, rinse everything in a mixture of seawater and kosher salt, and freeze it as quickly as possible so they don't begin to deteriorate. If you can afford one, the new vacuum baggers are worth the investment, too. They remove all air from the packages before freezing, ensuring that they won't "burn" in your freezer.

Bunker, butterfish, and herring are all excellent chunking and chum baits. My favorites are the butterfish and herring. When fresh, it's hard for tuna to turn up their noses at these.

If you have any bait left after the season is over, don't throw it away; simply grind it up for chum for next year and refreeze it. You can mix everything together this way, and be that much further ahead for next season. Just remember to keep your baits as fresh and naturally colorful as possible when handling and freezing them. This will result in more hookups during the season.

BAIT TYPES

Just about any type of baitfish indigenous to the location you're fishing will work well when you're trying to catch tuna. I have caught them on butterfish, mackerel, herring, whiting, bluefish, and hake when fishing with conventional tackle. On light tackle the same baits work well in smaller pieces, as do spearing (silversides or shiners) and sand eels. Sand eels used as baits or cut into chunks are particularly deadly on tuna, but for some reason are rarely used. I always try to net at least a few bucketfuls in May prior to the season for chunking.

WORKING YOUR BAITS

When you're anchored or tied up and chunking for tuna, the usual method is to put out your baits at different distances from the boat and at various depths. Another option is to work your bait in with the chunked baits to further disguise it and give it additional appeal.

This technique is very simple and, when fish are shy, will often result in hookups. With the rod placed in a rod holder, and the reel's drag relaxed or in free spool, clicker on, simply spool line off the reel by hand, allowing your bait to drop in with the chunked baits. After you've pulled off 30 to 50 lengths of line (this depends on the depth you're fishing), slowly retrieve the line by hand, placing it either in a spackle-type bucket or neatly on the cockpit floor, out of the way so it won't become tangled in cleats or your feet. You can also slowly reel the line in while keeping the clicker on and a hand on the line; stay alert for a strike. Many times if the bait is not taken on the way down, tuna will strike as it's swimming backward toward the boat.

When the fish strikes, it'll take the line out in no time at all. Simply lift the line up above the boat's gunnel in your palm, allowing it to run off as you or someone else takes the rod.

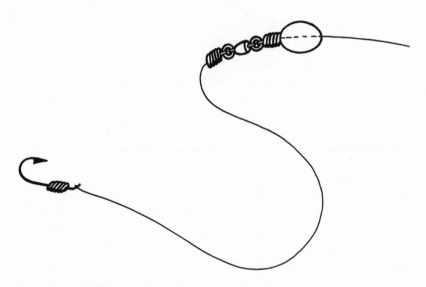

A good rig for chunking with an 8-foot leader.

At this point you should take the rod out of the holder, point it toward the fish, and place it in your gimbal belt or in the fighting chair's gimbal. Always have someone ready to fight a fish, with the belt on, harness in place or set up for the fighting chair. It'll then take only a few seconds to set up the angler with rod and reel, giving a considerable advantage over the fish.

Rigging butterfish chunks, either through the head-half or tail-half.

Working your baits is a very effective method of increasing your hookup percentages. It can also alleviate the boredom that sometimes sets in when no fish are being caught, particularly about 2:30 in the morning when you're 100 miles offshore.

SINKERS AND CORK

Ocean currents, winds, and the movement of your boat can affect the positions and presentations of your chunk baits. At times when there is little current, they may sink *faster* than your chunks and not look as realistic. When there's a stronger current, they may sink *slower*—again not looking right to a wary tuna.

You can make your baits look more realistic regardless of the conditions by using rubber-cored sinkers or pieces of cork. The latter will help float your baits, which is useful in light currents; on the other hand, rubber-cored sinkers attached to your leader will sink it faster in heavy currents.

They're also good for keeping your baits consistently at a particular depth—important if you've spotted tuna there on your color scope.

There are no set guidelines for how much flotation or weight to add in which situation. Experiment and see what works best for you.

10

LIVE BAITING

FOR

TUNA

A.J. McClane's *New Standard Fishing Encyclopedia* defines live baiting as "the use of any natural organism that can be employed to catch fish." This includes live baits ranging from insects to earthworms to small tuna, such as the blackfins used for marlin baits.

Live baiting for tuna has proven itself very effective here in the Northeast. This method can be used for all sizes of tuna, from schoolies to giant bluefins. Until recently, chunking and trolling natural baits in daisy chains was about the extent of the live baiting done here. It wasn't until 1986 that I first noticed one particular Montauk tuna fisherman who was having an exceptionally hot year. On days when the fleet was slow—only a handful of fish among the 200 or more boats anchored up—this captain more often than not headed back to the dock with a fish. After witnessing this numerous times I decided to charter his boat for a day of fishing and hopefully learn something.

To my delight the captain turned out to be not only a first-rate tuna angler but an excellent teacher as well. His method—which he generously revealed to me that day, and which has since dramatically improved my hookup ratio—was the use of live swimming baits in his floating rigs. It's a technique that doesn't require a great deal of expense to set up or to maintain. The nucleus of the system is the bait well, used to keep the tuna baits alive and fresh.

Many of the larger sport-fishing boats today come equipped with these live wells as standard equipment. In most cases they are placed out of the way below the cockpit floor in a readily accessible place. Smaller boats used for tuna fishing may not have an installed well system but can be equipped with one with little effort.

SELECTING YOUR LIVE BAITS

Your bait choices will depend on the regions you're fishing, but a major consideration should always be the hardiness and freshness of the baits. My favorite live baits are bunker and snapper bluefish, both of which are available in abundance here in the Northeast from June through September. Both are especially appealing to the giant bluefin tuna here, and they produce consistently. I've found snappers to be particularly hardy, living up to three days in a bait well with good circulation. And when rigged as baits, snappers outlast any other species of fish I've tried. They're also very lively, making a lot of commotion and attracting the curious tuna.

Bluefin and yellowfin tuna are also very fond of live bunker, but these fish are fragile and very hard to keep alive for any amount of time. They must have very fresh seawater and need to continuously swim upcurrent with water passing over their gills to supply them with oxygen if they're to survive. For this reason a live well with good circular current is ideal for them. I try to catch my bunker with a cast net on the way to my fishing grounds. They'll live longer in the bait well and also be fresher.

Other baits that I've used live with success are squid and tinker mackerel. These are often found at night swimming under our cockpit lights when we're anchored up in the canyons. A squid jig or a small hook with a piece of butterfish will snag one for you, and putting it immediately on a rig will increase your hookup chances dramatically.

HOOK POSITIONS

I use three hook positions for live bait and find that all produce well. My first choice is through the back, placing the hook through the meaty area of the fish just forward of the dorsal fin (as shown). This allows the bait to swim strongly for a long time.

Hooking through the nose and lower mouth (as shown) will give you a longer-lasting bait. If a deep-swimming bait is preferred, I place the hook through the meat, at the anal vent near the aft end of the stomach (also shown), causing the fish to swim deeper, though not for very long.

I usually use only one live bait in my rig; all the others are rigged as chunk baits. It's been my experience that multiple live baits almost always tend to swim together, creating a gigantic tangle of lines! When a live bait dies, use it right away as a chunk or hook bait. It will be fresh and not wasted.

REEL-DRAG SETTING

When you're live baiting, use just enough drag to keep the reel spool from turning into a mouse nest. Place the clicker on and, when the reel begins to scream upon hookup, push the drag lever to the strike position, at the same time lifting the rod's tip into the air to properly set the hook. If you know that you're going to release the fish, don't wait so long to set the drag into the strike position. This quick action will in most cases give you a lip-hooked fish that can be safely released after the fight. If you intend to keep the fish, wait a couple more seconds before setting the hook to let the fish swallow the bait and gut-hook itself.

Try live baiting the next time you're tuna fishing. It has put fish in my boat on those days when a lot of other folks went home with empty fish boxes. I'm sure it'll do the same for you.

11

TROLLING
FOR
TUNA

Although many think of it as the lazy man's way of fishing, trolling requires large amounts of patience, work, skillful use of tackle, and knowledge of existing fishing conditions as well as of the fish you're seeking. It may not always be your chosen method of fishing, but there are many times when it's the only productive way to catch tuna.

Trolling for tuna is not a new technique; research shows that the ancient Polynesians trolled for tuna from their outrigger canoes while making their voyages across the Pacific Ocean. They trolled at speeds ranging from 6 to 9 knots, with lures made by hand from mother-of-pearl shells attached to handlines woven from straw and local grasses. It seems they were quite successful. I like to think that we've refined and improved this technique somewhat today, but basically it is very similar. Simply put, trolling presents the illusion of real baitfish to tuna, hopefully enticing them to strike.

Planning is the most important factor in setting out for a day of trolling. Cockpits should be neat, with gaffs, tailropes, coolers, tackle, baits, tagging sticks, rods, and everything else you need stored away properly. On the way to the fishing grounds, baits can be prepared, rods rigged with lures, and hooks sharpened. We also put out our harnesses and fighting-chair seats, place rods in the rod holders, and do anything else that may make things run more smoothly.

TROLLING TACKLE

For trolling, my tackle ranges anywhere from 20- to 130-pound test. As a very general rule, 20-pound tackle can be used for tuna of up to 50 pounds; 50-pound tackle for tuna of 50 to 80 pounds; 80-pound tackle for fish weighing 80 to 120 pounds; and 130-pound tackle for any tuna over 120 pounds. These are generalities, of course, and I often fish for tuna larger than 120 pounds with 50- or 80-pound test.

NUMBER OF RODS TO TROLL

When trolling for tuna, I use anywhere from seven to nine rods, depending on what type we're trolling for and how many capable people are aboard. I've seen anglers troll as many as 11 rods—which is fine if you have the cockpit room and crew, but it's too many for me.

Before you place your rods in the holders, it's a good idea to first drop in a golf ball or a few larger egg sinkers strung together with monofilament line. This will leave you with enough depth to hold your rods safely yet still reduce your chances of losing a fish upon hookup if the fish runs across the boat's transom or wake with the lure. This is because the rod will be able to turn in the direction of the fish, preventing the line from being pulled across the rod's tip. This is also particularly helpful when trolling with the shorter-butted stand-up rods.

I usually troll two rods from each outrigger, placing the lure that runs from the end eye the farthest back—on the seventh or eighth wave. The line on the short rigger is fished through the second eye usually on the fourth or fifth wave, depending on the sea conditions. In rougher seas I'll fish these lines farther back. The two flat lines—run from either the gunnels or the fighting chair—are run to the third wave and clipped down with the aid of transom clips if the seas are particularly sloppy. The seventh line is fished the farthest back from either the center rigger or a rod holder mounted on the bridge. This line is often hit by passing stray fish and has also resulted in a few blue marlin catches for me.

TROLLING FOR BIGEYES

It wasn't until about five seasons ago when I was trolling for yellowfins in a canyon early one morning that I had my first "accidental" hookup with three bigeyes. From that moment on I've been hooked on bigeyes myself. These powerful fish will give you a great battle, and if you're trolling properly and practicing the right techniques you can often turn one hookup into multiples—really increasing the adrenaline level in the cockpit.

Where to Find Them

Bigeyes are generally found in depths ranging from 80 to 150 fathoms, especially on or in the immediate area of underwater structure. Like other tuna, bigeyes respond strongly to water temperatures. Cool surface water temperatures in the 64- to 66-degree range have worked best for me according to my logs, but temperatures of up to 72 degrees will also produce fish—just not as well. It seems that as the water temperature rises above 66 degrees your chance of taking a bigeye drops considerably. Be on the lookout at all times for water temperature changes due to currents, underwater structure, and the like. Called gradients, these changes are crucial when you're trolling for just about any type of tuna, but especially bigeyes. Once you find a gradient, work it back and forth over and over again, all the time keeping your eye on your chart recorder or video fish finder for changes in the ocean floor structure that might attract bigeyes. Bigeyes are found at various depths, so I recommend multiple lines, either weighted or used in conjunction with downriggers.

Tackle to Use

Because of the bigeyes great strength and stamina, as well as its evasiveness, I exclusively use 80- and 130-pound-class rods and reels when trolling for them. While it's not as "sporty" as some may like, heavier tackle is a great asset when you have multiple hookups—often the case with bigeyes.

When I previously used 50- and even 30-pound-test tackle, I lost too many bigeyes due to broken lines, stripped reels, and the carelessness that results from long battles. Primarily, though, I choose heavier tackle because of the dwindling numbers of these fish, and because of their great strength. As anyone who has been lucky enough to hook into one of these monsters knows, they're big, strong, and excellent fighters. You're going to need as many factors in your favor as you can get! I prefer bent-butt rods with roller-type guides, but I use straight butts as well.

TROLLING SQUID

Trolled squid appeal to the majority of offshore species, particularly tuna. For that simple reason it's one of my principal choices when I'm trolling natural baits.

Squid baits vary in size from a few ounces to a couple of pounds; the size you select depends on the species you're after. Try to choose a bait that's large enough to attract your quarry, yet small enough to be swallowed easily.

Squid are soft baits, and as such must be prepared and cared for carefully to prevent them from collapsing on the hook. For this reason never store them in or wash them down with fresh water. This will only cause them to soften, lose freshness, and turn an unnatural purplish color. To avoid this when you're storing squid in a cooler, wrap them in a plastic freezer bag first; before putting them in the cooler, cover the ice with a waterproof cover such as canvas or plastic to keep them from becoming moist. When it comes time to thaw one, place the squid in a bucket of seawater. Because squid should never be refrozen, use them as soon as possible.

While at first the squid's softness may appear to be a drawback, it makes the bait easier for a predator to swallow and also simplifies proper hook setting. I've seen billfish and tuna make multiple passes at properly prepared squid baits, and they held up to this foreplay before being inhaled. Still, I change my squid baits depending on the sea conditions and never try to stretch out the useful life of a bait—this is always counterproductive.

Squid are rigged in a number of different ways depending on the target species as well as who's doing the rigging. The important thing to remember when rigging one is that you don't want it to run up the leader when a fish strikes, nor do you want it to disintegrate or break up when being trolled. I'm going to describe a simple one-hook rig with minimal sewing that I use as a single bait for tuna and billfish.

You'll need your leader material, a hook of the correct type and size for the fish you're after, and a small cork like the ones used by bottom anglers.

1. If you're using stainless-steel leader material, attach it to the hook using a haywire twist followed by a barrel twist, leaving a tag end on the wire about 1 foot long. Slide the cork down the leader and lay the bend of the hook alongside the eye of the squid. Measure the distance from the eye to the tail. You want the cork to remain just inside the tail, so it's important to keep the cork in position. To do this, make a few barrel twists in the wire at the determined length, leaving a short tag end to prevent the cork from sliding back to the hook.

2. Slip the free end of the leader under the squid's collar and out through the tail, making sure that the wire passes through the center of the tail so that the squid will troll properly. Then pull the entire length of the leader through the tail until the cork is seated. Be gentle enough that the cork isn't forced through the body, and that the squid maintains its natural shape.

3. If you've correctly measured the distance between the cork and the hook, the bend should now be lying just opposite the squid's eye. Bending the head, insert the point of the hook through it. Once the hook is properly seated, the squid will straighten out again, and the hook will keep the head from separating from the body.

4. To keep the cork in place, use a regular bait-sewing needle rigged with some light braided line. Insert the needle forward of the cork and to one side of the leader wire. Pull the needle through, leaving about 4 inches of line outside the squid to be used later to tie off. Then continue with a series of stitches until you've formed an X on either side of the cork.

5. With the cork now sewn in place, wrap the remaining braided line four or five times tightly around the squid's tail just in front of the cork, then tie it off and snip the excess ends cleanly.

6. The finished bait is ready to be frozen for use later on this season.

Daisy-chain teasers are a valuable addition to your rig and should be used whenever possible. I use seven artificial squid, in varying colors depending on sun conditions and either 7 or 9 inches long. Don't rig all of them in line from one piece of mono leader. Instead place 2 ounces of egg-shaped lead in the trailing or last squid and attach the others on break-away lines off the mono leader, keeping each one just ahead of the other. This will allow the individual squid to swim independently, making the maximum commotion and resembling more closely a school of real squid. A tuna will more times than not strike at the last squid, breaking it off, but it'll then almost always return to continue hitting and breaking off the other squid. Finally in frustration and anger it'll hit one of your lures.

I rig this daisy chain to a length of 400-pound monofilament leader material, passed through the first eye of the outrigger pole, and snap it onto one of the teaser reels mounted on the bridge. This way I can tease the fish more from my position on the bridge as I drop the daisy chain back or reel it in. It adds to the tuna's frustration and makes it all the more determined to get hold of something.

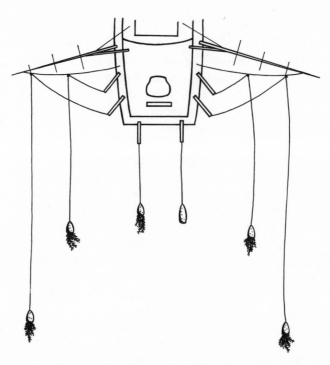

An excellent 6-rod trolling setup for yellowfin, bluefin, bigeye, or albacore. I would use generic lures.

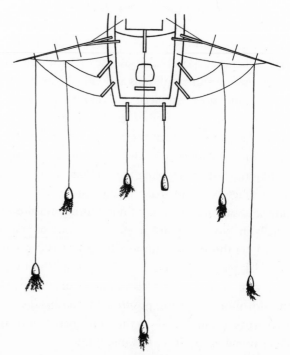

An excellent 7-rod setup.
Again use generic lures.

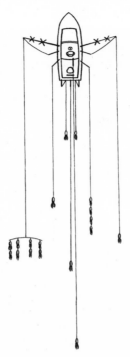

An 8-rod setup for bigeye and yellowfin with a teaser mounted on the #8 line. This is the setup I use most often on my boat.

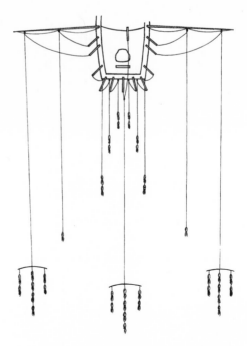

*For the more aggressive,
an 11-rod setup.*

LURE PATTERNS

I see the best percentages of hookups when I use a W-pattern. I fish this pattern with seven or eight rods, positioning one line off each outrigger back to the fifth and sixth waves (see diagram). I use taglines in many situations, especially rough water, to decrease the drop back and help in hooking up.

The two flat lines from the forward rod holders are placed on the third wave; put the two flat lines from the rods placed closest to or off the transom in close on the second wave, sometimes with taglines rigged through the scuppers and always with at least one teaser.

The center rigger lines are placed 150 to 200 feet behind the transom, with teaser birds rigged in front of the lures. These lines usually result in the first hookups; watch them constantly.

If you don't want to fish seven, eight, or more lines use six—but that should be the absolute minimum. To do this, simply delete the center rigger lines and fish your outrigger and flat lines.

Another pattern I use when I have a couple of competent mates fishing with me is the nine-rod pattern. Here I'll run two lines off each out-

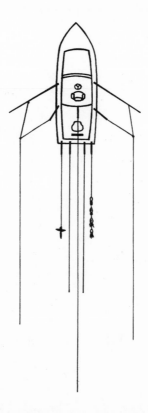

W trolling pattern.

rigger but close to the transom. The outside lines are placed on the third or fourth wave, and the lines close to the boat or the inside lines are placed on the second or third wave. My flat lines are then run to the third or fourth wave, while I place my center rigger or bridge lines (see diagram) on the fifth or sixth wave—or even farther back. Remember to run some birds with the lines set farthest back as well as at least one on the close-up flat lines.

Now that you've got the lures out in the basic spots that you're going to be trolling them, you need to fine-tune the rig and set each lure in its proper place on the wave. All lures should be placed so that they sit on the interface or front of the wave sliding downward. This will allow them to swim properly and be in the water the majority of the time. And as the lures move through the water, you and your mate will clearly see the stream of bubbles or "smoke" that they create. Thus both of you can scan the rig at all times—monitoring such things as proper action, seaweed accumulations, or approaching tuna.

PROPER TROLLING SPEED FOR LURES

Each boat has its own best trolling speed. Some say that a single-screw boat produces more hookups than a twin screw; others will disagree. Then there are captains of twin-screw boats who swear that they catch more fish while trolling with only one motor running. I think that no two boats are alike, even if they're the same model from the same manufacturer. Too many factors—prop size and condition, through-hull fittings, trim tabs, and many more—can change a boat's performance and the underwater sound it gives off (another very important consideration).

You need to become intimately familiar with your own boat's performance at different trolling speeds. Keep accurate records of things such as speed, rpms, lures, colors, wind speed, wind direction, depth, loran numbers, presence of surface baitfish, and bottom configuration. These records will soon become invaluable as you see patterns begin to develop.

Two things determine a particular boat's trolling speed: the boat itself and the sea conditions. Usually if you set your boat's speed fast enough to form a wake that a lure can set in you'll be in the area of the right speed. This will in most cases be about 7 to 10 knots, but more often 7 to 9. If your lures are jumping out of the water, you should slow down. Each boat will be different, and each captain will feel comfortable at different speeds. Just try to keep your engines synchronized and your lures running properly, and you'll find a comfortable speed.

RECORD KEEPING

Record keeping is an integral part of being a productive angler. While it may seem tedious at first, you'll soon begin to see patterns developing. Water temperatures, depths, currents, weather conditions, dates—all these will end up giving you a better overall picture of your angling activities, while helping you focus on areas and species to make better use of your time offshore. A good captain will always keep a notebook in the helm station to keep track of such things as the coordinates of hookups, lure or bait used, colors, weather conditions, trolling speed, and any other information pertinent to your hookup.

While this is clearly inconvenient at times, force yourself to do it and it will result in more productive and efficient future trips. I keep a loose-leaf notebook on my flying bridge, inside a plastic bag, and write down information each hookup. It has paid off immeasurably for me over the years as I've chased tuna around offshore, and helped me to realize things about the tuna's habits that have made me a more productive angler.

Then, after a day of fishing, I enter the information in a computer program called FISHbase. It is a very user-friendly program that keeps track of all the information I just mentioned plus a lot more. It includes a trip planner; allows you to keep track of the maintenance of your reels, line, and drag replacements; and much more. FISHbase is fully customizable and allows you to configure all your fishing data into a report that will help you keep catching fish.

Trim tabs are boat features that can and do make a big difference. When placed full down, they will give you the maximum amount of white water—something that tuna are very fond of. Add this to the hull, lure action, and lure noise, and you've got a combination that'll attract tuna to your boat. I've caught tuna right up at the first and second wave while letting out or retrieving line.

PICKING A SPOT

How and where you troll are also important elements in tuna fishing. Underwater ground structure, drop-offs, wrecks, and so on are all important considerations. Usually when you find one of the above you'll also find a concentration of bait, and where you have a concentration of bait you have the possibility of finding tuna. When you begin to troll a particular spot, don't make the mistake of leaving it too quickly, especially if all signs point to fish but nothing seems to be happening. I've made this mistake many times, due to just plain impatience. I'll spot an area that looks promising on my way to the canyon; there may even be other boats trolling. So I slow down, put my lines in the water, and begin trolling. If nothing happens in 15 or 20 minutes I'll pick up and go, all the time anxious to get to where the fish are—the canyon. Inevitably I find out later, by radio or dockside chatter, that that particular spot got hot shortly after I left and all other boats there went back to port satisfied.

So stay and work an area thoroughly once you're there. Troll a grid pattern, circles, or even figure-eights back and forth over and over again, covering the maximum amount of water. As a guide, if you're trolling at 8 knots, you're traveling 800 feet per minute. At that rate you can cover a lot of area a day.

DAISY CHAINS

In 1938 sport fishing for giant bluefin tuna was still in its infancy. Yet this same year saw the development of what was to become perhaps the best-known and most consistently used method of catching giants for many years to come—the mackerel daisy chain.

At first used as a sort of decoy bait or teaser, the daisy chain was rigged together hookless, then trolled behind a boat to resemble a small school of bait. After attracting a hungry fish, which inevitably would strike at the chain time and again in a feeding frenzy, the angler would drop back a rigged herring for the tuna to inhale. One fortunate angler, fishing this method soon after it was developed, boated nine giants in one day, losing at least twice as many. Today, like so many others, this method has been refined and improved upon. Anglers now rig the daisy chain with numerous baits in addition to mackerel and squid; all work well depending on the regions fished and the baits present.

When a tuna strikes a daisy chain it will usually take the last bait first, coming to it from underneath or from the side. If the fish misses, it may take one of the teasers without the hook in it, causing it to break off harmlessly when rigged right. Then now that its attention is on the rig, the tuna will usually return again to take the trailing bait. You'll know when the fish hits: The rig may come right out of the water with the tuna attached, and from there on the true fun and work begins.

Rigging the Mackerel Daisy Chain

The most important thing to consider in rigging daisy chains is that you want to use the freshest mackerel possible. Frozen is okay as long as the life hasn't been frozen out; you want your baits to still have some crispness and body left in them rather than feeling like a piece of wet toilet paper in your hand. This rig is made using a 15-foot piece of 400-pound-test monofilament leader material.

1. Rig a rigging needle with a length of either 25- to 30-pound mono or waxed rigging wrap. Insert the needle into a mackerel's nostril, then downward until it comes out the lower jaw. Leave some of the rigging sticking out of the nostril.
2. Reinsert the needle again through the jaw, coming up through the other nostril of the bait.
3. Make sure both strands are equal in length, then tie them together on top of the mackerel's nostrils, which will close the bait's mouth.
4. Using the slack mono or leftover thread, attach the bait securely to the leader material, leaving about 2 inches of play between the bait and leader. Winding the thread in opposite directions around the leader and then tying it off will prevent the bait from sliding. A crimp placed on either side of the attached line will also help.
5. Space the baits far enough apart on the mono leader that they don't hang up on each other—a little more than one body length is fine.
6. Rig the final mackerel bait with the 400-pound mono leader through the body and a 10/0 or 12/0 Mustad 7691 or 7698B hook implanted inside. The hook should be crimped or attached with a snell knot so it won't break off upon hookup.

Rigging the Squid Daisy Chain

This is essentially the same rig. To hold the squid in place and keep the from sliding, I use a small egg sinker held in place with a crimp, which I then hide inside the squid. This also gives the rig a bit more action on the water's surface.

Again, use a sharp 10/0 or 12/0 hook inserted into the squid's body on the trailing bait.

SPREADER RIGS

Until 1971 the daisy chain was the only known way to offer multiple baits to a fish. Then during the 1971 season Capt. Bobby Wood and his mate Les Shaw, fishing out of Provincetown, Massachusetts, on their boat the

Dixie, took the daisy chain one step further. Trying to imitate a school of baitfish, they rigged natural squids across a coat-hanger-sized straight bar and added the proven daisy chain down the center. Now they had something that really imitated a school of swimming squid. They tried this rig as soon as the giants showed up off Provincetown that year and caught 24 of the first 25 put on the docks! Of course the success of Captains Shaw and Wood raised more than a little curiosity; soon they were being accused of all sorts of illegal fishing tactics. Some boats even followed the *Dixie* out to the grounds each day like good bird dogs. The most innovative or

The spreader rig, invented in 1971 and a consistent standout performer ever since.

desperate of these baffled anglers actually hired a plane and followed the boat by air, trying to figure out what they were up to.

Luckily, tuna anglers don't have to resort to these tactics today, because an innovative tuna angler from Cape Cod has taken this idea of Bobby Wood's and Les Shaw's one step further, with some astounding results. Fully aware of the advantages of offering multiple baits to giant bluefins, Steve Moreton of Hyannis, Massachusetts, designed, tested, and introduced the first mass-produced spreader rig to sport anglers in 1983. In that same season Moreton successfully boated 20 giant bluefins off Cape Cod!

Then in September 1984, Marlene Goldstein, fishing on her husband Jerry's boat the *Rookie,* captained by Moreton, hooked and boated a 1,228-pound bluefin on a Moreton spreader rig, the largest bluefin caught in U.S. waters to date. This was enough to set off a rush on spreader rigs, which today are standard equipment on all serious tuna boats. Since then these rigs have boated numerous species of tuna and billfish in places like Hawaii, Block Island, Venezuela, and the Caribbean.

Looking somewhat like an overgrown version of the umbrella rig used for catching bluefish, the spreader rig is made from a stainless-steel rod about 3 feet long and the diameter of a coat hanger. Off this rod eight 12-inch artificial squid or mackerel are mounted in a V-pattern. At its longest point the leader stretches to 6 feet, with four trailing squid. All the squid are rigged with either 400-pound monofilament or 400-pound cable; the other teaser squid are rigged so that they will part from the spreader rig with less force, thus ensuring a long life for it. When finished, the rig closely resembles a school of live squid or mackerel. Only the pattern's trailing bait contains a hook, usually a 10/0 or 12/0 Mustad 7698B. The reason for this is that after much onboard research Moreton determined that giant bluefin usually strike a school of bait from the rear; putting hooks in all or part of the squid inevitably resulted in foul-hooked fish or tangled rigs. Squid are available in natural, glow, or amber colors, as well as blue, smoke, green, and purple metalflake colors. The two best-producing colors for me have proven to be amber and natural, with amber closely resembling a nervous or frightened squid and working best on bright, natural days. Natural is good on cloudy, overcast days.

These artificial rigs work well when trolled at speeds of 3 to 4 knots, although I have trolled them at up to 7 knots with no problem while fishing for yellowfins. When you place them in the water, be careful not to allow the leaders to wrap around the spreader bar, and place them far enough behind the boat that the squid all lie on top of the water with the swivel and leader out of it. They should skip across the top of the water, splashing as they go to create a commotion that will attract the curious and always hungry tuna. Tackle should be 80-pound or heavier, with drags set at a third of the line's breaking strength in strike position, and a quarter of its strength when trolling. If a drag scale is not available, simply set the drag tight enough that you need two hands to pull line from the reel. This will ensure a solid hookup without allowing the fish to break itself off. After the fish is hooked up, move the drag lever forward to the strike position to fight the fish. When the double line appears and you have the fish alongside the boat ready to wire, push the drag lever even farther up to aid in maneuvering the fish. After gaffing the fish, back off the drag sufficiently that a thrashing fish won't break off.

The advantages of these rigs are many. Trolling is always the best way to catch giant bluefins when they first show up in an area early in the season and are feeding. You can cover a much larger area, thus increasing your chances of a hookup, and at 4 knots will burn very little fuel. In addition, these artificial rigs won't soften and lose color like natural baits; nor do they have to be kept iced. They are always available, often result in multiple hookups, and can be easily repaired if necessary to be used over and over again.

I've had my best luck when trolling two of these rigs back on the third and fourth wave on the outside lines. It's far enough back to keep them away from the prop wash, and as a result they ride properly on the water's surface. Closer up I can then put out two artificial daisy chains. In the 1988 U.S. Atlantic Tuna Tournament held at Montauk, my boat the *Flashback* used spreader bars and daisy chains all made by Moreton to boat not only the first bluefin tuna of the tournament, but also the first bluefin to be brought into Montauk that season. The only other boat in the USATT that caught another bluefin (unfortunately just larger than mine) was also using Moreton's spreader rigs. Try them yourself—just keep them away from the bluefish!

Spreader Bar Variations
I've experimented with different types of artificial lures and teasers on spreader bars. I've found that Green Machine spreaders work great, but are not cheap to build. I had a giant bluefin hit one off Block Island one day that pushed it at least 6 feet into the air! Tuna Clones and the soft Mold Craft lures with teasers or birds also attract tuna. So try experimenting yourself with your favorite lures or teasers.

TROLLING SPREADER BARS AND DAISY CHAINS
Attach spreader bars and daisy chains with either 400-pound-test Jinkai monofilament or stainless cable. I find the former less conspicuous in the water. The thing to remember when you troll spreader bars and daisy chains is that you want to present the baits in the best possible manner to the fish: moving through the water at a speed just fast enough for them to remain skipping across the surface. This way they'll hopefully make enough of a commotion to attract the unsuspecting tuna.

I place mine between 200 and 300 feet behind the transom off my outriggers or center rigger. This keeps the line out of the water, and the baits, which are heavy, riding on the water properly. You can also troll bars and chains on flat lines using rubber bands, taglines, or outrigger clips mounted on the transom's gunwales, but I don't feel this works as well on my boat.

Experiment with different speeds inshore first—but make sure no schools of bluefish are around, because they'll destroy your rigs. Once you've gotten a feel for these incredibly productive setups, give them a shot offshore.

TEASERS

For years innovative anglers have experimented with various types of teasers—from automobile hubcaps and tires to bowling pins to "birds"—primarily when trolling for billfish. Some of these, such as the car tires, were very crude, while others like the birds were more refined. All had one thing in common, though—they all worked to some degree.

That's fine, but can teasers be used successfully when trolling for tuna? Well, if you take into consideration the four emotions that make a fish strike—*anger, hunger, curiosity, and competition*—the answer has to be a resounding yes. And while trolling for tuna, I've often seen the fish strike the teaser itself repeatedly, leaving the baits or lures alone. That should be enough evidence for even the most skeptical of us.

The primary purpose of any teaser is to attract fish to the lure area, or at least the area that your baits or lures are trolling through. By doing this you put the fish into a situation where any one of the four above-mentioned emotions may be evoked, thus hopefully resulting in a hooked fish.

Today there are three types of teasers on the market: artificial single-bodied teasers, artificial multibodied teasers, and natural fish teasers. Single-bodied teasers include such things as automobile hubcaps, large hookless lures, birds, and bowling pins. Multibodied teasers include artificial daisy chains and multiple bird rigs (see below), and natural fish teasers include whole squid, mullet, ballyhoo, bonito, bluefish, and natural bait daisy chains. All of these are hookless.

Natural Bait Teasers

When you're using any fish individually as teasers or collectively in a daisy chain or spreader rig, it's imperative that the gills and mouths be sewn shut to prevent water pressure from tearing the baits apart. To rig daisy chain baits, use 400-pound-test monofilament leader material for the main line, but avoid using this heavier line for the baits. Instead use the lighter tests of 150, 130, or even 80 pounds. This way the baits will break free when a tuna or other fish attacks without ruining the entire rig, giving your teaser a longer and more useful life, as well as the advantage of remaining functional. The daisy-chain teaser also allows tuna to tear off the baits individually without ruining the rig. These daisy chains should always be used in calm, flat waters and trolled at slow speeds to avoid tearing them up. I use them a lot when light-tackle fishing to raise fish. I can then cast or present a lure or fly to the inquisitive and eager tuna.

How to Troll Teasers

The designated mate should always be responsible for those teasers trolled off the transom, while the captain is responsible for the outrigger teasers. These are moderate responsibilities as long as both parties are paying attention to what's happening, which they should be anyway. The cockpit teasers may be attached to a rod-and-reel setup or simply to a length of heavy monofilament line to be let out by a gloved hand and tied off to a cleat. It's a good idea to wear gloves to avoid burning your hands, and also because you may want to tie knots at intervals on the monofilament to help you maintain your grip while you pull in the teasers.

Outrigger teasers are a bit more complex to rig, but still don't require the services of a rocket scientist. One or even two lines can be run off each outrigger when properly rigged. Pass the line through the eyes of the out-rigger and attach it to a reel set in a spot that's easy for the boat's captain to reach. This is preferably above the wheel or console on the tower supports, or to either side of the bridge on the hand railings. Many tackle stores such as Murray Brothers in Palm Beach sell complete teaser reel setups that you can install simply on the bridge. I use two older 6/0 Penn Senator star-drag reels filled to capacity with monofilament line on my boat for this. By keeping the reel filled to capacity, you make it easier to work or quickly retrieve the teaser when necessary. I've seen shiny Internationals and even Fin-Nors used for teaser reels on sport-fishing boats but could never understand this. I'd much rather spend that money on new rods or reels to catch fish, especially since the star-drag reels are more than adequate for running teasers.

The drags on the teaser reels should be set as tight as possible to keep the teaser in the exact spot you want it and to assist you in positioning it correctly. This will also help you to retrieve the line as fast as possible when necessary.

When you set out teasers, set the one closest to the boat first, with others in order of their distance from the transom. This way, if you should hook up right away, the time spent retrieving the set is minimized. On the other hand, if you've got the entire lure and teaser set out and hook up a fish, try to retrieve the farthest line first to help avoid dangerous tangles with other lines that may result in lost fish.

Birds

No trolling rig for tuna is complete without at least a couple of birds, orig-inally developed by the Japanese as part of handlining systems for tuna trolling. They've now been refined and developed for use in trolling for tuna and billfish from sport-fishing boats. They're made from wood, plastic foam, or injected plastic and come in sizes from a few inches to about 1½ feet in length. Their design always calls for a short set of "wings" that allow them to skip over the water's surface while making a commotion like a fleeing baitfish. To the tuna this must look like a fish (your lure) chasing a baitfish (your bird). The action will attract tuna to your trolled rigs and, because of the tuna's competitive instinct, will hopefully result in a hookup for you. Many times you'll see a fish hit the bird repeatedly until it tires of the thing and switches to your lure.

I place my birds all over the trolling patterns, depending on sea conditions, lure placements, and the like, but *always* on the center rigger line way behind the rest of the trolling rig. This one is usually a larger bird, but I've also rigged numerous small birds in a daisy-chain-type pattern ahead of a Green Machine, jethead, or hexhead lure off the riggers, or on flat lines.

Three companies make what I feel are the best birds on the market. The Boone Bird was the first I ever saw years ago, and the one that comes in the most sizes. It's made from foam and has a tough outer coating, a 300-pound mono leader, and many color options. Orange and yellow are my favorites, but others work well, too.

Frank Johnson of Mold Craft makes an excellent soft injection-molded plastic bird, with the wings molded into the head. It is the lightest of the birds, but made so that you can rig it with egg-type sinkers to give it the action you want.

Not to be outdone, Murray Brothers makes a painted wooden bird that also works great. It comes in numerous colors, and has aluminum wings that are epoxied in place. It is a well-thought-out and durable piece of equipment, rigged with a lead weight on its underside that gives it excellent action, and a 300-pound mono leader for strength.

Keep a good selection of birds on your boat, and experiment with colors to see what works best in different conditions. The bottom line, though, is that they *do* result in hookups and should be used often when trolling.

12

DOWNRIGGERS

A few years back I was fortunate enough to be invited by some friends to fish in what has now become a major international marlin tournament off the Cayman Islands. These are serious marlin people, and between the two of them have over 50 years of fishing experience. I enjoy fishing with them for many reasons, and each time leave amazed at the extent of their knowledge regarding all aspects of offshore fishing.

Upon arriving at their boat this time I noticed two downriggers mounted aft on the port and starboard gunnels. Until that day I had seen downriggers advertised in fishing magazines and described in articles on trolling in the Great Lakes or Northwest, but I had never seen them used in any type of saltwater fishing. Nevertheless here they were, mounted on a beautiful, shiny sport-fishing boat used almost exclusively in the pursuit of blue marlin. Boy, was I at a loss for words! Of course I didn't let on that I was totally baffled by the downriggers' presence or ask any questions. Instead I stowed my gear and waited to see just how these contraptions fit into the whole plan of things. That didn't take long to discover, and as usual I walked away from one of my fishing trips with these folks all the wiser. You see, not only did we hook up two blue marlin on the downriggers, but we also caught eight dolphin, two wahoo, and one king-sized barracuda.

I immediately bought a pair and had them installed on my Bertram. They have now become a vital part of my fishing equipment. When I'm trolling, I usually have at least one line fishing off each one.

WHAT ARE DOWNRIGGERS?

The downrigger is a simple concept basically intended to put the bait where the fish are most likely to see it. It can be traced back to the use of such crude rigs as the handline/drail sinker combination with a clothespin line-release clip that was dropped off a boat's transom. That early rig was used almost exclusively in the Northeast by commercial anglers trolling for striped bass and bluefish, and through time evolved into what we now call a downrigger.

The components that make up a downrigger are:

- A boom or arm with a small guide-pulley combination on the end.
- A reel-type spool that stores stainless cable.
- A hand crank and/or electric motor to retrieve the cable.
- A cannonball-shaped lead weight ranging from 8 to 12 pounds.
- A counter or meter that lets you know the depth at which the cannonball and your line are mounted on the downrigger's arm.
- A release clip. These come in a myriad of choices, many of them closely resembling outrigger clips. Experiment with a number of them and then decide which one best meets your needs.

At first downriggers were used primarily in freshwater lake or river fishing, and today they're the primary method of fishing for Pacific Northwest salmon. Saltwater anglers initially used them for sailfish off Palm Beach. They proved to be deadly effective when trolling at depths of 10 to 20 feet on those days when surface trollers zeroed out. Today downriggers are gaining rapidly in popularity and can be found on boats used for almost any type of fishing that involves trolling, drifting, or chunking.

Until the development of the downrigger, the use of wire line and trolling sinkers was the only method of deep trolling. This technique was full of problems, such as the wire line's tendency to kink and break, and the nightmare backlashes that resulted when the wire wasn't spooled off the reel properly. Now you can fish with any strength of line, working the waters effectively due to the downrigger's release clip. Once a fish strikes or is hooked up, the fishing line releases in a way very similar to that of an outrigger. You're able to work the fish without cumbersome wire line or leaders.

WHERE TO MOUNT THEM

Where you ultimately mount downriggers depends primarily on how many you plan to use, the layout of your boat, the thickness of your boat's gunnels, whether or not you have flush-mounted rod holders already installed, and—most important—fishability and a strong mounting location. You want to be sure that you mount the downriggers on a beefy section of the boat's gunnel, with a strong backplate if at all possible. Failure to do this could result in the downrigger ripping from its base due to the stress created by the 3-foot boom with a 10-pound lead weight hanging from it, as well as the drag created by 10 pounds of lead being pulled through the water.

The permanent mounts available are either fixed or swivel. I prefer swivel bases that are able to turn a minimum of 180 degrees. These offer more versatility in fishing as well as a greater ease of handling when you're rigging the downrigger and/or fishing line. With swivel bases you can swing the boom to tend your gear, then return the downrigger to the trolling position easily simply by loosening the set screw. This same set screw allows you to remove the downrigger at the end of a day's fishing for easy cleaning and storage.

If your boat is equipped with flush-mounted rod holders and you don't want to install a permanent mount, you can buy a gimbaled base for your downrigger that will fit into the rod holder. Again, be sure your rod holders are solidly mounted, and be careful when you're trolling with downriggers set at right angles to the boat. You can rip the pins in the rod holder's base by putting excess stress on them. With temporary mounts you're better off running the arms straight back rather than at an angle. This will help reduce the stress the rig creates on your boat and tackle.

HOW TO USE DOWNRIGGERS FOR TUNA

I use two downriggers when trolling for tuna set at depths ranging from 25 to 150 feet, depending on where I've spotted fish on the color scope or where they've been taking trolled baits in the past. If nothing happens or I simply want to experiment I'll adjust the depths or change the lures until I get a strike. But use your color scope or fish finder. It's an essential piece of equipment when you use downriggers and will give you the advantage of always knowing where the fish are.

To use a downrigger, simply let your lure or bait out behind the boat to the desired distance, then place your line into the release clip and lower the cannonball to the desired depth. When a fish hits it will hook itself and, in doing so, pop the release clip, freeing the line and allowing you to fight the fish unencumbered by sinkers or planers, exactly like an outrigger or flat line.

Be careful when you work with the lead cannonball, though. It can act as a miniature wrecking ball, rolling around or swinging into your boat when not secured properly. And be sure when you lower the cannonball that there's no slack in the cable. These weights generate momentum very quickly. If you drop the ball with slack in the line, you may break the cable, and 10 pounds of expensive lead will quickly drop from sight.

Unless you're trolling very slowly in water with no current, your weight and cable will drop at an angle that doesn't reflect the depth registered on the downrigger's meter. Keep in mind when you're letting out cable that in most cases water resistance from a combination of trolling speed and currents will put an angle in it, making the depth on the meter just a bit deceiving.

A reasonable complaint often associated with downrigger trolling concerns the drop back that occurs between the time that a fish strikes and the time the line becomes taut. This short period of time can result in a lost fish, since you're unable to solidly hook it on its initial strike. This problem can sometimes be resolved by adjusting the tension on the release clip, or by creating a variation on a tagline, but usually when a tuna strikes a bait or lure it will hook itself.

In the tagline variations, half-hitch a size 64 rubber band to the reel's line (not the leader) just above the swivel that attaches the line to the leader. Lock the loose end of the rubber band inside the snap swivel that connects the downrigger weight. This assemblage will in most cases result in a solidly hooked fish by the time the rubber band breaks. It works well with all the tuna lures I fish with and is worth trying.

You can troll any artificial lure used for tuna effectively with downriggers at the same speeds you would on the surface or subsurface. But remember that the higher your trolling speed, the more steeply angled your cable will be; you'll have to release more cable in order to get to the desired depth. You can also troll two or more lines from a single downrigger by placing release clips at different depth intervals. This requires a particular familiarity with the downrigger system and should be done only by those experienced in the system's use.

When you're trolling live or dead baits, your trolling speed should be reduced to 3 or 4 knots—again to reduce excessive drag that may damage your bait's effectiveness.

CHUMMING WITH THE DOWNRIGGER

On those days when strong ocean currents prevent a thorough dispersal of your chum—putting you at a severe disadvantage—downriggers can put the chum and bait deep enough to produce fish. I sometimes secure a mesh bag of chum to the weight tightly enough that it won't interfere with the fishing line above it. Then I strip off 50 to 75 feet of fishing line before I attach it to the release clip. This keeps the bait far enough away from the chum bag to avoid any tangling, but at the same time it's close enough to remain in the enticing chum slick.

I've had occasional problems with sharks attacking submerged chum bags, and I quickly learned to use my downrigger's drag system to reduce the chance of damaging the downrigger itself. In addition, put your chum in a mesh onion bag; a predator will either rip the bag open, releasing the chum, or (after feeling resistance) will drop the bag entirely. The safest alternative is to tie the chum bag onto the downrigger's cable with line so light that it'll break away if attacked.

WHAT TO LOOK FOR WHEN BUYING A DOWNRIGGER

When you're selecting a downrigger for tuna or any other type of saltwater fishing, it's most important to keep in mind that it will be used in a corrosive environment. For that reason make sure the model you select is made of materials that stand up to salt water.

Downriggers now come available in crank or manual models as well as electric powered. If you choose an electric model, make sure the motor is powerful enough to produce a high torque while drawing a low amperage. Also make sure that all parts and connections are effectively sealed to keep out salt water. The best electric models have a motor with an overload cutoff that prevents the motor from burning up if too heavy a load is put on it. In addition, your electric downrigger should be able to operate manually in the event that the motor should fail due to a burnout or any corrosive action in the electrical system.

In whatever model you choose, make sure that the downrigger features a slip clutch similar to that on a fishing reel. This will keep the handle from spinning and possibly injuring anyone nearby when the weight is released. It also allows you to control the speed at which the weight is lowered—a very important feature.

Some of the newer electric models now feature a programmable computer chip activated through a keypad. This allows the weight to be lowered to a predetermined depth time after time. Some models will even raise and lower a line continuously in a jigging motion.

The cables on the downriggers should be at least ³⁄₁₆-inch stainless steel and be long enough for your fishing needs. To avoid breaks in the cable, check it and its connections often for frayed spots.

For tuna fishing I feel that two downriggers per boat is plenty. Any more may result in nightmare tangles by strong currents or an overactive fish.

Today downriggers are just beginning to be used in offshore fishing. Still, they are already showing promise, and word is rapidly spreading. Their potential is limitless, and as they continue to be experimented with they will surely open up new doors as well as improve old fishing techniques.

13

MORE TUNA
TECHNIQUES

OUTRIGGERS

Capt. Tommy Gifford was instrumental in the development of the outrigger. His simple but effective bamboo poles have now given way to the high-tech but still basic aluminum riggers made by Lee, Rupp, Schaffer, and Rybovich (to name a few). They come in various lengths depending on your boat's size. Some are single-pole style, resembling the old bamboo poles, while the larger outriggers use spreaders to keep the poles stiffer and eliminate snapping or bending.

While outriggers do make a boat look sharp, they are used for tuna and other offshore fishing for three simple reasons: They spread your baits or lures out over a wider area, make them look more realistic, and give your lures or baits an automatic drop back upon hookup.

The outriggers are rigged with halyards or lines that go through the eyes and a small pulley mounted on the covering boards. It returns in a complete circle to be fastened to the other free end. Smaller riggers generally use one halyard, the larger ones two. The halyards are made from stronger monofilament leader material—up to 400-pound test—or braided cord that's sold especially for this. The mono is easier to rig and use, requiring only crimps to secure its ends, but it eventually stretches and gets cooked in the sun, becoming fragile and breaking. Nevertheless it's easy to replace each season, and is my choice. The braided cord is much more durable, but I've found that it doesn't slide as smoothly through the pole's eyes. Try to make sure when you rig the poles that when they're dropped to the trolling position, no adjustment in the halyard is needed. This is a nearly impossible trick, but by using bungee cords you can easily adjust your tension, taking up any slack when the poles are dropped.

To the halyards you attach an outrigger clip. These come with either roller guides or clip releases, and again are made by a number of manufacturers. I use the rolled type, because I feel it cuts down on any chance of the line chafing. However, if you use the regular clip, you can attach it to the outrigger by using a size 64 rubber band. This will give it just enough tension to help in hooking up when a tuna strikes. Both styles work very well if they're kept oiled and cleaned after each trip.

The pulleys are sold by all good marine supply or tackle stores, and many such as Murray Brothers and Outer Banks sell a complete outrigger rigging package that includes everything you need to do the job properly.

When using your outriggers, experiment to find the best placement of your lures. While most of us do put them all the way out at the end of the rigger just to maximize the spread of the trolling rig, this isn't always necessary. Some lures track better from different boats in other positions, so try out a few. Also remember that sea conditions will affect your lures' or baits' action at various points away from the boat.

TAGLINES

The outrigger concept was developed to allow the trolling of multiple baits in a pattern that more realistically resembled a school of baitfish. Used at first primarily with natural baits, they gave billfish anglers the added advantage of the drop back—the period of time from when the fishing line is released from the outrigger clip, creating a slack line until it becomes taut again. This short but crucial interval ideally allows the bill-fish to swallow the bait and hook it.

In some conditions or categories of fishing you may want to eliminate any drop back—for instance, when you plan to release any fish you've caught. The drop back only gives the fish an additional time to swallow a bait, usually resulting in a gut-hooked fish, which in most cases will die when released due to stomach damage and the resulting bleeding. Another instance where drop back is not wanted is when you're fishing artificial lures, simply because a ravenous or enraged fish striking a lure will quickly realize that it can't be eaten and give up. Finally, trolling for tuna is a special case when drop back is undesirable. These extraordinary game fish crash your artificial lures with such fury that the drop back just isn't necessary.

In order to eliminate the drop back, taglines were developed, successfully moving the break-away point aft. They do this by carrying the fishing lines out of and back from the cockpit with a minimum of additional line.

Installing Taglines

Taglines are simple to install; it can be done right at dockside in about an hour. Bring your boat alongside a dock or bulkhead where you can extend your outriggers and have clear access to them. Then, using 300-pound monofilament, attach a line to each outrigger's running line just above the clip. I do this by simply looping and crimping the line where I want it. Attaching the line to the outrigger's running line gives you the extra advantage of being able to retrieve the tagline at any time. Additionally, if your outriggers are double-rigged you can rig two taglines to each pole. Initially I think it's best to try one from each pole until you get used to using them.

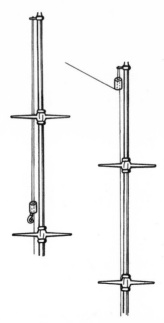

A tagline retrieval system, with the tagline set to the fish (left), and retrieved (right).

After the line is connected to the extended outrigger pole, measure out a length of it that reaches the cockpit's transom corner. This will ensure that the ends of the taglines are easy to hold when you attach your fishing line. It also allows you to clip off the line when you're changing lures or clearing the cockpit.

I've added a tagline sleeve to each line. These are available from any good offshore tackle store or directly from C&H Lures, Murray Brothers, and other stores. These sleeves serve the invaluable purpose of ensuring that your tagline returns safely to the bottom of your outrigger line after each release, rather than flapping around in the breeze and possibly injuring someone.

To install the sleeves, simply release the outrigger line from the bottom of your clip. Then pass this line up through the bottom of the sleeve and refasten it to the outrigger clip. Now pass the free end of the tagline through the top of the sleeve and pull it through. When done it should look like this (picture). As you set your lines out when fishing it will simply rise to the outrigger clip, falling safely back down the outrigger line to the boat when the fishing line releases.

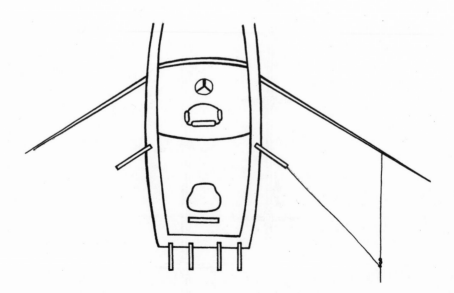

Tagline system.

At the free end of the tagline I crimp on an 18-inch section of 400-pound Dacron with a 400-pound-test ball-bearing snap swivel attached. I have also used 0 or 00 stainless or brass marine snaps, but I feel that the ball-bearing snap swivels eliminate the problem of line twisting (more on this later). Using Dacron line gives taglines better action and, because of its rigidity, may aid in solid hookups.

Attaching the Fishing Line to the Tagline

This part takes a little practice. You want to position the lures in the correct areas of your boat's wake as accurately as possible, because adjusting their position after you attach them to the tagline is going to be difficult. First set out your lures in the correct position, then take the line from the reel and wrap either a 64 or 84 rubber band around it. Your choice of rubber bands will depend on two things: the class of tackle you're using and the size and amount of drag caused by your lure. Most times the 64 rubber band will be more than sufficient for tackle rated 50 pounds and over. They break at 22 pounds of pressure, and that can be pushed to 44 pounds if doubled. For tackle in the 20- to 30-pound range, downsize to a band that will give you the proper break-away strain. Insert the loose end of the band into the tagline snap and you're ready to set out your rigs.

Check from time to time to make sure the trolling line isn't twisting or wrapped around the tagline and snap swivel. If this happens and a fish strikes, the wraps will grasp the tagline, causing chafing or breakoffs. This is why I've begun using ball-bearing snap swivels.

Assuming that your lures are set out in the positions and pattern you want, you can now set out the taglines. To do this simply release the fishing line by carefully backing off your drag, which will cause the tagline and fishing line to extend to their optimal position. Since you won't be able to adjust your lures easily once the taglines are set, try to position them allowing for the difference the taglines will make. You may have to try this a few times in order to determine the proper placement in your wakes, but this should come quickly, so don't get discouraged. After a while you'll get accustomed to how far back the tagline will shift the lure. Just don't forget to return your reel's drag to the strike setting.

One more thing I've discovered that works well is marking the fishing line with a Magic Marker at the point where the rubber band is. This way if you have to reel up due to a strike on another line, you can easily reset the lines later on.

SNAPPER POLES FOR GIANT BLUEFINS

One day while fishing for giant bluefins on Stellwagen Bank, I noticed that the crew of the boat next to me, which was chunking away like the rest of us, seemed to have no fishing lines in the water. This was a bit odd, to say the least, and in no time theories about what was going on next to us swept around my boat with no real conclusions.

After almost 2½ hours of what appeared to be a free meal for any giants in the area, there was a flurry of activity on the boat, followed by a member of the crew standing in the rear of the cockpit with what looked like a giant snapper pole. Then all hell broke loose as a fish hit whatever was suspended from the pole, hooking itself up solidly, and the boat released from its anchor and began fighting the fish. Backing safely through the fleet, we watched the battle off in the distance for almost two hours as we continued chunking with no luck. Finally the fish was brought to gaff and we watched the crew head back to the dock with it.

We stayed in the fleet for the rest of the day without seeing a run or another fish boated, but wondering among ourselves between cold beers and leftover Chinese food just *what* was responsible for hooking that big fish.

That night back at the marina in Green Harbor I spotted the boat tied up near us. Determined to find out what the hell was going on, I walked down and introduced myself. At first these guys were reluctant to divulge their secrets, but after talking (and celebrating) for a while they began to loosen up—and I started to learn about a simple new technique for tuna fishing that has since proven very productive.

The "pole" we had seen turned out to be just that—a bamboo pole about 20 feet long with one of the older clothespin-type outrigger clips attached to the end. This combination is used to position a live bait on the surface before a tuna that has been brought up near the boat by chunking. It's very much like kite fishing (see below), except you can position your bait more precisely. When the tuna hits the bait, the line is released from the clip and the fight begins.

I talked to these guys late into the night about their system. They had hooked and boated numerous tuna over the years using this seemingly unsophisticated technique, which was developed back in the 1960s and used very successfully by the fishing team of Ed Murray, Hy Jacobson, and Joe Rinaldi on the famous *Cookie*. They showed me the simple yet effective setup and explained how easily it hooked tuna after you'd gotten them into your chunking slick.

In addition to your usual tuna fishing setup, there are only three components needed:

- A bamboo pole 16 to 20 feet in length with a tip about ¼ inch in diameter.
- An older clothespin-type outrigger clip that will be mounted to the pole's end.
- Electrical tape or duct tape.

Using the pole rig is just as simple; none of your tackle has to be altered or changed at all, although because the leader remains out of the water (and thus out of sight) for the most part, you are able to use a wire leader or heavy mono. This eliminates the chance of the tuna chafing through your leader. Should you decide to use a monofilament leader, which is a lot more sporting anyway, simply attach a Tuna Bullet Rig to the rod's tip and you're in business.

Once you've sighted a tuna in the slick, attach the baited hook with a rubber band. Strip off enough line to reach the fish, then wrap the line three or four times in a loop and attach the loop into the outrigger clip (a rubber band release can also be used). Put some extra coiled line in a dry bucket, and set the reel's drag to the strike position. Then secure the rod in a rod holder or—if you're using a chair—get the angler strapped in and give him the rod.

As the fish swims up to take a chunk of bait, place the hooked bait in its path right on the water's surface and hold on. When it takes the bait, the line will release exactly like an outrigger, and with the added pressure of the reel's drag the fish will more often than not hook itself, especially if you're using sharp hooks. Then it's up to you to bring the fish to gaff.

Since first using this rig I have experimented with many variations on it. Although live baits always work best, natural chunks can and do work well, too. Because bunker heads float naturally and don't require an added piece of Styrofoam, they work extremely well for us when fishing for yellowfins. I now also use a Rupp outrigger clip instead of a clothespin so I can adjust the tension settings, but this is a personal choice.

As I mentioned earlier, with this technique you can use a more durable wire leader. The pole will also keep the baits where you place them, a particular advantage if you're experiencing strong tides or winds, which always seem to leave the lines around the anchor line or under the boat.

One last thing: If you're not using live baits, it's important to use the freshest baits possible. If not, the fish are likely to turn up their noses at your offerings and seek out another boat with fresher baits. Also, use the sharpest hooks possible at all times to ensure a quick and solid hookup. For that reason I usually use Gamakatsu hooks when chunking.

TUNA ON CEDAR PLUGS

My recollections of offshore fishing begin at about five years old on my family's sport-fishing boat. We spent at least one day of each summer weekend (weather permitting) slowly cruising off Montauk, Block Island, or Martha's Vineyard looking for swordfish. There was always a colorful group of local characters who shared my uncle's enthusiasm for harpooning these then-abundant fish. Adding to the day's excitement, we always trolled a couple of Japanese feathers and cedar plugs for yellowfin tuna, which were also much more abundant then than they are today. One day off Nomans Land—an uninhabited island south of Martha's Vineyard—we came across a school of yellowfin tuna that was literally two acres in size. The good old days indeed!

These feathers and cedar plugs were the artificial baits of choice back then in the 1950s and early 1960s simply because at the time that's all that was available except natural baits. We could always count on at least one tuna per trip, usually by accident. This was my favorite part of the trip. As soon as we had a run, I was put into the fighting chair and, with the aid and encouragement of those aboard, allowed to do battle with these "football" tuna. At the time they looked like giant bluefins to me.

Even with today's mind-boggling choices of artificial lures and tuna fishing techniques, I still honor this tradition by keeping a half-dozen or so rigged cedar plugs on board my boat for tuna fishing. I continue to have excellent luck trolling them on school yellowfins and albacore here in the Northeast. These unsophisticated, cigar-shaped plugs with lead heads and cedar bodies still sometimes outproduce some of today's better-known plastics.

Rigging the Cedar Plug

I rig my cedar plugs in many variations, some with wire leaders but most with monofilament. I paint them in color combinations of red/white, green/yellow, green/yellow/orange, and more, but also troll them unpainted with great success. My hook sizes range from 5/0 to 9/0 with long shanks that set up inside the cedar body. I feel that these keep the hook a bit stiffer, resulting in a better hookup percentage.

When you rig with wire leaders, be very careful not to kink the wire at any time or you'll weaken its effective strength. I use size 7 to 9 brown or black wire, but monofilament leaders are my first choice. They don't hold up well in the schools of gorilla bluefish you sometimes encounter but do produce more hookups than wire. I choose my mono leader strengths based on the spookiness of the fish, but generally I won't use anything over 250-pound test or under 100.

To rig a cedar plug, simply insert the leader through the top leaded part of the plug's hollow body and out the bottom. Then either use a haywire twist (for wire) or a simple crimp (for monofilament) to attach the hook to the end rig.

For added enticement I sometimes dress up some plugs with plastic skirts in various colors and combinations. They make these plain-jane lures even more tempting. My favorite colors and combinations for use here in the Northeast are green, green/white, green/yellow, green/yellow/orange, and orange/white. I always soak my cedar plugs in my chum mixture on the way out. This keeps the porous plugs smelling attractive to tuna, and I feel results in hookups, too.

Trolling the Cedar Plug

I place my plugs off flat lines just behind the prop wash, where small hexheads would usually go. On my boat that's usually around the fourth or fifth wave, depending on trolling speed. I troll them anywhere from 4 to 7½ knots and have had hookups at all speeds. One thing I've noticed from looking over my records is that my hookup ratios are much better with cedar plugs when they're not trolled off the outriggers or center rigger. In addition I often run taglines out through my scuppers or off the transom and attach them to the flat lines pulling the cedar plugs. This keeps them tracking straight and much more enticing to the tuna.

From the looks I sometimes get when I pull one of these cedar plugs out of my tackle box, it seems these lures have a lot more appeal to tuna than to style-conscious anglers, who take great pleasure in selecting colorful artificials. This quite often changes by the end of a trip. I've found myself more than once sitting up on the bridge on the way home with a tuna in the cooler and a few more swimming around with tags in them, explaining to these same skeptics the benefits of trolling cedar plugs.

KITES

Kite fishing was developed and used exclusively for sailfish off Palm Beach and other hot sailfish spots. It is indeed a particularly deadly method of attracting and catching sailfish, and it now has been refined for other species, including tuna. This method effectively presents the live bait on the surface, where its splashing attracts the attention of predator fish. I've used it with great success in the Northeast, and recommend it to all those who want to increase their hookup percentage.

Kites can be bought from a number of well-known tackle stores such as Aftco, Murray Brothers, Capt. Harry's, and Outer Banks. All sell good-quality kite systems and accessories designed to work in light, moderate, or heavy winds. They aren't initially expensive, but you can really go overboard spending money on these systems if you add a lot of accessories. For instance, custom short rods with special wooden or even electric reels to hold the kite and line are available. I use a stiff 5-foot bluefish rod with a 4/0 Penn star-drag reel rigged with 130-pound black Dacron line. I think it works better than mono, is lighter, doesn't stretch, and helps the kite fly better.

To set up the basic kite-fishing rig, insert a barrel swivel about 75 feet below the end of the kite's line and reel this right onto the spool. To use the rig offshore, simply pass the Dacron line through the bluefish rod's guides. Then slip a release clip over the end, and attach a snap swivel to the end of the line.

Now snap the kite onto the line, pass your fishing line through the release clip, and let out your kite. As the kite plays out, the release clip will fall down the line until it hits the barrel swivel and stops in place.

In the meantime your fishing line, with the bait rigged to it, will pass through the release clip until your kite is in position. Adjust your fishing line so that your bait splashes right on the surface. Too much line will allow the bait to swim deep, and too little will suspend the poor bastard out of the water, so keep an eye on it as weather conditions and your boat's drift change.

With the bait in its proper position splashing around on the surface, place your fishing rod in a rod holder. I place my kite rod on the flying bridge in a rod holder, but each boat and captain will have their own techniques. Keep your drag loose with the clicker on. When the fish strikes, the clip will release. Put your drag into strike position and you're ready to battle the fish. Just make sure to retrieve your kite so it's out of the way.

I don't drop back to tuna since, unlike billfish, they crash the bait and hook themselves. I think the brief time it takes to grab the rod, set up, and set the drag is more than enough for a fish to hook itself.

HANDLINING

The oldest fishing method is the use of the handline. Handlines are referred to in biblical passages and many of the early accounts of fishing. Handlining retains its basic form today, though with the additions of floats or barrels, monofilament leaders, and other minor improvements. It is a very effective and inexpensive system for catching fish, simple to make, store, and maintain. The handline can be built for a fraction of the cost of a rod-and-reel setup. It's still used to catch tuna commercially, with excellent results.

However, a handine setup lacks some of the features of a rod and reel that take the work out of boating a tuna; thus an increased effort is needed to properly and safely boat a fish. Using a handline often forces your back and hands to become the drag system, and hand-over-hand retrieval always replaces the high-tech, two-speed reel. That's not to say handlines don't work. On the contrary, many large tuna have been caught on handlines, and continue to be.

The handline can be used for either trolling or chunking. It is just as easy to present a bait with a handline as it is with a rod and reel, but the chances of it becoming fouled when a fish hits are greatly reduced because of the attention you must pay to it. Handlining is a very labor-intensive method of tuna fishing that requires two people to work at all times. One person works the line with gloved hands, and another stays close to the basket, ensuring that any retrieved line is packed back in carefully so that in the event of another run no tangles occur. The latter crew member also has to run the boat if needed. Unless there's a third person aboard, this puts an increased responsibility on the crew members. One thing you don't want is a tangled handline or any other line being pulled off by a tuna. It's serious business, and getting caught up can result in serious injuries, lost fish, or much worse.

The typical handline setup consists of a 10- to 15-foot monofilament leader made from 200- to 300-pound test. This is attached by an improved clinch knot or crimps to a 250-foot length of ⅛-inch braided nylon line with a large 1,000-pound-test barrel swivel. This 250-foot length of line is then connected to a larger ¼-inch-diameter nylon line up to 800 feet long, again with a 1,000-pound barrel swivel. At the end of this long length of nylon line I attach a large orange ball buoy so that I can easily find the handline if the tuna takes it all. I store my entire handline setup in a plastic fish basket. First I put the orange buoy in, then I carefully wrap the line around the outside to avoid any tangles. When the tuna hits you'll have to hold the line in your gloved hands to make sure that it runs out without becoming tangled or knotted. I use either a 10/0 or 12/0 tuna or circle hook crimped onto the mono leader.

When fishing a handline, set your baited hook at the depth desired. Then attach a length of 100- to 200-pound mono line to the handline and cleat it off on the boat. This will act as a shock cord, helping hook the fish when it strikes and then breaking off under the force of the run. A 10- or 15-foot length is fine, but again fasten it so that it's out of the way of anyone in the boat.

When the tuna strikes, the first angler should pick up the line carefully in gloved hands. Keep just enough pressure on the line that you don't burn yourself, and hold the line thumbs-forward, keeping it pointed in the direction of the fish's run. Stay out of the way as the tuna is running; when retrieving line is necessary, do it hand over hand as your other crew member carefully repacks it. If the fish runs again, you can let go if you must simply by opening your hands without worry of tangling.

If you fish from smaller boats like center consoles, the fish may actually pull you around, which will tire it out rapidly. You may want to take a couple of wraps around a cleat or other object to take some of the pressure off your hands and increase the drag on the fish. Just be careful not to put so much pressure on the line that you break the fish off. This is a matter of intuition, and requires a sense of when to increase and decrease pressure by a focused and experienced angler. On larger boats you won't be pulled around by the tuna as easily, so you'll have to maneuver to keep up with it. You can also transfer the handline setup and anglers into a much smaller boat to fight the fish from. But when the handlined fish is tired out and brought alongside the boat, the rewards can be much more amazing than if you'd caught it on rod and reel.

In any event, handlining is not easy fishing. It is truly for the most rugged and experienced. Tides, currents, winds, and the fish will wreak havoc with you, as they do in all situations. If it interests you, be ready to put in a lot of time getting a feel for it—not to mention getting yourself in physical condition to do it.

PART 4

BOATING YOUR TUNA AND BEYOND

14

HOOKING AND BOATING YOUR FISH

HOOKING UP

There is nothing more exciting than hooking up with a tuna—well, almost nothing. This is a crucial time, especially if there are schools of tuna around and you're hoping for a multiple hookup. But it's also a time that you and your crew should rehearse over and over again in your minds, or—if you're lucky enough—in the cockpit of the boat. Teamwork is now more crucial than ever, and in the excitement of hooking a fish all hell can and will break loose, so work out a plan for fighting the fish and try to stick to it. It won't be easy amid the excitement, but the alternative is often a lost fish.

The first thing that should happen upon hookup is the captain should either hit the SAVE button on the Dytek, loran, or GPS, or immediately write down the coordinates of the spot. This way you can come back and work it again after landing the fish. As this is happening, the designated angler—who should already have the harness on—is ready to battle the fish. Move to the rod, pick it up out of the holder, and make sure the fish is still on. Then set the hook yourself and get into either the chair or stand-up gear. At the same time the mate or mates should be clearing the cockpit and watching the other rods for signs of multiple hookups.

While all this is going on, the captain should maintain trolling speed, or even goose the throttles and turn the boat from side to side. This will create "blue holes" as well as making your lures dance in imitation of frightened baits, more often than not resulting in multiple hookups. A method used a lot on the West Coast very successfully is that once schools of tuna are found near a trolling boat, someone begins to throw chum overboard while the boat continues to troll. This keeps the fish's interest, holding them around the boat and working them up into a feeding frenzy, but it requires a lot more planning and sometimes manpower in the cockpit.

With multiple hookups, I reel one or two fish up close to the transom and leave them swimming around there while at the same time slowly bringing the other lures up in my chum mixture and placing them behind the fish. This, too, will result in more hookups at times. West Coast tuna anglers will also stop the boat in the water while continuing to chum and then jig the tuna using a heavy feather, a butterfish jig, or the new tuna jigs. The important thing is to be constantly analyzing the conditions and forming and re-forming your fishing plan. Communication is crucial.

But I'm getting ahead of myself. As you begin to fight the fish, and once you're sure you've hooked every tuna you're going to hook on this pass, the captain should back off the engines enough to just keep the boat moving ahead. You can kick the gears in and out as needed, but keep the boat slowly moving and determine where your fish is headed.

While this is going on, your cockpit crew will be readying the gaffs or tagging stick, clearing the other lines, and supporting you. From here on there is no set pattern. The boat will have to be maneuvered by the captain as he sees fit for the fish. Backing, spinning, running, quartering, and variations on all of the above will have to take place to bring the fish alongside. Each fish is different. The important things are to be familiar with your boat and how it responds, and to keep open lines of communication and a clear view of the cockpit from the bridge or pilothouse. You won't get every fish alongside the boat, but with a good captain, crew, and angler combination your chances will increase greatly.

BRINGING THE FISH TO THE TAG OR GAFF

Okay. You've been fighting the fish for about an hour now on stand-up tackle. You're standing at the boat's transom, trying to steer the fish to a corner of the boat. It's a large yellowfin, in the 175- to 200-pound range, and it's beaten the hell out of you. You know the fish is close to the boat. It's

Bigeye tuna being wired by Capt. Tred Barta. Gaffers are Eddie Larsen (left) and Roger Tollofsen (right). Courtesy Capt. Tred Barta.

Boat positions to gaff a large tuna, for right and left-handed gaffers.

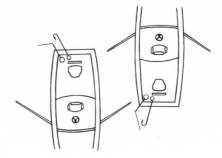

swimming in a circle not too far down, and your instincts tell you you've got it—but don't get overconfident. Here's where every move becomes very important. While you're bringing up the fish with quick, short pumps of the rod, the captain should be closely watching your progress in the cockpit, and the designated mates relaying information to him.

It's imperative that the boat be used to help bring up the fish at this point—kicking it in and out of gear, keep it moving forward. This will lift the fish toward the surface while at the same time maintaining pressure on the hook so it can't be spit. It will also keep the fish from going under the boat and breaking off. More important, it will keep water running through the gills, so that the fish can be released with a better chance of survival.

You've got the fish up and can see it on its side or belly as you begin to bring the leader in. At this point the leaderperson grabs the leader with a gloved hand and takes a couple of wraps on it, again as the boat slowly moves forward. The fish is maneuvered up alongside the boat as the angler backs off on the drag in case the fish decides to give it one last run. If the fish turns away from the boat, the leader will have to be released, and if tension on the drag is minimal the fish will move away safely without breaking off. Too much drag tension here will result in a broken-off fish.

LEADERING OR WIRING THE TUNA

Wiring or leadering a tuna always involves real risks, and for that reason it should be attempted only by someone who has practiced the method beforehand or watched someone else do it enough so that he's familiar and confident with the entire responsibility. Otherwise tangles or wrapped lines can lead in a split second to an unwanted swim for the wireman—or damaged or lost limbs. Even experienced mates always practice extreme caution when handling a powerful tuna. It may look easy as they double-wrap the leader with each hand, but believe me, it's not. For most of us a single wrap will be enough to skillfully guide the fish to gaff, so initially try it that way.

The three basic rules to keep in mind when you're leadering a fish are:

- Always wear a good-quality glove made for the task.
- Wrap toward the fish without exception.
- Be ready at any point to let go if the fish lunges. Never try to be a hero and hold the fish. The fish will always win, and you'll always suffer as a result.

As the designated wireman, you'll "steer" the fighting chair for the angler, watching the progress of the fight the entire time. You've already donned your gloves; wait until the leader or double line is in sight before leaving the chair to take up your wiring duties. Only then should you try to control the fish. This is done by reaching for the leader with your hand open, letting the leader or wire lie across the center of your palm between the thumb and next finger. Then as the wrap is made, be sure that the line falls across the center of your palm, not across the fingers and not across the heel of your hand. Keep your thumb outside the wrap, and the leader itself well away from the glove cuff. At this point you don't want anything to hang up or tangle on a part of the glove's surface. Next, with your hand still open, turn it over and in the direction of the fish, again keeping the wrap free from your fingers. Now you should be able to cinch up on the leader while at the same time being able to release it quickly if you have to.

It is imperative to always maintain a firm grip on the line, especially if you happen to be giant-tuna fishing with a wire leader. If the wire should slip across the surface of your glove, it will quickly heat up and possibly curl. This could result in a weak line that might later kink or break, and you don't have to be a rocket scientist to know what that means.

As all this is going on, things in the cockpit will be very hectic. People will be yelling back and forth, and your heart will most likely be beating 200 times a minute. This is why it's imperative that you stay aware of what you're doing so that you don't lose the fish or injure yourself. The first few times you try wrapping the leader, make only one wrap; as you become more comfortable with it, go ahead and make a second. Whatever you do, though, don't rush it; you'll only make mistakes, which will result in lost fish or personal injuries. Don't be afraid to practice. If it's possible, each member of the crew should have a designated responsibility as well as an alternate one that he's practiced alone as well as with the group. A group of people who fish together frequently and know each other's capabilities is a hard combination to top in any fishing situation.

One more thing: As in any aspect of fighting a tuna, don't allow the fish any slack line while you're wiring it. The least bit of slack will give it the opportunity to shake the hook free from its mouth or lunge powerfully away from the boat. Always try to maintain firm pressure on your fish.

After the Wrap Has Been Made

Now that you've made the wrap and established a firm grip, start working the fish in toward the side of the boat to the waiting gaff or tag stick. To do this you'll use a motion very similar to that of the pumping-retrieving action an angler makes when fighting the fish.

Working hand over hand, gently pull the fish in toward the boat. As you complete each retrieve, release the wrap on the hand closest to you, reaching up and gaining on the leader again. In other words, when you're sure the leader has been released from your rear hand, reach that hand forward to take another wrap while pulling the forward hand into the rear position. If you work hand over hand like this, the fish will soon be in

Always try to bring the fish alongside the boat rather than across the transom.

position to be gaffed or tagged. Try to avoid jerking or yanking on the leader, which often results in a spooked fish that will use its last reserves of energy to take off on one last run. Instead keep the fish coming in nice and easy, and don't let it get under the boat where it may break off on barnacles, a prop, or a trim tab. Also be careful of hanging up the line on any deck hardware that might break the tuna free.

If the fish does start to go under the boat, yell or motion to the captain to maneuver the boat away from it. Again, previous practices or drills can be helpful. If the fish should become spooked and start to run, simply release the wrap and let it go as the angler backs off the drag. It's better to do this than to try to force him out, which may result in a broken-off or injured fish or even a man overboard.

In any event, always try to bring the fish alongside the boat rather than across the transom. There are just too many ways to lose a fish behind a boat, including inboard prop wash and exhaust noise that may unnecessarily spook a fish. If you should be fishing from an outboard, you'll make the gaffer's job a nightmare if he's forced to reach over the tops of outboards as he tries to sink the gaff into the fish.

GAFFING THE TUNA

If you're the angler or wireman, yell "color" when you see the fish, so that the designated gaffer can step into place. Now you must keep your eyes on the fish at all times and be ready to back off the drag a bit if the fish lunges, or even to dip the rod's tip into the water if the fish heads under the boat, which they so often do.

SPECIAL CONSIDERATIONS FOR FLYING GAFFS

When I use a flying gaff, I take a good wrap on the line with my right hand, pull tight, and hold the end of the handle. I guide the gaff with my left hand, and when sticking the fish I hold on to the line with my right hand, passing the handle off to someone in the cockpit with my left. Because the line of the flying gaff and not the handle is responsible for controlling the fish, try to avoid excess slack in the line at all times, even though you are allowed up to 30 feet.

The gaffer should be ready with the gaff standing right next to him, hook up. If this is your job, keep the gaff line about the same length as that of the gaff handle—*plus* your anticipated reach over the side of the boat. Any more than this will just give the fish an opportunity to run after being gaffed, possibly tearing the hook free or ruining part of the meat. Cleat the unattached end of the line off on a stern cleat or fasten it to the stanchion of the fighting chair. The latter is my preferred method because it allows me to predetermine just how much line I'll need to gaff the fish from either side of the boat. Equally important, by fastening the gaff to the fighting chair's stanchion I'm able to easily move back and forth from port to starboard as well as forward without having to waste time tying and retying the line on a cleat.

Once the wireman has the fish alongside the boat, he should call for the gaff. Now step up to the side or transom and take a moment to make sure that the fish is close enough to the boat that you can easily reach out over it and sink the gaff. At this point the tuna will be either facing forward (if the angler pumped it in) or facing the transom (if it was backed down on). After you've determined the fish's position and distance from the boat, grip the gaff with both hands on the handle hook facing up and away from the boat. Now reach the gaff and hook out and over the fish in the head area. Spin the handle so that the hook is at a right or left angle and ready to be sunk into the head area. When you're confident that the time is right, stroke the handle firmly toward you and follow all the way through. This will set the hook and hopefully secure the fish. Don't jerk the gaff when you're trying to set it; more often than not this will result in a poorly secured fish that will probably get away due to a broken leader, and in all likelihood die. Also be careful not to set the hook too high or too low on the fish's head or you may not have enough meat to hold it, again allowing it to get away. Never pull the fish's head out of the water. It will go nuts, and you'll risk losing it.

By the way, be careful with longer gaff handles when it comes time to gaff the fish. Long handles sometimes give you a false sense of security, resulting in rushing the gaff and losing the fish. This occurs due to the refraction and water resistance misleading you as to where the gaff hook is. Wait instead for a clean shot.

If the fish is facing the bow it's not inconceivable that upon being gaffed, it will come out of the water and possibly hit or land in the boat. The captain should be paying particular attention to what's happening now so that if he sees a situation such as this happening, he can immediately move the throttles and clutches forward to properly maneuver the boat.

Here's another scenario: If the tuna is facing the stern, its surge could carry him away from the boat. This may cause you to miss the gaff or, worse, to gaff the fish in the tail section. Whatever you do, *never* gaff a fish in the tail. This takes away none of its strength, but gives the fish the chance—and the motive—to beat you or the boat to hell with its tail. The rope may break, too, or the hook may straighten out, resulting in a lost fish.

If the fish still has any strength left, when gaffed it'll simply go nuts, thrashing about and beating its tail while throwing water all over you and the boat. This is an exciting sight, but not yet a time for congratulations. The fish must now be properly secured and brought aboard.

Gaffing a tuna or any other species is an art, and like all art forms takes a lot of practice to master. More fish are lost at the boat than anywhere else, and this is one of the major reasons why. Practice as much as you can; experience is truly the best teacher. I know of one mate who was so dedicated that he used to gaff grapefruits out in the bay as practice. Today he's on one of the top private boats in the country, and can work pretty much anywhere he wants to.

GAFFING DO'S AND DON'TS

Don't:
- Use a gaff that's too long.
- Try to gaff a fish that's too deep or beyond reach. Be patient!
- Select a gaff hook that's too big for the fish.
- Place the gaff in front of the leader or line. You could be pulled overboard or break the line if the fish makes a sudden move.
- Gaff a fish in the tail.

Do:
- Keep the cockpit clean and organized. Stow unnecessary gear and equipment out of the way.
- Communicate! Make sure everyone in the boat understands their responsibilities.
- Back off the drag as soon as the fish is alongside the boat.
- Make sure the gaff hook is facing downward.
- Gaff from over the top of the fish for better control and protection of belly meat.

TAILROPING THE TUNA

Tailropes are an enormous aid in securing the fish as well as maneuvering it into the boat later by either a gin pole or a pulley system. Tailropes should never be considered a substitute for gaffs, but there are circumstances when they may be used carefully in place of or in conjunction with a gaff, particularly when a fish is to be tagged and released. In most cases they won't cause any injury and may be an excellent means of controlling the fish. Mine are all about 15 feet long from the top of the eye splice to the free end of the line, in diameters of ⅜ and ½ inch. They work simply by creating the equivalent of a cowboy's lariat; you pass the free end of the line through the eye splice to form a sliding loop that you'll then slip over the fish's tail.

Applying the Tailrope

Before placing the tailrope, it's imperative to get some degree of control over the fish's head. If the fish isn't particularly big or is tired, you may be able to do this simply by leadering it alongside the boat. A tuna can be a real challenge, though, if it still has a fight left in it. More aggressive or larger fish may demand a gaff, but again this poses a problem for the angler who intends to release the fish. However, if care is taken and the fish is handled properly, a lip gaff may be put through the lower mouth. This will cause a minimum of harm to the fish, allowing it to be released in relatively good health.

Designate someone to be responsible for tailroping the fish, and be sure that he's in the background watching the action in the cockpit until the time comes to apply the rope. Then before trying to secure the fish, make sure that the tailrope's free end is fastened to a cleat or around the fighting chair's pedestal. With this done, you don't have to worry about holding the fish or losing it if it should turn and try to get away. It's also crucial to pay attention to the other crew members' progress, patiently waiting for the ideal moment to maneuver the loop around the fish's tail before pulling it tight and recleating the line so the fish is immobilized.

After the tuna has calmed down and you're sure the first gaff is set properly, your job then becomes holding on to and securing the fish. You may find that you need to put an additional gaff into it if it's particularly big or if the first gaff looks like it might not hold for some reason. Be very careful not to mutilate the fish when you do this. A gaff put into the meat will only cause it to hemorrhage and possibly introduce bacteria, not to mention ruining its commercial value. But since we're all conservation minded now and not interested in selling fish, this shouldn't be a factor.

Once the fish is securely gaffed and you've determined whether or not it needs another gaff, gently begin to pull the fish alongside the boat with the gaff line and/or leader. With a gaff line use the hand-over-hand method, and have someone take up the slack line on a cleat as you go. This will eliminate the chance of damaging or losing the fish if it surges, which is common. When you get the fish within your reach, slip a tailrope over the tail and tighten up on it as quickly and firmly as possible. The greatest problem you'll find in using the tailrope is actually getting the loop to fit over the fish's caudal fins. Ideally you should be able to slip the loop under the fins' lower lobe, then upper lobe, before tightening it, but if you're like most of us, you'll most likely get the tailrope on and the fish secured in any way you can. Once in place a tailrope will give the angler maximum control over the fish, because it renders the tuna's "motor" inoperative, thus hindering its ability to swim. Just be sure to secure the tailrope on a cleat, too.

Once the fish is secured with the first tailrope, you can add more as needed. Many times a second line will be placed between the dorsal and pectoral fins, ensuring total control over the fish. Referred to as a belly rope, this is the best means of securing a large shark or billfish along the outside of the boat, and not often used on tuna. In any case, tailropes are fairly easy to use, particularly for a seasoned crew of anglers. Just remember to handle the fish as carefully as possible, and to keep only those fish that you can eat—tagging and releasing the rest!

BEATING THE TUNA

After you're sure that the tailropes are secure and the tuna can be handled safely, maneuver the fish to the boat's transom. You can now further secure the fish and, if necessary, tow it backward for a few minutes. This is a good thing to do after gilling the fish, because it allows the fish to bleed out as the water travels through the gill area. Also, when towed backward the fish will suffocate in a very short time, which will allow you to then bring it inside the boat.

When you're sure the fish is ready to be brought aboard, use the gin pole, block-and-tackle setup, or transom door, or carefully lift it over the gunwale. If you're short of muscle, use the VHF radio to try to raise another boat in your area that has a gin pole or even extra hands to help you. If you find one with a gin pole, the captain can come alongside you and lift the fish into your cockpit safely. Otherwise you may be forced to tow the fish back to the dock, which I've seen done many times by center-console boats. I once watched a boat off Montauk in a fleet of about 200 trying an innovative approach to bring in a 300- to 400-pound tuna. It was a center console about 26 feet long with no transom door or gin pole. The six guys in it took all their coolers and equipment and stored them in the rear starboard corner of the boat. Then they all stood in the same corner themselves with the tailrope in hand. The boat's rear corner was now dropped much lower than before, and each time a wave brought the boat into its trough these guys, screaming and cursing, would pull on the fish and manage to get it a little closer to coming inside. This went on for about 20 minutes with other boats watching and yelling chants of support. Finally, the exhausted crew got the fish up far enough on the covering boards that it could be dropped into the boat. The boat's name was the *LunaSea*.

TOWING THE FISH TO THE DOCK

If you do have to tow your fish back to the dock, never tow it from behind the boat. The turbulence created by the prop wash will severely damage the meat, making the fish effectively worthless. Instead tie it alongside the boat with its head and tail as far out of the water as possible, and its stomach pointed in toward the boat. This will keep the fish in the best possible condition.

RELEASING TUNA PROPERLY

Responsible anglers have always believed that all illegal or unwanted fish should be released. Granted, there are exceptions to this, but as the stocks of our saltwater fish continue to be depleted by overfishing and pollution, sport anglers are given the added responsibility of doing their part to help ensure that population levels of fish are at the very least maintained, and if possible increased. The most effective way to accomplish this is by first tagging and then releasing any fish caught.

Of course this doesn't mean that a fish that's obviously going to die should be wasted by throwing it back overboard. But what it boils down to basically is this:

- Do we have a method to catch fish that will assure their survival if released?
- Do we know how many fish actually survive being released?
- Can we recognize the signs of a fish about to die?

In all cases we would have to honestly answer no. Still, the bottom line is that released fish stand a better chance of survival in the water than they do in your cooler.

How does an angler handle a fish without causing it injury? Fortunately for offshore anglers, saltwater fish are a lot tougher than their freshwater counterparts—with the possible exception of their gills. The gills of any fish are as sensitive and delicate as the human lung. Always avoid them during handling to ensure the fish's survival. The vast majority of fish that don't survive being released die because of injured, torn, and/or bleeding gills. Also be aware that many species of saltwater game fish have razor-sharp gill covers that will severely cut your fingers if not handled properly.

Many fish can be held out of the water long enough to be measured or photographed without danger of injury if they're handled properly. When handling a manageable-sized tuna, grab it by the "neck," pressing in the gill covers with your free hand (see illustration). If it's a particularly large fish, you'll need your other hand to grab it at the stem of its tail. Now carefully lift the fish out of the water horizontally. Always avoid lifting a heavy fish out of the water vertically because of the enormous weight the internal organs have when out of water. If you lift a big fish vertically from the water, chances are that the internal organs could rip loose from the blood vessels that hold them in place, causing the fish to hemorrhage internally and die. A horizontal removal provides a much greater chance of survival.

If the fish is too big to lift you'll need the help of a gaff and tailrope. To do this correctly, put the gaff's hook through the lip of the fish and secure the tailrope as explained above. Then lift the fish carefully aboard. If no gaff is available, pass the leader or fishing line through the fish's lip and use it to pull the fish in. Always avoid grabbing the fish by its back or you'll get a quick lesson in dorsal spines.

Once you have the fish out of the water, avoid laying it on the cockpit floor, where it can injure itself by beating its tail and thrashing about. Instead try to hold it gently while taking pictures or measuring, then lay it gently on the boat's covering board while maintaining a slight pressure so that it won't be tempted to start beating about.

As soon as you're ready, return the fish into the water carefully by holding it by the head and the stem of its tail. Instruct the captain to kick the boat in and out of gear, keeping it moving in a forward motion, while you hold on to the fish. This will pass water through its gills, providing it with fresh oxygen and helping rebuild its strength. After a minute or two of this the fish will most likely have gained enough strength back to be set free.

Hook Removal Versus Cutting the Leader

Another aspect of the debate on whether or not to release fish has to do with the relative merits of hook removal and cutting the leader. There are proponents of both sides of this issue, with some arguing that it's less stressful to cut the leader than to spend the time and energy necessary to work out an embedded hook. Still others claim that a cast-iron hook deteriorates more rapidly than a stainless or aluminum one, so leaving it in the fish's lip or mouth is not harmful. The truth is that nobody really knows how long this deterioration process takes, although studies should certainly be undertaken.

The fact is that a healthy tuna will react to a hook in its body a lot better than we would. White blood cells will wall off the hook, eventually forming scar tissue. Should the tuna swallow the hook, internal fluids will encapsulate it much like a pearl, or dissolve it altogether. Eventually the hook or what's left of it may be passed, and at this point it's pretty much assured to be a harmless event.

There are countless verifiable reports of tuna caught on longlines with hooks already embedded in their jaws. And who knows how many billfish are released by sport anglers with longline hooks embedded in their stomachs?

What I do when releasing a fish for purely commonsense reasons is simply to cut the leader as close to the hook as possible, unless the hook can be removed or snipped easily. Putting myself in the place of the fish, it clearly makes more sense to do this than to twist, turn, and try to pull the hook out of the mouth. I put this method in the same category as an unpleasant trip to the dentist, but with the added risk of enlarging the fish's wound or damaging a gill arch. This would surely result in a fatal hemorrhage.

Another concern has to do with injuries caused by raising the fish to the surface too fast. The effects of decompression often prove fatal to humans. The "bends," as the phenomenon is commonly called, is a result of gas coming out of the blood causing a large bubble in the bloodstream, which can then travel to the brain or another organ and lead to excruciating pain, paralysis, or death. This occurrence is quite rare in fish. However, something that is very common and usually mistaken for decompression in a fish is the gas bladder protruding from the mouth or intestines protruding from the anal area. The National Marine Fisheries Service has done at least two studies in different areas of the country on this. One done off the Atlantic coast indicated that up to 90 percent of fish caught at depths of 70 to 100 feet survived when released. These results changed, however, when fish were caught and released in deeper water, suggesting that decompression may have killed these fish. Particularly susceptible were the smaller species. The second study was done in the Gulf of Mexico near offshore drilling rigs. Here 55 red snappers were caught in 165 feet of water on high-speed electric reels. When brought aboard they were tagged, measured, and placed in metal cages overboard so that they could be studied further. They were then returned to a depth of 115 feet, where scuba divers made the following observations: Two-thirds of the fish survived the entire two-week observation period, while of the third that didn't survive, 95 percent died within the first two days. Just what did they die from, you might ask? Surprisingly enough, it wasn't from protruding bladders or innards. Seventy-two percent of the fish with bladders sticking out survived and only 59 percent of the fish without them made it. In fact it was stress, heavy bleeding, and torn gills that killed the majority of the fish, all the result of being pulled rapidly to the water's surface.

For years commercial anglers have been puncturing fish's gas bladders. This releases the gas held inside and returns the bladder to its usual size, allowing the crews to put the fish in live wells until they can get to port, thus ensuring their freshness. Studies have shown that such fish can survive for a few days—but how about longer periods of time? The National Marine Fisheries say that by no means is puncturing the bladder always cause for eventual death. In autopsies of fish that survived the experiments as well as those that didn't, *both* showed signs of the bends—gas around the heart, in the body cavity, in the gut area, and in the eye. However, the survivors also had torn or punctured bladders that had healed.

Nevertheless, the bottom line is the same: No matter how weak it may appear after you've battled it to the boat, the fish stands a better chance of surviving to fight again for someone else if it is released back to its own environment carefully. It stands no chance at all in your cooler!

15

AFTER THE TUNA'S BEEN BOATED

CARE AND HANDLING OF THE TUNA

Any fish's physiological makeup begins to change immediately after it's hooked. The great exertion involved in the fight begins to deplete the energy reserves stored in the muscles. This change will continue until after death, when an irreversible spoilage process begins. Tuna are perhaps the most extreme examples of this phenomenon because they have such high metabolic rates and fat contents, as well as a body temperature that may reach 10 degrees or more above that of the surrounding waters.

Because this higher body temperature encourages the proliferation of bacteria that will then produce histamine, it is essential to lower the tuna's body temperature as quickly as possible after you secure it. This is especially true after a long battle or in particularly warm weather, when the tuna's metabolic rate changes rapidly in order to obtain stored energy. When this occurs enzymes and acids in the tuna begin to break down or digest, resulting in the edible flesh becoming soft, mushy, and inedible. If you're to maintain the highest quality of edible meat possible, you must know the proper tuna care and cleaning techniques. Otherwise the combination of the tuna's high body temperature and the acid wastes that build up from overexertion during a battle or after death will result in the tuna actually cooking the protein in its muscles. This phenomenon has become known as burnt tuna syndrome, and it's becoming more and more evident at dockside as more of us participate in tuna fishing.

Tuna, mackerel, bonito, and skipjacks all contain large amounts of free histidine in their muscles. In a poorly handled fish histidine is converted rapidly by bacterial action into histamine, a small molecule associated with allergic reactions and tuna poisoning. This bacterial reaction will occur within one to two hours in an improperly cared-for tuna and usually leaves the contaminated fish with a telltale peppery taste or foul odor. Ingestion of such a fish may lead to such symptoms as cramps, diarrhea, vomiting, thirst, hives, a swelling of the lips, and a burning sensation in the throat. Such waste can be avoided by simply educating yourself in the proper care and handling of boated fish.

To the inexperienced eye the flesh color of a tuna is generally a reliable indicator of how that fish has been handled and what kind of shape it's in. Fresh flesh is typically a rich red color, slightly translucent, and possessing an iridescent sheen. Spoiled tuna will display an opaque, pale beige color.

The availability and type of food as well as the length of time since its last feeding determine the oil content of a tuna's flesh. A high oil content is desirable for dockside buyers, and if the fish is in good physical condition, will result in a higher purchase price.

Dockside buyers are for the most part very well trained and extremely knowledgeable concerning the tuna as well as very aware of what characteristics to look for when buying. At Montauk Marine Basin we are fortunate to have as buyer Tommy Edwards, who knows as much about tuna and tuna grades as anyone I've run across. He has been doing it for more years than he'll admit, but he has also visited various fish markets in Japan to learn more about the grading process and what these insatiable buyers are looking for.

While a high oil content is desirable, buyers also look for a well-rounded fish with a good overall shape, thick belly flesh, and thin skin—a good indication of an all-around healthy fish that has been cared for properly. Upon determining that the fish has a worthwhile oil content, the buyer will check the flesh colors of its meat by inserting a long metal core—usually made of copper with a diameter smaller than that of a pencil—through the thickest part of the fish. By examining this core sample, the buyer will be able to see the various color contrasts that make up the internal layers. These layers are good indications of the fish's fat content, which now can be more precisely determined by feel, smell, and taste.

Finally, in order to establish if the fish has been bruised at all during the battle or in the boat, the buyer will often run his hand over the entire surface of the tuna, feeling for soft areas often associated with bruises.

BOATING A TUNA

After you fight a tuna it's imperative that you boat it and prepare it for icing as quickly and carefully as feasible. The basic goal should be to reduce the tuna's internal body temperature to a minimum of 45 degrees F as soon as possible. This is the temperature at which histamine production is minimized, ensuring a better-quality fish for the table or the market.

GAFFING AND BOATING REVISITED

Proper techniques for gaffing and boating tuna are covered thoroughly in Chapter 14. Some pointers for presenting your tuna's meat deserve reemphasis, however.

Whether your fish is big or small, always attempt to gaff it in the head. This will subdue it as quickly as possible, allowing you and your crew to begin the dressing process but also ensuring that no flesh is damaged and thus wasted. Gaffing the fish in its flesh or meat area will only cause it to hemorrhage as well as damage the edible meat. If the fish is too big for the cockpit crew to handle, leader it and bring it alongside the boat as gently as possible. After gaffing it through the head, slip a tailrope over the tail, tighten it down, and cleat it off securely. This will keep the fish in the water and allow its body temperature to gradually cool as you begin the bleeding process. Next, rig another tailrope to the gin pole or—if you have a transom door—to a pulley system in your cockpit and bring the fish into the cockpit carefully. If there are gaff wounds to a side of the tuna or noticeable bruises caused by handling the fish prior to boating it, make sure that that side is down when you pull it through the transom door. This will eliminate the chance of causing further damage to the edible flesh. It's also a good idea to have a large stainless tuna hook on board with a length of line spliced to it. This hook can be inserted in the tuna's mouth, head, or gill area, with the line cleated off, as an extra protection against loss during the boating or cleaning process.

After the tuna has been gaffed, tailroped, and secured, begin the bleeding process right away while in the water. Because the water temperature is usually lower than that of the surrounding air, it will allow the fish's body to cool gradually rather than dramatically.

Using a knife or cockpit harpoon, puncture and rake the gills under the gill plate to begin the bleeding. The tuna will still be alive at this point, and the heart's beating will push the warm blood out, keeping the flesh from cooking itself. After a few minutes of this it's time to bring the tuna into the boat.

When the fish is boated, if it is still alive and wants to beat around, stun it as quickly as possible with a blow to the forehead or by inserting an icepick there. This will keep the fish from beating around in the boat's cockpit, which will only result in a damaged fish. I once watched in horror as two anglers on a boat next to me beat a tuna senseless with stun clubs for about five minutes while trying to subdue it, the whole time cheered on by crews from surrounding boats. I'm sure that the fish was rendered worthless after this unnecessary carnage.

After the tuna is safely aboard and subdued, place it on a smooth, flat surface—ideally atop an old blanket, a piece of foam rubber, or even a rug scrap. Wearing rubber or latex gloves is also a good idea to keep your warm hands from marring the fish. The oil and heat from your hands will leave impressions on the skin that will remain even after the fish is iced.

FURTHER BLEEDING

While keeping the fish moist with your saltwater washdown hose or buckets of salt water, the next step is to bleed it using a tail and throat cut as well as a cut behind his pectoral fins. This pectoral fin cut is the most important, because it will bleed the remaining blood quickly, reducing the body temperature even more.

To do this correctly, insert the knife's blade approximately one hand's width behind the base of each pectoral fin and about two inches deep. Done correctly, this will sever the fish's major arteries and cause the blood to flow out easily. If this doesn't happen, calmly try making additional cuts in the same area without prematurely preparing the fish for the sushi restaurant. When you're cutting the tail, slice between the second and third finlets to the bone. This will cut that primary artery and induce bleeding. Insert a knife into the fish's throat as shown and wait until all of the blood has been drained. The entire bleeding process for a big fish should take between 5 and 10 minutes. Just remember to keep hosing the fish down with salt water the entire time, if you can.

I usually bleed a smaller tuna over the boat's side or transom after attaching the fish securely to a tailrope and cleating it off. I then make the previously described cuts and keep the tuna hanging over the side for about five minutes while it bleeds out. This allows the fish to remain in the water—which is cooler than the boat's cockpit. A fishing buddy of mine swears that the smell attracts other tuna to the area as well.

Proper bleeding keeps the tuna's warm blood from coming in contact with its warm oily flesh, which would turn it rancid in short order. It also increases the contrast of the flesh's colors, making it easier for the buyers to determine the fish's quality.

GUTTING AND GILLING THE TUNA
Gutting
As soon as the tuna is bled, it must be gutted and gilled. To do this, make a 6-inch belly cut by inserting the knife in front of the anus and cutting toward the head. *Do not cut through the anus.* Instead, insert the knife through the flesh and cut a circle around the anus, removing it when you're done.

Now pull the intestines out through the open belly cavity and disconnect them from the fish's body wall and meat carefully, using a knife where necessary.

Gilling
Make a cut at the top of the gill cover toward the eye. Now pull the gill cover back and cut the muscle that connects it to the head. Don't completely remove the gill cover, however; hold it back to expose the gill arches.

These arches must now be removed by severing the throat and skull connections at the gill arch bases. Don't cut through the throat, because this would distort the flesh and make it less valuable if you're planning to sell it.

Now remove the fish's innards through the gill openings by making cuts behind the gill membrane. Extend this cut toward the rear as close as possible to the backbone. Then remove the gill membranes inside the covers as well as the spoiled skin around them, or else they'll turn brown and slimy in the ice. Remove all skin from the gill area and all leftover innards from the belly cavity. Finally, thoroughly rinse and gently scrub all leftover blood and other tissue from the fish, being especially careful not to bruise the flesh.

ICING THE TUNA
Once the fish has been properly bled and gutted, it must be chilled immediately. The best way to do this is inside a Canyon Products insulated tuna bag. These bags keep your catch fresh for hours when iced and prepared properly.

The best mixture to use is an iced seawater slurry that will lower the body temperature as quickly as possible and preserve the fish. Crushed or flaked ice is preferable, because it won't bruise the flesh. When you're icing small tuna you can make this mixture right in your cooler by mixing 2 parts ice to 1 part seawater. Otherwise fill your Canyon Bag with the mixture before leaving the dock. It will temper the bag to the colder temperatures, and thus keep your catch as fresh as possible until you get back to the dock.

If this method is impractical due to space limitations, simply pack the fish in crushed or flaked ice. Don't let any of the ice lie under the fish, which again might bruise it. When you ice the tuna, first fill its stomach cavity with ice, then cover the fish with as much of the remaining ice as possible to ensure balanced cooling. In addition, you can wrap the iced fish in a sheet or piece of plastic to add a bit of insulation.

DRESSING THE TUNA

Back at the dock, and assuming you've properly bled and iced your tuna, you'll want to continue the cleaning process by separating the edible meat and slicing it into steaks for the barbecue grill, oven, or tuna salad. This is a simple process that requires a good sharp, long-bladed knife and some seawater if available. A second choice is tap water, but it will detract from the flavor.

1. Lift the pectoral fin and make a vertical slice behind the head and fin from top to bottom without cutting through the backbone. At the tail, do the same thing at the second finlet.
2. Slice a straight line down the backbone of the tuna from head to tail, similar to a filleting cut. Then make another slice just above the fish's lateral line, again from head to tail. Then trim as necessary, without wasting meat, until this slab of meat is cut free.
3. Slice under the lateral line and parallel to the tail finlets, trimming as needed to remove the bottom section of meat.
4. Turn the fish over and repeat these steps.
5. Trim away any of the strong-tasting red bloodline from the slabs of meat.
6. Slice the slabs into 1- or 2-inch steaks from top to bottom, and turn the knife blade down and along the skin to separate the flesh from the skin.
7. Vacuum-bag or wrap the steaks for freezing and storage. But remember, don't freeze them for more than three months, and less is better.

Dressing the tuna.

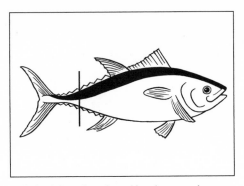

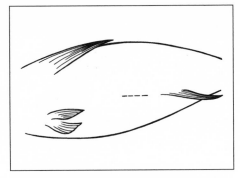

Kill the fish with a sharp blow between the eyes. Then make the tail cut as shown.

Using a short blade, insert the knife four inches in front of the anus, and make a shallow cut toward the anus, making sure not to cut the intestines.

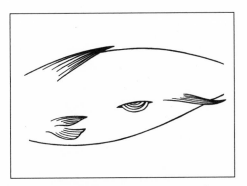

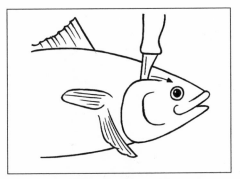

Pull out the intestines and cut them near the anus.

Insert the knife at the top of the gill cover and cut toward the eye.

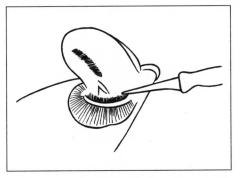

Cut the lower end of the attachment between gill and head.

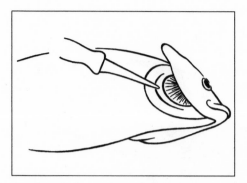

Cut through the membranes behind the gills.

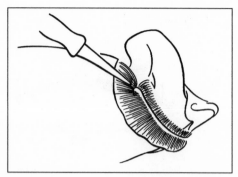

Cut the upper end of the attachment between gill and head.

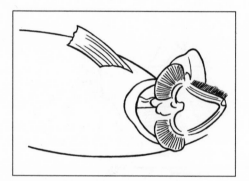

Remove gills, innards, and any remaining intestines.

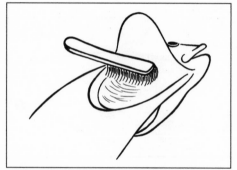

Remove the kidney by scrubbing the spine through the gill opening.

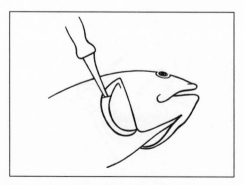

Trim the membranes lining the gill collar.

FLESH TEXTURES AND COLORS

Each species of tuna has its own distinctive flesh color, texture, and flavor as well as its own fat content. Albacore is the lightest-colored tuna with the lowest fat content; it's the only member of the tuna family allowed by the FDA to be labeled "white meat." It's most often canned and reaches your table as a tuna salad sandwich. Yellowfin tuna is the next lightest in flesh color, with a slightly higher fat content than the albacore but a still-delicate flavor. Bigeye tuna have an even darker meat with a higher fat content. Their flavor is more pronounced, although not gamy or strong at all.

The bluefin tuna's meat ranges from intermediate to dark red in color, depending on the fat content, which is usually higher than other tuna species. It has a good all-around flavor and texture and is the most sought-after tuna for sushi or sashimi.

Little tunny or false albacore has very dark meat, unlike its cousin the true albacore. This meat is not sought-after for the table, because it has a very strong oily flavor.

The bonito is usually considered the least desirable for consumption of any of the tuna. It has very dark meat and a strong flavor much like a mackerel.

BRINING

In the case of some of the stronger-tasting tuna, brining the meat will help lighten the flesh color as well as removing some of the oily taste. To properly brine a tuna before cooking, dissolve approximately ½ cup salt in 1 gallon fresh water. Place the meat in this solution and keep it in a refrigerator. The soaking process may take up to two hours, depending on the fish's oil content and flesh color. Cutting out the dark strip of meat in the tuna steaks will also reduce the strong taste. The meat can now be cooked or packaged and frozen for a later meal.

STORING THE MEAT

Because tuna meat deteriorates so rapidly when it's stored, use your fresh or frozen meat as soon as possible. Never leave tuna in the refrigerator for more than three days or in the freezer for more than three months. Frozen tuna will take on a strong fishy taste if you leave it too long, and it's very susceptible to freezer burn. For the best flavor, eat tuna meat within a day or so of catching it. The same day is best, though.

PART 5

THE COMMERCIAL FISHERY

16

TSUKIJI MARKET, TOKYO

The ties that link Japan and the sea are ancient and abiding. The sea has always provided the Japanese with the mainstay of their diet—fish, and great amounts of it. Even in modern times, with meat in the form of fast foods readily available in Japan, consumption of seafood remains important. Those familiar with Japanese society agree that traditions die hard there. Despite McDonald's, Kentucky Fried Chicken, and even Taco Bell outlets all over the country, seafood will always remain an integral part of the Japanese diet.

It should come as no surprise, then, that the people of this island nation have developed a love of the sea every bit as rich as France's love of the grape. Japanese descriptions of fish are as evocative and metaphoric as descriptions of fine French wine. Even the Japanese language, which reflects the concerns of the culture as a whole, possesses an extraordinary vocabulary of fish names and fish-related terms.

Consider these numbers: The Japanese eat 6 million pounds of fish each day, six days a week and 52 weeks per year. This equates to 1 million tons or 2 *billion* pounds of fish sold and consumed by Japan each year. In dollars and cents that's over $10 million U.S. spent each day on fish in *wholesale* markets, making the seafood business a $3-billion-per-year enterprise.

With over 60,000 restaurants, seafood stores, and other food outlets feeding Japan's 110 million people each day, supplying these fish is in itself a huge task. In fact, in order to harvest and preserve all this fish the Japanese maintain an extensive, modern, and varied fleet of commercial fishing vessels that travel the oceans of the world in search of seafood. The most highly regarded of these is the tuna fleet, which catches staggering amounts of tuna each day.

A typical tuna fishing fleet may consist of several longliners, purse seiners, and one huge "mother ship." This 400-foot-plus boat accommodates an entire fish-processing factory that prepares tuna at sea in various ways while the fishing fleet continues to fish tuna for up to six months at a time.

The process of flash-freezing was invented by the Japanese and is used extensively on their longliners and purse seiners in preserving tuna. The procedure freezes fish at temperatures between 80 and 140 degrees below zero and preserves the quality of the fish so satisfactorily that the untrained eye cannot tell the difference between flash-frozen and fresh tuna meat. Fresh tuna are always sold in the market first, with flash-frozen fish brought out for sale only when the demand is greater than the supply, in order to prevent erratic price fluctuations.

These fleets are in turn sustained by other fleets of supply ships that continually bring fresh crews, food, and fuel, and take fish back to Japan to be sold. It is a well-orchestrated effort that is stripping our waters of tuna and other fish. After filling their holds the fleets return to Japan, where the tuna are then sold at one of the 10 major wholesale fish markets throughout the country. The largest and best known of these is the Tokyo Central Wholesale Market.

Established in 1932 and one of three in the capital city of Tokyo, this wholesale market sits alongside the Sumidagawa River on nearly 150 acres of land. It is the largest fish market of any kind in the world and is operated by the city of Tokyo, which takes a small percentage of each sale to cover operating expenses. On a typical day over 63,000 people and 22,000 trucks will pass through its 2 million square feet of space, home to over 1,200 specialty fish shops that sell over 2,000 different seafood products—and 400 which sell only tuna. The most significant part of this market and the one that deals in the tuna is the Tsukiji (pronounced tsu-kee-jee), a

Newly caught and flash-frozen tuna at the Tsukiji Fish Market, Tokyo.

55-acre market within a market. It is named for the water-front neighborhood where it is located that is also home to Tokyo's most famous geisha house, hundreds of restaurants, theaters, hospitals, and the main office of Japan's biggest newspaper, *Asahi Shimbum*. Vast amounts of tuna are sold here at Tsukiji each day, so vast that this market accounts for 50 percent of the tuna sales in Japan. In fact, in 1995 alone 80,000 tons of tuna were sold at Tsukiji!

But the market at Tsukiji actually is part of a much larger food distribution system that dates back to Japan's Kamakura

Dressing the tuna at Tsukiji Market.

Dressed tuna undergoing inspection, Tsukiji Market, Tokyo.

period (1185–1333). Impressed by the huge amounts of money being brought in by trade with China's Sung dynasty, the Japanese feudal lords took control of the existing barter-type markets and centralized their operations, turning them into huge sources of taxable income.

The central fish market at Edo (Tokyo) got its start in 1590 when Shogun Ieyasu Tokugawa began to successfully organize the supply system he needed to feed his army, civil servants, and family. He brought a fisherman named Magoemon Mori in from Osaka to set up the market in what is now downtown Tokyo. When the catch exceeded the demand, Mori was allowed to sell the surplus to the general public.

During the Genroku period (1688–1704) the population of Edo passed the one million mark, and the expansion of the fish market began to attract other fishermen and farmers with their goods.

In September 1923 the fish market in downtown Tokyo burned down, and that December it was moved to the Tsukiji district, where it remains. Then in 1935 in order to centralize activities, the Tokyo city government brought Tsukiji and three other markets together to form the Tokyo Central Wholesale Market.

A visit to Tsukiji today puts into stark perspective what is being done to our waters every day. Prior to the day's auctions, fish of all types and sizes are hauled on thousands of motorized carts and wagons from the wharves to the marketplace. The enormous and sanitary market is filled with astounding and artistic displays of seafood ranging from edible seaweed to giant bluefins. Everything that swims or lives in the oceans of the world is represented here, including salmon from Norway, lobsters from Maine, octopus from the Pacific Northwest, and giant bluefin tuna packed in ice-filled coffins and flown in from the United States. Row after row of seafood products, many unrecognizable, can be seen neatly arranged according to type, quality, grade, category, method of preservation, wholesaler, and consumer demand.

Pallets of flash-frozen striped marlin are stacked in one section of the market for as far as the eye can see—a remarkable sight yet at the same time frightening, when you think that all these marlin were taken from the world's oceans within only the past few days. But it's the tuna that are the aristocrats of fish sold here. They're called *maguro* in Japan, but Tsukiji merchants refer to them with the generic term *omono,* which means "the big ones." Strolling through the tuna section, even the untrained can recognize six different types of tuna. There are *mebachi* or albacore, and *Indo-maguro*— tuna from the Indian Ocean, also known as *minami-maguro* or southern (bluefin) tuna. The true bluefin is called *hon-maguro,* the yellowfin *kiwada-maguro.* Local tuna from nearby waters are *kinkai-maguro.* Even the vanishing swordfish, *kajiki-maguro,* is represented here. Most of these fish will be auctioned off whole. For now they lie in the market like giant cold cadavers, row after row giving off a gentle white vapor in the warm morning air.

THE DAY

A typical workday at the Tsukiji Market begins at 2:30 A.M. with shopkeepers arriving to open up and prepare for the day's business. At 4:30 A.M. live fish from aquaculture farms and inshore fisheries that have been kept in pens are offloaded. Others might come in special tanks to keep them fresh; unfamiliar species are actually sent to a testing area where they are fed to stray cats to see if they are fit for human consumption.

This is also the time when wholesalers will begin to inspect the tuna unloaded during the night. Middlemen and other bidders take notes on each fish they are interested in, checking the eyes and the shape of the tuna's body to determine freshness and care. Walking past row after row of darker tuna that have not been frozen but shipped from the United States in a chilled brine solution, they'll look at the meat where the tail was removed, checking its color. A deep red is good; anything lighter is less desirable. They also check the stomach cavity of the fish, and use a small core-sampling device—along with a trained eye—to check fat content.

At 5:20 A.M. sharp the market opens and the tuna auction begins. This is the highlight of the day at Tsukiji, an event full of emotion and yelling as bidding goes on rapidly and prices rise quickly. Trained buyers flash hand signals recognizable only to the two auctioneers' eyes as together they scan the crowd watching for the next bid. These men work together every day, and many are close friends. Yet this is no place for friends or even small talk. This is the single most significant fish auction in Japan each day, and the men know that their day's income depends on this crazed activity.

Within 30 minutes the auction is over. Half the tuna that will be consumed in Japan that day have been sold, and in excess of $2 million has changed hands for tuna alone. A single fish of good quality might sell for more than $20,000 to a wholesaler, with fish of exceptional quality going for much more. The buyers now resell the fish to sushi restaurants for upward of $350 a pound.

At 6:30 A.M. all the shopkeepers are back at their stalls and the market is opened to licensed retailers who will buy for their stores or restaurants, spending another $10 million during the next three hours. By noon everything is pretty much over as shops are washed down and owners mill about drinking tea or sake and discussing the day's business. On the surrounding docks throughout the day ships can be seen unloading massive amounts of seafood for the next day's business in Japan's never-ending harvest.

THE TUNA AND JAPAN

Since the Japanese depend on fish as their primary source of protein, and because the tuna is particularly rich in fat and protein, it has become one of the most important commodities sold in Japanese fish markets today. This was not always the case, however. During the 16th century the Japanese considered tuna a second-rate fish fit only for the poorest people. It wasn't until the mid-1960s that the real food value of these fish was discovered and Japan's commercial fishing interests and government joined forces to import them in huge quantities.

Today the preferred species of edible tuna are, in order, northern and southern bluefin, bigeye, and yellowfin. The meat of these different species is graded extensively. The business of buying and selling tuna is looked upon with great respect by Japan's citizens. A buyer or wholesaler must be able to quickly size up a fish as to its quality (and thus price range). This requires an experienced eye; it takes an apprenticeship of at least 10 years in the tuna trade to learn the basis of proper tuna selection. Only after 30 years of apprenticeship are you considered qualified to determine the grade and quality of a tuna by yourself.

The preparation of slabs of tuna meat for the market is looked upon as an almost spiritual process. Cutting a slab for sale is a separate skill that requires great experience and training as well as a mental attitude that some describe as a meditative state. The meat is cut with "quick, decisive, and clean cuts," using "proper breathing techniques and meditative phrases." According to one gentleman whose family has been in the tuna business for 11 generations, the tuna cutter "must first clear himself of any wicked thoughts, for if his mind retains any evil he will not be able to cut straight."

It's obvious that not only are these great game fish an integral part of the Japanese diet and culture, but the process of buying, preparing, and selling them possesses a spirituality all its own. Unfortunately, this is putting ever-increasing pressure on worldwide tuna stocks, resulting in their current precarious state.

17

HARPOONING TUNA

Although the technique of harpooning or "sticking" tuna had been practiced in an unorganized way prior to the 1950s, it was about then that it began to turn into an industry. Refinements in boat design, power, and technology in the 1950s were behind this change. Harpooning takes an incredible amount of patience and skill, and although it can be quite profitable, it does not adversely impact the tuna stocks. It gives schools of tuna enough time to rebuild themselves while at the same time letting anglers make a decent living. I hope that more commercial anglers will return to it in the days ahead.

Harpoon boats are serious pieces of equipment custom-designed to meet each owner's requirements and tastes. They usually feature downeast-type hulls built and designed to be as quiet as possible in the water. Engine compartments are well insulated, spray rails removed from the bow, and engine shafts, motor mounts, and exhausts designed and built to be noiseless so that the boat can move up on the fish without startling them. All stick boats feature a bow pulpit and tuna tower. The pulpit is essentially a walkway that allows the stick man to gain an advantage on the fish before it knows the boat is behind it. Today many boats feature pulpits up to 30 feet long that actually fold back over the wheelhouse when not in use. Towers, too, can reach 30 feet in height, and usually have a set of controls that allows the boat to be operated from high above the water's surface. They give the spotter a great advantage in finding and following the movements of fish, particularly in conjunction with spotter planes. These single-engine aircraft rigged with auxiliary fuel tanks fly grids over known tuna migratory routes during the season in an attempt to find the moving schools. But tuna are smart creatures, and while years ago a spotter plane might pass a school at 50 or 100 feet off the water, today's fish can sense the danger of a plane and get spooky when it's 400 or 500 feet up. Still, spotter planes remain an extremely effective addition to a harpooning crew, and in most cases will see the fish before anyone on the boat can.

Once tuna are spotted, the pilot radios the boat and the crew goes to work. The goal is to bring the boat up behind the moving school or in some cases to move the pulpit over a school of baitfish then wait for a shot at a tuna. There must be a real synchronicity of communication between the pilot, the tower man, and the pulpit man. The stick man in the pulpit must direct the boat up to the moving fish, which he does through hand signals to the captain or, more recently, with a wireless walkie-talkie headset.

The gear used for harpooning is very basic, and didn't change at all until only recently. Most harpoons today are about 12 feet long and made from fiberglass or aluminum; wooden handles are still seen strapped to the pulpits of a few stick boats. Lengths vary depending on personal prefer-ence of the man in the pulpit, but in general the point of the harpoon's steel shaft should just touch the water when it's hung from his bellyband or belt.

Attached to the end of the harpoon shaft snugly—but not so snugly that it can't release—is the "lily" or "dart." It's designed to penetrate the flesh of the tuna and then release from the harpoon, staying inside the fish. The dart is made from bronze in an arrowhead shape with a fish's tail. Its design has changed little since I was a boy and used to see bunches of them hanging in the cellar of our summer house. The dart is attached to about 50 feet of thin ⅛-inch nylon throwing line that in turn is attached to 600 feet of lobster-pot warp-type line. At the end of this is spliced a 30-inch plastic orange ball; a high flier is attached to this with another 8-foot splice. The ball was once used to slow the fish and keep a certain amount of pressure on it as it pulled through the water. This would eventually tire out the average fish so that it could be brought aboard. However, some harpooned fish are not "average," and until recently they were lost using this method—they pulled the ball and gear off into the horizon, never to be seen again. Unless it's hit through a vital organ or its backbone, a tuna can tow the line and ball for well over an hour before blood loss and trauma finally do it in.

Today we also have the electronic dart, which eliminates the risk of fish getting away. It has been used with great success and is now a part of all serious stick boats. The Zapper, as some call it, features the same type of dart end always used, but with a wire attached and fastened to the harpoon line. As soon as the fish is hit, the guy in the pilothouse or flying bridge hits a button wired to the boat's generator. The resulting shock kills the fish almost immediately, and in many cases ensures a high quality of flesh—in part because the ocean itself acts as the ground back to the boat. The harpoon fishery is now much more efficient and less wasteful, for stuck fish swim only 100 feet or so before rolling over belly-up.

It's important to keep the ball and line as straight as possible above the fish after it's dead. You can then bring the boat alongside to retrieve the fish slowly until it's brought alongside, gaffed, and secured. If the fish runs due to a Zapper failure, the high flier attached to the line system's end can really help you find the fish. Some crews even add a radar reflector to it.

Sticking tuna is a true art form that seems to be enjoying new popularity among anglers. If we could use methods such as harpooning, rod-and-reel fishing, and handlining for harvesting these great fish while also eliminating wasteful and destructive methods such as purse seining, longlining, drift netting, and pair trawling, the tuna should rebuild its population into the vast schools once found in our oceans.

18

TUNA CONSERVATION

Recently stocks of northern blue-fins have declined dramatically in the western Atlantic, and to a lesser degree in the eastern Atlantic and Pacific Oceans. According to some estimates this decline exceeds 80 percent since 1970. Equally alarming is the case of the southern bluefins, whose stocks have declined as much as 90 percent. Other tuna species are facing similar plights.

The total worldwide catch of wild marine fish has hovered at around 80 metric tons for years now, despite the ability of fleets to catch more. There are many reasons, though perhaps the primary one is the fact that our oceans are being strip-mined faster than they can rebuild themselves. The United Nations reported that by the early 1990s, 70 percent of the world's important fish species were already fully exploited or depleted; in U.S. waters, that figure was closer to 80 percent.

More and more the finger is being pointed at ocean pollution as a factor as well. Industrial contaminants like mercury and low levels of radioactivity from weapons fallout and the operation of nuclear power plants destroys the capacity of fish eggs to develop into the larval stage.

THE PROBLEM OF BY-CATCH

Consider this: Nearly 25 percent of the annual global catch of marine fish, and four times the number of total fish landed by American fisheries, is killed and thrown back into our oceans! This equals over 44 billion pounds of fish annually—a staggering figure that directly correlates to the precarious state of our oceans and our fisheries.

What is by-catch? It's the taking of nontargeted animals, and includes undersized or juvenile fish of targeted species as well as sea turtles, marine mammals, birds, and other forms of wildlife. The vast majority of these animals are discarded back into the oceans, either dead or in danger of dying. By-catch is not a product of all fishing techniques; it's closely related to indiscriminate, nonselective-gear fisheries such as longlining, drift netting, purse seining, and pair trawling, as well as fishing in areas known to support large populations of juvenile fish. These methods cannot target specific species or sizes of fish; anything unfortunate enough to be hooked or netted is taken, and is often a by-catch statistic soon after.

Shrimp trawling stands out as the largest culprit; it has both the most by-catch and the highest discard-weight-per-landed-target-catch rate. Still, high by-catch rates are associated with most indiscriminate forms of fishing around the globe. For instance, the Hawaiian longline fishery for swordfish and tuna catches over 100,000 sharks annually, and over 50 percent die.

By-catch results in a situation that both fisheries biologists and sport anglers find frightening—one in which fish are being caught faster than they can reproduce or replace themselves, with obvious consequences. This is particularly serious for slow-growing or less productive species. Atlantic blue and white marlin populations, for instance, have now been reduced to about 25 percent of the level needed to be self-sustaining. And in 1995–96, over 1 million pounds of dead marlin were thrown back by longliners—and that's only the reported figure!

The picture, although very bleak, does have a bright spot. Commercial fisheries that use selective gear, such as the Pacific pole fishery for tuna, limit their by-catch to less than 1 percent of the total overall catch. Additionally, the harpoon fishery for swordfish and tuna in the Northeast has essentially no recorded by-catch. Both fisheries were healthy for decades until the advent of nonselective gear. Selective fisheries discard fish only because of an inability to meet the minimum size requirements of regulatory agencies.

A CONSERVATION GLOSSARY

By-catch: The unintended catch or take of animal life associated with commercial fishing operations, including nontargeted species of fish, undersized and juvenile fish of targeted species, turtles, birds, and sea mammals.

Drift net: A large net up to 30 miles long and 300 feet deep that is set and allowed to drift through the night, catching all the fish, birds, and mammals that cross its path. Used primarily in the Pacific. It was first used for squid but now, because of its effectiveness, is used for other species as well.

Gill net: A net that is suspended vertically in the water column to catch fish by ensnaring their gills, eliminating any possibility of escape. Gill nets are a highly nonselective type of gear with high by-catch rates, especially when smaller mesh sizes are used.

Longline: Fishing gear comprised of a central mainline to which hundreds or thousands of baited hooks attached to leaders are set at regular intervals. Longlines are nonselective, hooking anything large enough to bite.

Maximum sustainable yield: The greatest amount of a species or population that can be removed without interfering with the species' ability to continue reproduction.

Pair trawl: When two large dragger-type boats string a large net between them and sweep a section of the ocean. This indiscriminate fishery catches whales, birds, and nontargeted fish. The target is usually tuna.

Purse seine: A large net used to encircle entire schools of fish. It is then closed or pursed at the bottom, creating a bowl-shaped net from which escape is virtually impossible. It's very effective in the tuna fishery on the West and East Coasts but also kills tens of thousands of dolphin in the Pacific each year.

Nontargeted species: Species other than the one being targeted by fishing operations, such as sharks being taken in a tuna fishery. Most are discarded as by-catch.

Nonselective fishing gear: Fishing gear that catches nontargeted species or undersized targeted species in addition to the one being targeted. Examples are drift nets, trawls, longlines, purse seines, and gill nets.

Target species: The species being sought by the angler, such as tuna by the purse seiner.

The logical thing to do in order to eliminate this mind-boggling amount of waste emptying our oceans of life would be for government regulatory agencies such as the National Marine Fisheries Service to greatly reduce the opportunities that nonselective-gear fisheries have to harvest fish. This would result in increased survival rates for reproducing species as well as an end to the destruction of turtles, birds, seals, whales, and other affected species.

SOLUTIONS

Treaties

The International Convention for the Conservation of Atlantic Tunas (ICCAT) recommends catch quotas for the bluefin in the western Atlantic. However, these quotas have always exceeded levels that would restrict the catch to maximum sustainable yield (MSY), placing ICCAT in violation of its own charter. In 1996 ICCAT *raised* the quota, even after its own scientific consultants advised that if bluefin populations were to recover over a 20-year time period, the quota would have to be cut by as much as 80 percent.

Australia, New Zealand, and Japan have established a Convention for the Conservation of Southern Bluefin Tuna (CCSBT) in an attempt to allow their regional stocks to recover. However, although Australia and New Zealand agree that catches must be reduced, Japan refuses to go along. Adding to the troubles in this region of the Pacific is that overfishing by non-CCSBT members is causing overall catches to exceed agreed-upon quotas.

Circle Hooks

The design of these hooks can be traced back at least 4,000 years to when they were laboriously handmade from animal bone or shells. Even then the features of these hooks were innovative and reflected the angler's knowledge of the hazards of the aquatic environment. Stone Age hooks have been found with a turned-in point to keep it from becoming lodged and lost on the bottom or a coral reef. Back then this would have been a drag (no pun intended) because of the time required to fashion one by hand. Today this same feature remains important to anglers, particularly longliners, who were first responsible for the resurgence in popularity of these hooks beginning in the 1960s. In the early 1980s the use of circle hooks took off after West Coast halibut boat anglers reported increases of up to 30 percent when using them.

Today the use of circle hooks are popular in both the recreational and commercial fishing communities. Studies by the Canadian Fisheries Department show increases in catches of up to 50 percent when using circle hooks, and recreational anglers are now using them for everything from tarpon to striped bass, redfish, bluefish, and tuna.

HOW THEY WORK

The amazing thing about circle hooks, and one that baffles first-time users, is that fish hook themselves. It happens when the fish takes the baited hook and begins to move off. The tightening line then pulls the hook from the fish's throat and up into either corner of its mouth. Then, as the eye of the hook clears the fish's mouth, the resistance of the line makes the hook turn in the corner of the jaw, and the fish hooks itself by putting the point into his jaw and cheek area (see diagram). Once this happens there is no way the fish can free itself. Equally as important, circle hooks keep the hook shank and line out of a tuna's mouth. As a result the usual concern about chafing from the mouth is not an issue.

Tuna fishing with circle hooks is unique in that the hook must be set. Usually this isn't necessary with circle hooks; simply raising the rod tip and reeling will result in a hookup. With tuna and particularly bluefins, however, a hard hookset is needed. When properly done it will result in a 95 percent hookup percentage, and a hook firmly planted in the fish's jaw corner, lip, or cheek area is conducive to a safe release.

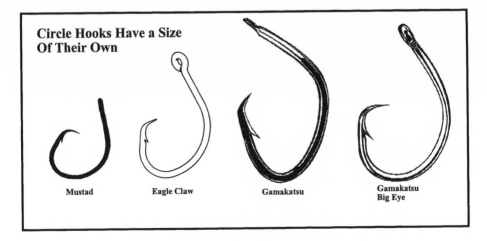

Circle Hooks Have a Size Of Their Own

Mustad   Eagle Claw   Gamakatsu   Gamakatsu Big Eye

Circle hooks, in use for some 4,000 years, have become hugely popular in recent years both for their effectiveness and ease of safe release of the fish. Check sizes carefully: the hooks shown above, from different manufacturers, are all described as 10/0 hooks.

GOOD FOR THE FISH

Longline captains have reported as many as 3,000 tuna in a row jaw- or lip-hooked with circle hooks, and although they probably weren't released, for the more conservation-oriented angler this means a much higher survival rate. Some fisheries such as the salmon fishery off northern California are now required by regulatory agencies to use barbless circle hooks because of their safety for fish.

GOOD FOR THE ANGLER

Circle hooks are also ideal for anglers who practice tag-and-release fishing. As previously mentioned, they not only result in increased hookup ratios but also make release easy; the chances of internal damage, such as with a gut-hooked fish, are nonexistent.

They are also perfect for anglers chunking tuna because it is easy to hook a fish safely in the jaw area. Just try cutting your chunk bait a little thinner at one end to make it easier to slip between the hook's point and shank. You can also use lighter leaders with circle hooks, thus fooling the more leader-shy tuna.

HOOK SIZE

Here is an instance where size does matter. Because circle hooks are sized differently than conventional hooks, you will need to familiarize yourself with them. For instance, if you're using a 6/0 regular hook for tuna fishing, don't order the same in a circle hook. An 11/0 circle hook would be a close match. You must also be careful when buying from different manufacturers; one may sell an 11/0 that's different in size from another's 11/0. An Eagle Claw F2000 size 6/0 is almost the same size as a Mustad 39960ST 12/0! Confusing? You bet, but using circle hooks is worth getting used to the crazy idiosyncrasies of the manufacturers. One thing circle hooks do share, though, are the points. All are needle or cone shaped.

TAGGING STUDIES

A new tagging system that doesn't depend on the fish being recaptured is giving scientists and the angling community valuable information on the bluefin tuna's biology and behavior after the fish leave New England and mid-Atlantic waters, including such specifics as stock structure, spawning areas, and migratory patterns. The program is being spearheaded by Dr. Molly Lutcavage, a marine biologist from the New England Aquarium who has been studying the bluefin since 1993, when she first began conducting aerial surveys of bluefin populations off New England.

The new pop-up tags cost about $3,000 each. When a bluefin is caught, either by rod and reel or commercially by purse-seine boats such as the infamous White Dove Fleet, a tag is placed in the dorsal-fin area of its back. Fish are tagged during the fall run, and the tags release in the spring. They then automatically transmit data to orbiting satellites that are transmitted to Dr. Lutcavage as e-mail. Other species currently being tagged with these innovative tags are sharks and marlins, including a 1,000-plus-pound giant off Madeira.

This data will hopefully clarify the previously mentioned issues and also provide us, for the first time, with accurate information instead of statistical assumptions, which are so much a part of the inexact science of fisheries management. Concerns of course are that in the wrong hands—such as those of the purse-seine and longline industries—the information could result in increased fishing pressure on already-precarious stocks.

New England was chosen this time as the region to tag bluefins because of the well-established bluefin fishery there featuring many different size classes of fish, as well as its proximity to Boston.

The tags feature a satellite transmitter and a short whip antenna attached to an egg-shaped float. The transmitter is programmed to release from its anchor system, holding the entire tag in place in the fish's flesh at a predetermined time. On that day it electronically releases, and the float carries the transmitter to the water's surface, where its transmitting begins. First reports are of the tag's location and water temperatures.

Scientists are now beginning to believe that one stock of bluefin tuna roams the Atlantic, but it could be a boost to conservation efforts here in the United States if this became an undisputed fact. In this case, international fishing nations with quota systems far less stringent than the United States' would have to adhere to the same quotas that anglers here do. With stocks in the western Atlantic thought to have been depleted by about 80 percent since the late 1970s, and eastern Atlantic stocks dropping by 50 percent in the same time period, this would be a welcome development, and one that could add to the rebuilding of the bluefin population in the Atlantic.

RESOURCES

BIBLIOGRAPHY

In a book like this, all the sources of information can never be given full credit. Over the years I've been fortunate enough to have met, fished with, and listened to many anglers who have influenced me. I've also read everything I could get my hands on in a long list of excellent magazines listed on page 232. The best learning tool, however, is to just get out and fish. You'll always learn something and return to the dock each time a more knowledgeable person—what more could you ask for?

Beacher, Capt. Greg. *Fish the Chair if You Dare.* 1993.

Ben-Yami, M. *Tuna Fishing with Pole and Line.* 1980.

Bond, Carl E. *Biology of Fishes.* 1979.

Borgstrom, Georg, and Arthur Heighway. *Atlantic Ocean Fisheries.* 1961.

Coleman, Tim. *Offshore Fishing.* 1988.

Connett, Eugene, ed. *American Big Game Fishing.* 1935.

Eschmeyer, Herald and Hammann. *A Field Guide to Pacific Coast Fishes.* 1983.

Farrington, S. Kip. *Atlantic Game Fishing.* 1937.

Freeman, Bruce. *Gamefish Profile: Thunnus Thynnus: The Bluefin Tuna.* 1988.

Gall, Ken. *Handling Your Catch.* 1986.

Garrison, Chuck. *Offshore Fishing Southern California and Baja.* 1981.

Gifford, Capt. Tom. *Anglers and Muscleheads.* 1960.

Grey, Zane. *Tales of Swordfish and Tuna.* 1927.

Heilner, Van Campen. *Salt Water Fishing.* 1953.

Hill, Capt. James. *Tuna.*

Holder, Charles F. *The Gamefishes of the World.* 1913.

International Game Fish Association. *World Record Game Fishes.* 1986–1995.

Marshall, N. B. *Explorations in the Life of Fishes.* 1971.

McClane, A. J., ed. *McClane's New Standard Fishing Encyclopedia.* 1974.

————. *Field Guide to Saltwater Fishes of North America.* 1978.

McClane, A. J., and Keith Gardner. *McClane's Game Fish of North America.* 1984.

Migdalski, Edward C. *Saltwater Game Fishes of the Atlantic and Pacific.* 1958.

Migdalski, Edward C., and George S. Fichter. *The Fresh and Salt Water Fishes of the World.* 1983.

Moss, Frank T. *Successful Ocean Game Fishing.* 1971.

————. *Modern Sportfishing Boats.* 1981.

Murawski, S. A. *Biological Implications of Bycatch.* 1995.

Nakamura, Hiroshi. *Tuna Distribution and Migration.* 1969.

Preble, Capt. Dave. *Sportfishing for Yellowfin Tuna.* 1988.

Reiger, George. *Profiles in Saltwater Angling.* 1973.

Robins, Ray and Douglass. *Atlantic Coast Fishes.* 1986.

Smith, Christopher F., and Richard Grog. *Tuna Handling Tips.*

Taylor, Fred. *Tuna Fishing for Beginners.* 1934.

Vesey-Fitzgerald, Brian, and Francesca LaMonte. *Gamefish of the World.* 1949.

Woolner, Frank. *Modern Saltwater Sport Fishing.* 1972.

MAGAZINES

Salt Water Sportsman
263 Summer Street
Boston, MA 02210
The best all-around fishing magazine in the U.S.

Marlin
Box 2456
Winter Park, FL 32790
Best coverage of billfishing anywhere.

Sport Fishing
330 West Canton Avenue
Winter Park, FL 32789
407-628-4802
Excellent offshore fishing magazine.

The Fisherman
14 Ramsey Road
Shirley, NY 11967
516-345-5200
(five regional editions covering East Coast)
Well-rounded weekly publication for beginners, novices, experts.

The Edge
1800 Bay Avenue
Point Pleasant, NJ 08742
Excellent how-to magazine for offshore fishing enthusiasts.

Fly Fishing in Salt Waters
2001 Western Avenue, #210
Seattle, WA 98121
Excellent articles on inshore and offshore fly fishing.

WHERE TO FIND TUNA
Massachusetts to Montauk Point

The Banana	14080/25125/43588
The Star	14180/25238/43695
The 31 Fathom Hole	14280/25375/43697
NW Corner—The Dump	14390/25375/43697
The Fingers	14360/25490/43712
Nomans/19 Fathom Bank	14305/25458/43775
SW Corner Coxes Ledge	14411/35610/43783
Little Fishtail	14474/25661/43745
24 Fathom Bank	14480-523/43771/43789
Stellwagen Bank	
Butterfish Hole	14638/25908/43789
West Bank Butterfish Hole	14692/25944/43746
The Horns	14610/25825/43720
	14575/25775/43695

| The Fishtail | 14645/25730/43340 |
| The Dip | 14785/25905/43295 |

Montauk to Cape May

Texas Tower	26313/43268
Chicken Canyon	26400/43235
	26485/43325
Glory Hole	26520/43355
	26612/43375
The Wall	26460/43185
	26475/43045
20 Fathom Bank	26735/43445
The Thumb	26720/43400
The Star/20 Fathom Fingers	26675/43175
35 Fathom Slough	26375/43100
28 Mile Wreck	26825.5/42803.7
50 Fathom Ledge	26500/42790

Delaware to Cape Hatteras

Elephant's Trunk	26775/42510
20 Fathom Lumps NE	26800/42240
SW	26885/42125
The Hill	26880/41925
The Rockpile	26904/40072

INDEX

A

Albacore, 8, 39

  Characteristics of, 39, 40

  Coloration of, 40

  Distribution and Behavior of, 40, 41

  Features of, 40

  Fishing methods of, 41

  Growth rate of (chart), 41

  Size of, 40

Allothunnus fallai, see also, slender tuna

Almadrabras, 16, 17

Anchor retrieval system, 88, 89

Angled head lures, 116

Aristotle, 16

Atlantic Bonito, 42

  Characteristics of, 42

  Coloration of, 42

  Distribution and Behavior of, 42

  Fishing methods of, 42

  Size of, 42

Australian Bonito, 42

  Characteristics of, 42

  Distribution of, 43

  Fishing methods of, 43

  Size of, 43

Auxis rochei, see also, bullet tuna

Auxis thazard, see also, frigate tuna

Avalon Tuna club, 21–23

B

Bahama Mama, 72

Bait types, 137

Bait well, 86

Bait, catching and preparing,
    136

Baits, working your, 137

Bay of Biscay, 49

Beating, tuna, 193

Bigeye Tuna, 44

Characteristics of, 45

Coloration of, 45

Distribution and Behavior of,
    45, 46

Fishing methods of, 46

Bigeyes, trolling for, 147

Birds, 161, 162

Blackfin Tuna, 43

Characteristics of, 43

Coloration of, 43

Distribution and Behavior of,
    44

Fishing methods of, 44

Bleeding the tuna, 202, 203

Block-and-tackle system, 85, 86

Bluefin tuna, 3, 8, 46

Characteristics of, 46

Coloration of, 47

Distribution and Behavior of,
    47, 48

Eastern north atlantic stocks,
    49

Features of, 47

Fishing methods of, 50

Growth rate of (chart), 51

Population of, 50

Size of, 47

Spawning of, 50

Western north atlantic stocks,
    48

Bluefins, juvenile, 51

Boating tuna, 201, 202

Boats, tuna, 71–80

Bonito tuna, 3

Boone teaser, 85

Brining, 207

Bucket harness, 83, 84

Bullet heads, 116

Bullet tuna, 3, 52

Characteristics of, 52

Distribution of, 52

Fishing methods of, 52

Burnt tuna syndrome, 200

Buying a downrigger, 168

By-catch, 224–225

C

Camouflage, 7

Campbell, W. Greer, 21

Cape Cod, 49

Care and handling, of tuna, 199

Cat Cay Club, 28

Cat Cay Tournament, 28–30

Cat Cay, 48

Catalina Island, 21–23

CCSBT (Convention for the Conservation of Southern Bluefin Tuna), 226

Cedar plugs, 176

Center console, 77

Center rigger, 84, 85

Characteristics and behavior, of tuna, 6

Chicken of the sea, 39

Chum bags, 134

Chum container, 134

Chumming, 133–139

Chumming, with the downrigger, 167

Chunking rigs, 129

Chunking, 88, 123–133

Circle hooks, 226–228

Cockpit, 73, 74

Color scopes, 111, 112, 128, 166

Color sounder, 80

Colors, of tuna, 207

Commercial fishing, 15, 211

    Ancient Rome and Greece, 15

    California, 19

    Japan, 18, 19

    Spanish, 16

Commercial value, of tuna, 8

Conservation, of tuna, 223–229,

Controls, 77

Coolers, 105

Cork, 139

Corselet, 6

Crimps, 99

Cupped face lures, 116

Cutting the leader, 195–197

Cybiosardo elegans, see also, leaping bonito

D

Daisy chains, 31

Daisy-chain teasers, 149, 155, 156, 159

Distribution, of northern and southern bluefin (chart), 11

Distribution, of yellowfin and skipjack (chart), 11

Dixie, 157

Dogtooth Tuna, 52

    Characteristics of, 52

    Distribution and Behavior of, 52

    Fishing methods of, 53

    Size of, 53

Door knob lures, 116

Double-hook rigs, 120

Downriggers, 163–168

Drag washers, 93, 94

Drails, 121

Dressing, tuna, 204, chart, 205, 206

Drift net, 225

Drifting, 124

E

Eddies, 110

Electronics, 79, 80

End loops, 99

Engine choice, 77

F

Fair Play to Game Fishes, 22

Farrington, S. Kip, 26, 27, 32, 33, 36

Farrior, Michael, 23

Fighting chair, 81–83

Fish bags, 104

Fish boxes, 86

Fishing the Atlantic, 27

Flat head lures, 116

Flat lines, 85

Flesh textures, of tuna, 207

FloScan gauge, 79

Flush-mounted rod holders, 74

Flying gaffs, 102, 189

Flying wedge, 35

Forecasting services, Roffer's Ocean Fishing, 110, 111

Frigate tuna, 3, 53

   Characteristics of, 53

   Distribution of, 53

Fuel capacity, 78, 79

Fulton Fish Market, 20

G

Gaff hooks, 101

Gaff, bringing fish to, 184–186, 188

Gaffing, 189–191, 192, 201

Genroku period, 214

Gifford, Capt. Thomas, 25, 169

Gill net, 225

Gilling, 203

Gimbal Belts, 81

Gin pole, 85, 86

GPS (Global Positioning System), 79, 109, 111

Gray, Capt. Bill, 27

Grey, Zane, 3, 24

Guides, 93

Gutting, 203

Gymnosarda unicolor, see also, dogtooth tuna

H

Handlining, 179, 180

Harpooning, tuna, 219–221

Heilner, Van Campen, 20

Helm station, 77

Hemingway, Ernest, 25, 27

Hex-heads, 115

Histamine, 199, 200

History of Animals, 16

Holder, Dr. Charles Frederick, 20–22

Hook positions, 142

Hook removal, 195–197

Hook-and-line fishing, 9

Hooking up, 183, 184

Hydrodynamic refinement, 4

Hydrostatic pressure, 8

I

ICCAT (International Convention for the Conservation of Atlantic Tunas), 226

Icing, tuna, 203

IGFA (International Game Fish Association), 23, 30

Intercollegiate Tuna Cup, 37

International Tuna Cup, 32–37

Istiophoridae, 4

J

Japan, 13, 211–217

Jetheads, 114, 116, 117

K

Katsuwonus pelamis, see also, skipjack

Kidney harness, 81

Kite fishing, 178, 179

Kona heads, 116

Kyle, Capt. Clay, 28, 29, 72

L

Leadering, 186

Leaping Bonito, 53

Characteristics of, 53, 54

Coloration of, 54

Distribution and Behavior of, 54

Fishing methods of, 54

Lerner, Michael, 30

Lever-drag system, 94

Life cycle, tuna, 4

Little Tunnies, 54

Characteristics of, 55

Distribution and Behavior of, 56

Fishing methods of, 56

Growth rate of, 55, 56

Live baiting, 141–143

Live well, building a, 87

Longline, 225

Longtail tuna, 3, 57

Characteristics of, 57

Distribution and Behavior of, 57

Fishing methods of, 57

Loran, 79, 109, 111

Lure rigging, 114

Lure types, 113

Lures, 113–121

Colors of, 117

Patterns, 152, 153

Size of, 118, 119

Weight of, 118, 119

Lutcavage, Dr. Molly, 228, 229

M

Mackerel daisy chain, 155

Masey, Mr., 26

Maximum sustainable yield, 225

McClane, A.J., 141

Merritt, boats, 71–73

Migration, (chart), 12

Mitchell-Henry, Mr., 25

Mold craft teaser, see also, Boone teaser

Moore, Anne, 26

Morehouse, Col. C.P., 21,22

Mousetrap rig, 130, 131

MSY (maximum sustainable yield), 226

N

National Marine Fisheries Service, 196, 197, 225

Natural bait teasers, 160

New England Aquarium, 228, 229

New Standard Fishing Encyclopedia, 141

NOAA (National Oceanic and Atmospheric Administration), 109

Nonselective fishing gear, 225

Nontargeted species, 225

O

Oriental Bonito, 57

Characteristics of, 58

Distribution of, 58

Fishing methods of, 58

Outriggers, 25, 169, 170

P

Pacific Bonito, 58

Characteristics of, 58

Distribution and Behavior of, 59

Fishing methods of, 59

Growth rate of (chart), 59

Pair trawl, 225

Patillo, Thomas, 20

Perciformes, 3

Pollution, of the ocean, 223

Power, 77

Pulley system, 85, 86

Purse seine, 9, 225

R

Recessed rod holders, see also, flush-mounted rod holders

Record keeping, 154

Reel-drag setting, 143

Reels, 93–99

Regulation of, 91, 94, 101, 102

Releasing, tuna, 194, 195

Rigging, 139

Rigging, cedar plugs, 176

Rocket launchers, 84

Rod holders, 74

Rods, 91

Rope locker, 88

Rybovich, boats, 72–76

S

Safety lines, 76, 77

Sambo, 72

Sanchez, Julio, 28

Sarda australis, see also, australian bonito

Sarda chiliensis, see also, pacific bonito

Sarda orientalis, see also, oriental bonito

Sarda orientalis, see also, striped bonito

Sarda sarda, see also, atlantic bonito

Satellite-tag studies, 8

Scombridea, 3

Scombrodidei, 3

Seawater temperature gauge, 80

Sharp Cup, see International Tuna Cup

Shaw, Lee, 156, 157

Sheer, Otto, 23, 24

Sheer, William G., 23, 24

Shrimp trawling, 224

Single-hook lure rigs, 119, 120

Sinkers, 139

Skipjack, 8, 59

    Characteristics of, 60

Distribution and Behavior of, 60

Fishing methods of, 61

Size of, 61

Slender tuna, 3, 61

    Characteristics of, 61

    Distribution of, 61

Snapper poles, 174–176

Sounds, of tuna, 7

Southern Bluefin, 61

    Characteristics of, 62

    Color of, 62

    Distribution and Behavior of, 62

    Fishing methods of, 63

    Size of, 62

Spoon feeding tuna, 120

Sport fishing, history of, 19

    Bimini, 25–28

    California, 20–23

    Cat Cay, 25–28

    England, 25

    New Jersey, 23–28

    Nova Scotia, 30–32

Spreader rigs, 156–159

Squid daisy chain, 156

Squid, trolling for, 148

Stanchion collar, making of, 103

Stand-up rods, 92, 93

Star-drag reel, 93, 94

Stereoscopic vision, 7

Storing, tuna meat, 207

Straight gaffs, 102

Striped Bonito, 63

   Characteristics of, 63

   Fishing methods of, 63

Stuart, Capt. William Henry, 25

Surface temperature chart, 80

T

T. thunnus, 48

T.t. saliens, 48

Tag, bringing fish to, 184–186,
   188

Tagging studies, 228, 229

Tagline retrieval system, 171

Taglines, 170–173, installing,
   171

Tailroping, 103, 191,
   applying, 191, 192

Tales of Swordfish and Tuna, 3

Target species, 225

Teasers, 31, 160

Thunnini, 3

Thunnus alalunga, see also
   albacore

Thunnus albacares, see also,
   yellowfin tuna

Thunnus atlanticus, see also,
   blackfin tuna

Thunnus maccoyii, see also,
   southern bluefin

Thunnus obesus, see also,
   bigeye tuna

Thunnus thynnus, see also,
   bluefin tuna

Thunnus tonggoi, see also,
   longtail tuna

Towing, 193, 194

Transom, 86, 188

Treaties, 226

Trolling daisy chains, 159

Trolling location, 154, 155

Trolling rods, 92

Trolling setup, 150, 151

Trolling speed, 153

Trolling spreader bars, 159

Trolling tackle, 146

Trolling teasers, 161

Trolling, 113, 145–162

Trolling, cedar plugs, 177

Tsukiji Market, 211–217

Tuna Alley, 26

Tuna bag, 203

Tuna bullet rig, 132, set up, 133

Tuna family tree, 5

Tuna techniques, 169–180

Tuna towers, 71

Tuna, finding, 111

Tuna, fishing for, 109–111

Two-speed reels, 95
   types of, 104

U

United States, 13

V

VHF radio, 80

W

W-trolling patterns, 152
Water temperature, 110
West Coast rods, see also,
    stand-up rods
Wiring, 186
Wood, Capt. Booby, 156,
    157
Woods Hole Oceanographic
    Institute, 66
Worldwide distribution
    (Chart), 11
Wrapping, 187, 188

X

Xiphiidae, 4

Y

Yap lures, 116
Yellowfin tuna, 3, 8, 39, 63
    Characteristics of, 64
    Color of, 64
    Distribution and Behavior of,
        64
    Fishing methods of, 67
    Growth rate of (chart), 65
    Migration of, 66

Z

Zapper, 221